The Political Role of Palestinian Women in the 1930s

The Political Participation of Palestinian Women

Women's Oral Narratives

Dr. Faiha Abdulhadi

The Political Role of Palestinian Women in the 1930s
The Political Participation of Palestinian Women
Women's Oral Narratives

Translated from the Arabic Language by: Nitham Sais
English Editing by: Susannah May
Published by: The Palestinian Women's Research & Documentation Center, December 2006

Design and layout and printing by: Al-Nasher Advertising Agency

First Edition - Ramallah -February 2015

ISBN: 978-9950-345-19-5

Back Cover Photo: Eastern Women's Conference in Cairo -1938

All rights reserved©
Palestinian Women's Research and Documentation Center
Macca Bldg. 2nd floor, Al-Balo', Al-Bereh, WB
Tel: +970 2 2406468
Fax: +970 2 2406469

The designations employed and the presentation of material throughout this publication do not imply the expression of any opinion whatsoever on the part of UNESCO concerning the legal status of any country, territory, city or area or of its authorities, or concerning the delimitation of its frontiers or boundaries.

The ideas and opinions expressed in this publication are those of the authors; they are not necessarily those of UNESCO and do not commit the Organization.

Contents

Part One: The Political Participation of Palestinian Women 9

Introduction 11

The Research Method 14

    Theoretical Framework 14
    Mechanisms Used in the Research 18
    Practical Difficulties Encountered while doing the Research ... 21

Chapter One: The Political Participation of Palestinian Women before the 1936 Palestinian Revolt 23

    Introduction 23
    1933 Intifada 24
    The Comrades of Al-Qassam 24

Chapter Two : The Political Participation of Palestinian Women in the 1936 Revolt 29

    Introduction 29
    The Role of Women in the Revolt 29
    The Socio-Political Role 31
    The Role of Women in Providing Food 32
    Women's Role in Incitement 36
    The Medical Role 60
    The Role of Women in Postal Work 62

    The Establishment of Societies and Unions............................63

    The Participation of Palestinian Women in Conferences 67

    The Military Role 78

    Hiding Weapons 78

    Taking Care of Weapons...82

    The Transportation of Weapons..84

    Training to Use Weapons 85

    Bearing Arms and Participating in Battles................................87

Chapter Three: The Impact of the
Failure of the 1936 Revolt on Palestinian Women.................91

    The Impact of the Failure of the 1936 Revolt 91

Chapter Four: Women in People's Collective Memory..........97

    In the Narrators' Memories..97

    In Women's Memories... 105

    In the Memory of both Male and Female Narrators 111

Chapter Five: Social Changes
Accompanying the Political Struggle of Women 115

    The Changes in Customs and Traditions
    as reflected in the testimony of Fattoum Al-Ghurairi.............. 122

Conclusion 125

References 127

Part Two: Women's Oral Narratives

Maymanah Ezzedin Al-Qassam 143

Wadee'a Qaddourah Khartabil 171

Issam Hamdi Al-Huseini 201

Samiha Khaleel (Samiha Yusef Mustafa Al Qubbaj) 219

Najeyyah Barham 243

Hasnah Salim Masoud 243

Zahidah Ahmad M. Mustafa 243

Sobhiyyah Ismael A. Barham 243

Sanajeq Mohammad A. Barham 243

Annexes

List of Women Narrators 271

Index 275

Fattoum Al-Ghurairi

Sathaj Nassar

Salma Al-Huseini

Adala Al-Aseer

Sanajeq Barham

Zakiyeh Hulaileh

Amneh & Haijar Mustafa

Shahirah Muslihi

Hasna Masoud

Zulaikha Al-Shihabi    Milia Sakakini    Maymana Al-Qassam

Hilweh Jakaman    Wadee'a Khartabil    Khazneh Al-Khateeb

Issam Al-Huseini    Samiha Qubbaj Khaleel    Zahida Mustafa

Field Researchers

Palestine

North
1. Nida' Abu Taha
2. Sumaya Al-Safadi

South
1. Lamia' Shalaldeh
2. Maryam Ismail

Center (Ramallah)
1. Hala Abu Hashhash
2. Na'ilah Oudeh

Center (Jerusalem)
1. Muna Mahajneh

1948
1. Muna Mahajneh
2. Rabab Tamish

Gaza
1. Iman Radwan
2. Taghreed Abdulhadi

Jordan
1. Ruqayya Al-Alami
2. Sana' Muharram

Syria
1. Buthaina Al-Kurdi
2. Maha Al-Tamimi

Lebanon
1. Suhair Al-Uzom
2. Khadija Abdul 'Al

Egypt
1. Sabah Al-Khuffash
2. Amaal Al-Agha
3. Hala Mansour

PART ONE

The Political Participation of Palestinian Women

Introduction

In our attempt to study the role of Palestinian women in politics in the 1930s, we relied on narrations by both men and women. Our aim was to find answers to the questions surrounding a number of issues that have not been accounted for in the documented or recorded history of the political participation of Palestinian women.

We tried to examine and investigate the role of women using the feminist perspective accounted for by oral history. We examined the participation of women in politics, concentrating particularly on rural areas, given that previous studies have clearly indicated that there is a lack of specialized studies on the struggle of Palestinian women, and particularly rural women, before 1948. This led us to embark on a research study that would concentrate on a rather neglected, but very important, historical period, firstly examining what has been written about this period in history books[1] and subsequently attempting to make a contribution to a subject of real historical significance.

The key questions underpinning our research were 'Did women participate in politics during the period before 1948?', and if so 'Was their participation central, as our research study assumes, or was it as marginal as some history books have claimed?', and furthermore 'What was the role of women in rural areas in this period of Palestinian political history?'.

Whilst we have been careful not to minimize the role of women in urban areas our research has primarily concentrated on rural women. By focusing our research study in this way we have tried to discover and do justice to an issue which has unfortunately not received the same level of attention as other political issues in recorded history.

Recorded history has discussed the participation of urban women in demonstrations and has noted their great courage and perseverance in challenging the occupying British soldiers by carrying protest petitions and writing articles in local newspapers.[2] It has also examined their participation, through the women's union established in 1921, in Palestinian political conferences, as well as their role in

Part 1: The Political Participation of Palestinian Women

organizing women's political conferences. In addition, references are made to their contribution to the Arab women's conferences which were held in support of the Palestinian question. An example of their participation was the formation of a large delegation which participated in the conference that was organized by Huda Hanem Sha'rawi in Egypt in 1938.

With regards to rural women, we endeavored to discuss their roles and do a survey of those roles which were different from those of urban women. In this context we asked the following questions: 'Was the participation of rural women in the armed revolution significant and influential or was it marginal?', 'Was their participation restricted to specific forms of political activities or did it cover all forms of revolutionary activity?', and if recorded history has recognized one fundamental role for women - which was to supply revolutionary forces with food and water and to transport arms and ammunitions for them - we must ask the question of whether this was the only role that women played or were there other roles that they played which need to be researched and discovered? Additionally we wanted to consider how the women themselves assessed their roles. Did they consider their participation in the revolution as political participation or simply an extension of their normal roles? Would they even describe it as participation at all?

Our intention was therefore to use our research to rewrite what has previously been written in history books on Palestinian women during this period, this time attempting to understand their role through the eyes of the women themselves and allowing them to narrate their own experiences, given that we consider them to have played an active and fundamental role in the formation of the history of their societies. Finally our research has tried to combine the need for answers to specific questions about women's political participation and contribution to the making of their history - information which we would benefit from when writing about the history of this period - and the need to make a contribution of our own to the formation of a historical archive on Palestinian women. This represents an ambitious attempt to break the silence surrounding the accomplishments of women, to give recognition to the effective and active role that women have played and to redefine some of the terminology which is used by both men and women without due attention to its accuracy, negative associations or impact on the writing of the history of the Palestinian people. It is furthermore an attempt to bridge the gap between the hard work that women have done at key points in Palestinian history and those historians who have tended to neglect and marginalize their efforts in the writing of this history. Finally, this research is a contribution to the formation and development of Palestinian historical sources.

Part 1: The Political Participation of Palestinian Women

The Research Method

Theoretical Framework

There was a need in our study to apply a different research method in the hope of coming up with different results and information which could fill the various gaps that were found in research studies conducted on the historical period our work addresses. These research studies were not successful in challenging the stereotypical picture of the role of rural women in the 1930s, which was repeatedly discussed in many of the studies conducted on this period, and which can be summarized as follows: the role of rural women focused on supplying Palestinian revolutionaries with food and water, transporting arms and ammunitions and encouraging and raising the morale of fighters participating in the various battles that were taking place at the time. The ubiquity of this understanding of women's roles has led researchers active in the field of oral history to invite other researchers to follow and apply different research methods in their future studies. Ted Swedenburg, for example, realized that it wasn't possible for him to rely on the narratives that he managed to compile from women while he was researching the Palestinian revolution of 1936. He was not satisfied with the answers village inhabitants gave to his questions on the participation of women and their role in the revolution. Rather he felt that there was something missing in these answers and that the information given to him was hiding many forms of female participation during the revolution. Narrated stories talked about women and their role in hiding fighters and arms from the British army, in addition to the double burden that they had to take on as a wife, sister or mother. However Swedenburg suspected that the fact that the revolution was led by men meant that some of the activities of women who participated in specific fields were probably not recorded in popular memory or in these stories. He subsequently found it difficult to compile a full account of the various activities of women during that period.[3]

Our research has instead relied on the feminist perspective of oral history, which is gender oriented in analysis, and which approaches the issue of women through women themselves, consciously listening to their narration and allowing their narration to be heard. This approach is multifaceted; it has benefited from various epistemological fields and has uncovered the artificial division of academic knowledge which limits and disables the researcher from having a deep understanding and knowledge of women[4]. This research method gives more freedom and flexibility to the researchers and narrators and enables them as a result to get a deeper psychological understanding of women.[5] This method also deconstructs the prevailing values which do not consider the experiences of women to be a fundamental component in the construction of history and consequently seeks to form new values which allow for integration and compatibility between the experiences of men and women.[6]

Whilst we approached women with the specific research aim of writing the political history of the Palestinian people during the period spanning from the 1930s until the mid-1960s, having adopted the feminist perspective, we also tried to listen to the aims of the narrators, which might intersect with our aims but would not necessarily coincide with them completely. We learned to listen to the contradictory voices of women, the voice that she was brought up to express and the other hidden voice that she was taught to suppress. We tried to read the hidden voice while comparing the two so as to have an in-depth understanding of the thoughts of women, given that "what women reveal about themselves does not reflect an objective description of their lives, but tends to originate from a cultural background, and a cultural content that has a historical authority which limits and restricts the activities of women. Accordingly, the uncovering of the language and meaning that women utilize in their daily lives helps us become aware of the social forces and ideas that have an impact on them"[7]. Furthermore "Female oral historians do not constitute a radical paradox for oral history; they simply make their own self-reflection permeate through the interview, and thus it becomes clear and a part of the recording"[8].

We relied on reading the body language and the emotions that accompanied the narrations, requiring us to simultaneously record the body movement of the narrator and her emotions. We found it useful to pay attention to the movement of her hands, legs and head and then separately observe the movement of her eyebrows, lips and eyes, where there would be a form of human reaction expressing human communication. "Because non-verbal communication usually

Part 1: The Political Participation of Palestinian Women

surpasses verbal communication the female researcher starts to give signals and communicate through her eyes with the group of women. She sits in a position where she can observe every individual without any effort. She uses her ability to play with her voice (to raise and lower its tone when necessary) in support of her opening words or speech".[9]

It was also necessary to pay attention to the skill women exhibited in talking about their feelings and their private relationships, and the fact that they were more comfortable talking about the impact of events on their lives rather than talking about the events and actions themselves.[10] This consequently required the researcher to give the women the opportunity to choose the angle from which they would start talking about their past so that it would become clear from their choices the kind of experiences and emotions that they consider to be central and fundamental: "When people start to talk about important emotional moments in their lives, they reveal what is inside them. But if you have a pre-structured interview then you tend to impose it on them".[11]

In our research we were keen to ask women about the meaning of the terms that they were using especially those terms they used to describe themselves; for instance what do they mean when they talk about 'joint work', 'politics', 'support'...etc.

The female researchers were trained on how to conduct a preliminary interview with each narrator, how to be sensitive and develop a rapport with them and how to take notes and record the personal data of the narrators. This was designed to help create a sense of trust and affinity between the researcher and the narrator and lessen any worry or fear that the narrator might feel about being interviewed and recorded.

In the first session of the second interview the researcher was instructed to start the interview with an open question that would allow the narrator to talk freely, and then carefully and consciously listen to what the narrator talked about, whilst recording the interview using a tape recorder. The rationale behind such a method is to allow both the researcher and the narrator to meet their aims. The aim of the researcher is to get the information that will enable her to write the history of the participation of Palestinian women in politics during the period in which the narrator lived, but the narrator is also in need of someone to talk to about her life and the moments that she considers to be important in her childhood and she might sometimes have the urge to address her present sufferings by linking the events of the past with those of the present. This flow on the part of the narrator, even if it seems to be irrelevant to the research topic, is important as it allows the narrator to feel comfortable with the researcher and the research project, which will ultimately make the narrator respond better to the questions addressed to her in the second session of the second interview.

During the second session of the second interview, the topic of the discussion was more specific corresponding to the primary aim of the researcher. At this stage the narrator should be more comfortable talking about things and the researcher would also have listened to the recorded interview and would have made some remarks and noted some questions and specific points to inquire about. Occasionally the researcher might feel the need for a third session, or alternatively decide that she could do without if she felt that she had received answers to all of her questions.

The feminist perspective - which relies on the principle of participation, observation, patience and careful listening - led to a sense of trust between the narrators and the researchers, which, in consequence, enabled the narrators to open their hearts and minds to the researchers and be very honest and transparent in talking about their lives. This method enabled us to record the history of their lives and fill some of the gaps in the recorded history of the political participation of women in the 1930s, especially in rural areas, as well as investigating the existence of a group known as "The Comrades of Al-Qassam".

In general women were not hesitant in talking about the role of woman in the 1930s especially as the interviews progressed and they began to recollect the past and became more aware of the significance of their role. Whilst most of the women didn't talk about their role in politics during the first session, and some claimed to be ignorant of this specific historical period and told the researchers to seek information about specific facts from men, (as was the case with Ted Swedenburg when he asked women for information) the strategy of encouraging women to talk about their roles and the methods the researchers used to point out the historical significance of these roles, without minimizing the role of men, did eventually help encourage the narrators to talk about their experiences. As they opened up they began to discuss many issues of real historical significance not just for the purpose of this research but as material that would be useful in writing the history of a people during a very significant political period.

Mechanisms Used in the Research

This research project could not have been completed without the support of institutions believing in the necessity of recording the history of women using methods of oral history and gender analysis. The Women's Directorate of Gender at the Ministry of Planning and International Cooperation provided the field researchers with technical equipment. The Rsearcher/Supervisor began by doing a critical review of everything that had been written on oral history in general, and Palestinian women in particular, so as to determine the historical period the research would focus on. Research studies on the political participation of women during the period from the 1930s until the mid-1960s were found to be missing. Therefore this period was selected as well as the areas where the research was to be conducted and the gender of the narrators. The vast majority of the 155 narrators who were interviewed were women: this unequal ratio of men to women served the purpose of the project as we were able to record the political participation of women in the 1930s while recognizing need to record the narrations of some men who were their contemporaries especially during the 1930s. In our research we relied on populated areas, taking into consideration the distribution of narrators in each area in accordance with two age groups: over 75 years old and over 55 years old. In addition we took into account the division of women into urban, rural, educated and illiterate groups.

Our study tried to cover areas of Palestinian presence both inside and outside Palestine. Areas of the study included:

Palestine: (the West Bank, the Gaza Strip, the 1948 areas, Jerusalem), in addition to Jordan, Syria, Lebanon and Egypt.

The following table shows the distribution of narrators in accordance with age group and location, in keeping with the objectives of the research. (A percentage of men were selected as eye witnesses of the political participation of women. The men selected constituted 10% of the narrators).

Year	Age Group	West Bank	Gaza Strip	Palestinians of 1948	Jordan	Lebanon	Syria	Egypt	Total
1935 - 1948	Over 75	21	11	8	13	9	8	6	76
1948 - 1965	Over 55	21	11	11	13	9	8	6	79
		42	22	19	26	18	16	12	155

The research study required a large group of researchers. The group was made up of 17 researchers, distributed to the following areas of Palestine: North, South, Center and Jerusalem, the areas of 1948 and the Gaza Strip, in addition to Palestinians living in the diasporas (Jordan, Syria, Lebanon and Egypt). The researchers were carefully selected from among those who had a university degree in sociology or worked with women in a women's organization. To get to know more about them and select the most promising for the purpose of our research, the researchers were interviewed. They were then provided with theoretical and historical material to read on oral history and on the struggle of Palestinian woman. In addition a workshop was organized in Egypt to give them training on how to collect research material using the methods of oral history and gender analysis. The workshop was held in Egypt for a period of three days. Half of the workshop focused on theoretical issues, while the other half concentrated on practical training. Many female and male researchers participated in the workshop including female activists in Palestinian and Egyptian feminist movements.

It was important to write a research questionnaire that would reflect the method of oral history and its relationship to gender analysis. This was a difficult task which required many steps before it could be properly implemented. Firstly the Rsearcher/Supervisor developed the preliminary research questionnaire in accordance with the needs and aims of the research. The questionnaire was then sent to the field researchers in different areas, who tested it in the field and then provided the Researcher with feedback. An evaluation of the questionnaire was conducted in the locations of the research: Palestine, Jordan, Lebanon, and Egypt. No evaluation of the questionnaire was done in Syria due to the fact that Syria was not initially selected as one of the research areas. Later on, upon the recommendation of those who participated in the workshop that was held in Egypt, Syria was selected as a research area.

Based on the comments made by the researchers from the different areas of the research and the results that came from the tests of the questionnaire in the field, major changes were made to the preliminary questionnaire. The institutions that discussed the questionnaire included: The General Union of Palestinian Women, The Women and Memory Forum in Egypt and The Palestinian Association for Cultural Exchange, in addition to academics and professors from Jordan University, Birzeit University and Cairo University.

The field research began after researchers were provided with tape recorders, batteries and cameras. The researchers were asked to reach an agreement with some of those interviewed to make a video recording of their narrations. In addition they were asked to collect some old photographs and take new photographs of those narrators who agreed. With regards to tape-recording the interviews it was necessary for the researchers to try their best to convince the narrators of the importance of being recorded while answering questions, and if the narrator refused to allow the interview to be recorded they were asked to put their signatures on the notes taken from the interview.

All the interviews conducted were eventually transcribed, edited and archived. This took extra time as it required a high degree of accuracy in order to first of all produce a readable text and secondly to ensure that the narration did not lose its distinctive qualities.

Some of the information collected from the interviews was analyzed using the program Statistical Package for the Social Sciences (SPSS). This analysis gave indications of the importance of some of the information. The researchers managed to conduct 132 interviews (117 with women and 15 with men). 33 of the women interviewed were from the age group 'over 75 years old' whilst 84 were 'over 55 years old'. All of the men interviewed were from the age group 'over 75 years old'. It is important to pay attention to the relative accuracy of this information given that the percentages only account for the ratio of those narrators who answered the questions and not all the narrators. This is in addition to the multiplicity of answers given by the narrators, which required the calculation of ratios based on the number of narrations and not the number of narrators. It also proved necessary to record the number and gender of narrators who answered specific questions.

Practical Difficulties Encountered while doing the Research

There were difficulties with finding and selecting alternative narrators in the event that some failed to show up. Other difficulties were created by those narrators who had to go back home immediately after either the preliminary interview or the first session. This meant that the Field Researcher was required to conduct one interview with a narrator on a specific day and another one with the same narrator a few days later. Age was also a problem especially for those who were over 75. Their bad health and unstable mood made it difficult for some researchers to set up appointments for interviews and to convince narrators of the necessity of recording and in some cases videoing their interviews. As a result, the Field Researchers had to increase their efforts to convince some narrators of the significance of the interview and the necessity of the audio-visual documentation of their narrations. Additionally in some cases, to make the narrators feel more comfortable, interviews had to be organized differently. For instance a group of narrators and researchers had to be present at the same time to conduct a specific interview or a number of interviews. This, however, did not provide an ideal atmosphere for interviews to be properly conducted as it led to lack of concentration on the part of both the narrators and the researchers. The narrators also voiced fears about their security because of their previous political affiliations to The Ba'ath Party, The Communist Party and The Arab Nationalist Movement.

Some of the difficulties encountered during the research had to do with the field researchers themselves. Some of the researchers were working on a full-time basis while others were part-time and therefore some were able to complete all aspects of the research while others were not and in some cases interviews had to be carefully reviewed and new appointments with the narrators had to be arranged for a third

Part 1: The Political Participation of Palestinian Women

session. On some occasions the transcription of the interviews had to be checked more than once to ensure that the whole content of the interview had been properly transcribed, requiring the researcher to listen to the recorded interview multiple times. Additionally, some of the researchers had to leave before completing their work and, in fact, two of them got married and moved to a different area from where their research was being conducted. This required the Researcher to appoint new Field Researchers and to train them in order to complete the research.

The researchers also faced some problems in travelling to the various areas where the research was being conducted, and there were some difficulties with the nature of the method of oral history from a feminist perspective which required a high degree of accuracy and the need to do more than three or four interviews with each narrator. This is in addition to the inherent sensitivity of writing such a history from a feminist perspective which required increased effort throughout the entire research process.

Despite the training given to the field researchers in Cairo, much of their real training took place in the field while they were doing the interviews and then afterwards when they were transcribing them and presenting the collected material in a typed or written text.

Chapter One

The Political Participation of Palestinian Women before the 1936 Palestinian Revolt

Introduction

A survey of accounts of the pre-1936 political participation of women in current history books gives us little and sometimes contradictory information. Researchers point to a gap in the historiography of the period; whilst some historical sources[12] record the establishment of the Association of Arab Palestinian Women in Jerusalem in 1929 (whose activities were then stopped in 1932) there is no information about the role of women from 1932-1936, as noted by the researcher Rosemary Sayegh in the introduction to the book *Portraits of Palestinian Women*.[13] The history books mention the significance of the 1933 uprising but they do not acknowledge the active role that women played in it. An example of this active participation was the protest organized by Palestinian women against the visit of British officials on Friday, 15th April, 1933, which took place in spite of heavy rain. This protest represented a challenge to the watchful eyes of the British police and proved the women's courage and political intelligence. The demonstration marched forward to the Mosque of Omar, where a Christian lady, Mrs. Mateel Maghnam, delivered a speech from the rostrum of the mosque, an unprecedented event at that time. Likewise, when the procession reached the Church of the Holy Sepulchre, a Muslim lady, Mrs. Tarab Abdulhadi delivered a speech before the Christ's Sepulchre. Such events indicate the deep awareness and insight of the urban women's movement at that time.

As far as rural women are concerned, we were unable to find any historical record of their political activity and role during the period in question. Given that the activities and role of women, in particular rural women, has been overlooked in this way one aim of our research is to investigate the existence of a group known as "The Comrades of

Al-Qassam", and if it did ever exist, the nature of its work and the names of those women who were members of it. The group named "The Comrades of Al-Qassam" was revealed by a narrator from Al-Yarmouk Camp, Damascus to the researcher Rosemary Sayegh, and is mentioned in her introduction to the book *Portraits of Palestinians Women*.[14] However there is no evidence of this group in recorded history and therefore research and investigation is necessary.

1933 Intifada

The narrator **Bahjat Abu Gharbiyah** talks about a significant march of women in 1933 during which a confrontation between the women and the British police took place. This narrative, despite being the only one of its kind, has a special significance because of the importance of the event itself and because the narrator was an eyewitness to that march.

"I don't have further details. But as I told you, in 1933 a demonstration took place in Jerusalem, and the women also organized a demonstration guarded by young men. The police did not respect them, but rather hit them and tried to disperse them. However, they formed a delegation to meet with the High Commissioner as there was officially some democracy. They met the High Commissioner and handed him a memorandum, then they went to all the foreign embassies. These were some of the things I witnessed."[15]

The Comrades of Al-Qassam

The quantitative analysis of the interviews with 43 narrators (thirty-seven females and six males) shows that 39.5% of them (15 females and 2 males) have heard of a women's group called "The Comrades of Al-Qassam" or "Al-Qassam Comrades", and 60.5% (12 females and 4 males) have not.

The narrators **Su'ad Tawfeeq Abu So'ud** and **Haroun Hashem Rasheed** emphasized that they had heard of the group, saying:

"Yes, we have heard of the group called Al-Qassam Comrades."[16]

"I read about them, and I have an idea about their roles."[17]

Of the women who had heard of the group, none knew the date of its formation and only one of them knew how it was dissolved. Sa'adeh Al-

Kilani, who according to some female narrators was one of the group's members, accounts for its dissolution:

"The group broke up upon the death of Al-Qassam. We haven't heard of the group since then."[18]

Five female narrators and one male narrator mentioned members of the group: **Su'ad Abu So'ud, Samira Abu Ghazaleh, Awatef Abdulhadi, Sa'adeh Al-Kilani, Isam Abdulhadi and Ahmad Mahmoud Al-Zaben**:

"There was a woman from Al-Falouja who took part in the group. I don't remember her name, but most likely it was Um Ali or something similar! She was 60 years old. My father, may Allah have mercy upon him, used to tell us about her. He often said he had never seen such a great woman. Although she was from Al-Falouja, she would carry her weapon and go there."[19]

"Yea, actually I have heard of it. One of them was Fatima Ghazal, in addition to others, but I didn't read or find clear information about this."[20]

"As I told you, I only remember Zulaikha Al-Shihabi and Tarab Abdulhadi."[21]

"I knew Ruqayya Al-Houri who was a member of the group. She was from Haifa. Mrs Isam can tell you about her."[22]

"Of the Al-Qassam cell members we knew Ruqayya Houri from Haifa. Members were more from Haifa and Acre than from Nablus."[23]

"There was my cousin Nayefa Al-Zein who lived in the same town as Ezzedin Al-Qassam. I can't remember all the names, but they were all assistants of Al-Qassam. Of them, one was called Su'ad, she was from the Acre district and she used to come to see my cousin. There was also one from Safad, who lived in my town. I knew about seven or eight of them. In my town of Al-Teera, women were not allowed to go out and mix with men, except the old women who used to help with washing their clothes because they used to train in Mount Carmel, and they used to prepare food for them too. Most of them were over 50 years of age. Among them was Gharibah Al-Sheikhah and Alhajjeh Aisha Abu Gheida' Al-Shoukaneyyah."[24]

As for the nature of the activities of the group, only six out of the fifteen female narrators who had heard of the group could identify the tasks undertaken by the group members. Two narrators said they were military (Khadra Mustafa Al-Sari and Samira Abu Ghazaleh) and the other four said they undertook socio-political tasks, as seen in the testimony of Adala Touqan.

"It was them who used to transfer weapons to the young men."[25]

"I read some things but I have forgotten. For example, some of them used to train with the weapons and some took part, but I can't recall their names. I can remember that as a little girl living in Nablus where there are mountains, all the families used to cook food and send it to them, and money and clothes were collected. Quite a few of the group's members used to train with the weapons, and others functioned as supporters of the militants."[26]

"His comrades always offered him food and a place to rest, and they usually welcomed him into their houses."[27]

With regards to the male narrators, both of the two who knew of the group gave an explanation of the nature of the women's tasks. The narrator and eyewitness **Ahmad Al-Zaben**, spoke in his testimony about the significant role of women in food provision, and the other narrator, **Haroun Hashem Rasheed**, discussed in his testimony his understanding of that role and the nature of the tasks:

"In the town of the Sheikh, every woman used to offer assistance to Sheikh Al-Qassam, but I can't remember their names."[28]

"Those women were illiterate village women. Most of them had husbands who were fellows of Al-Qassam, and they supported them. Some of them acted as nurses. The Al-Qassam revolt did not have any source of support, so those women played the role of providing funds, medical care and being on watch for the rebels. Some women were usually on watch in certain places and would make a signal to alert the rebels to any danger. I have read about this, I'm sure I have. I have read about this in many sources but I didn't witness it. I also learnt of it from more than one old man who witnessed that period. Those women played a key role in making the mission of Al-Qassam successful. For instance, they managed on more than one occasion to prevent the British from capturing the rebels."[29]

When the female narrators were asked if they knew any woman from the Al-Qassam group, only one - Khazneh Al-Khateeb - gave a positive

Chapter 1: The Political Participation before the 1936 Revolt

answer. On the contrary neither of the male narrators gave a positive answer.

"No! No! I was in Haifa. I haven't ever seen any of the women, except the wife of Sheikh Ateyyah: the group's name was the Black Palm."[30]

Despite their inability to name any women who were members of these groups, the two male narrators were able to identify the nature of tasks undertaken by women within the group of Al-Qassam. One of them said the tasks were military in nature while the other said they were socio-political. Similarly of the six women who replied to the question about the nature of the group's activities four said they were military, and two said they were socio-political.

"They usually provided them with water and ran alongside them to help whoever fell down and attend to them. The daring women would carry a weapon whereas the timid ones would not. As I told you, I myself carried a weapon and fired it twice before my husband took it away. Although some women didn't have the nerve to carry weapons, they used to help with food and water, and travel with the rebels to help whoever might fall down to stand up again or sprinkle water onto his face."[31]

"I told you! My house was a shelter for the injured, the martyrs and the local weapons."[32]

When we read the testimonies of the narrators and investigated the existence of a women's group called "Al-Qassam Comrades" or "The Comrades of Al-Qassam", we discovered inconsistency in the narrators' statements as well as uncertainty concerning the existence of such a group. The research indicators pointed towards the existence of women who worked with Sheikh Ezzedin Al-Qassam without being organized into a specific group with the name "Al-Qassam Comrades".

Of those narrators who had heard of the group, most seemed confused about it and none could name more than five female members of it. When we examined these names, we excluded the testimony of a female narrator who mentioned the names of urban women – Zulaikha Al-Shihabi and Tarab Abdulhadi - who played political roles and had no relations with rural women. We also doubted the narrations that included the names of women who worked with Al-Qassam, but did not emphasize the existence of a particular group. An example of such a narration is that of the only female narrator who showed knowledge of how the group was dissolved - Sa'adeh Al-Kilani - but whose narration was, in fact, based on inference and intuition rather than information.

She said "I knew Ruqayya Al-Houri who was a member of the Al-Qassam group" however, she then referred us to another narrator for more details: "Mrs Isam can tell you about her and about Haifa." When the narrator Isam Abdulhadi was asked for further information, she replied: "Of the members of Al-Qassam cells we knew Ruqayya Al-Houri" Although this narrator corroborates what Sa'adeh Al-Kilani said, we discovered, once we investigated her narration, that her knowledge of this subject was based on hearing some talk about the group:

"People used to talk about Ruqayya Al-Houri. I gave you some examples. People used to say that Sathej Nassar was not one of the Al-Qassam Comrades, but rather a struggling writer at that time."[33]

When we sought further information from Sa'adeh Al-Kilani, her replies reflected limited information about the subject, a focus on the women who worked with Al-Qassam, and more generally activist women during the Revolt:

"My husband usually ordered us to prepare food because they used to supply the rebels with weapons."[34]

When we asked about the specific tasks undertaken by women in that group, we discovered that what we got was little more than suppositions from some narrators of what such tasks might have been, rather than an account based on information and testimonies from eyewitnesses. This was clear in the testimony of Haroun Hashem Rasheed who said "I have read about them, and I have an idea about their roles."[35]

None of the narratives emphasized the existence of a group called "Al-Qassam Comrades" although some emphasized the existence of women who worked with Ezzedin Al-Qassam. They were: Um Ali from Al-Falouja, Fatima Ghazal, Ruqayya Al-Houri, Khazneh Al-Khateeb, Nayefa Al-Zaben, and Su'ad from Acre district, Gharibah Al-Sheikhah from Safad and Alhajjeh Aisha Abu Gheida' Al-Shoukaneyyah, as mentioned in the interviews with Ahmad Ali Al-Zaben, Samira Abu Ghazaleh, Sa'adeh Al-Kilani, Isam Abdulhadi and Khazneh Al-Khateeb.

Chapter Two

The Political Participation of Palestinian Women in the 1936 Revolt

Introduction

Contrary to the pre-1936 period, recorded history has not denied the participation of women in the 1936 Palestinian revolt nor has it denied their participation in Palestinian economic and agricultural life. However some sources, including those which rely on oral history, have considered the participation of women to be marginal and subsequently they only mention their role in providing food for the rebels.[36] This narrow reading of the role of women encouraged the researchers to embark on an in-depth research study on the nature of women's participation and their various roles in the 1936 revolt. In addition, the research project adopted the feminist perspective as a method to write the political history of women during that period. Such a method enables researchers to do in-depth interviews with women and allows them to ask narrators about the meaning of the terms they use in their evaluation of women's work.[37] It further allows them to delve deep into the inner, silent and unrevealed thoughts and feelings of the narrators.

The Role of Women in the Revolt

Seventy-five female and fourteen male narrators (a total of eighty-nine narrators) answered the question on the role of women in the 1936 revolt. 98.8% of the narrators who answered the question asserted that there was a role played by women in the revolt, while only one narrator said that she didn't know (making up 1.12% of the narrators). Not a single female or male narrator denied the participation of women in the revolt. However the narrations showed that some narrators, particularly

Part 1: The Political Participation of Palestinian Women

those from rural areas, despite their recognition of the participation of women in the revolt, have nevertheless belittled their role. Prevailing cultural values have deepened society's negative perceptions of women and their stereotypical roles which has as a result made people underestimate the importance of these roles.

The researchers asked the narrators whether they were aware of the role of women when they were children (in the 1930s) asking the question "What did women do when you were a child?".

The narrators; Khadra Mustafa Al-Sari and Shams Al-Titi and Um-Kayed give quick answers along the same lines: "They didn't do anything: there were those who would milk the sheep, shake the milk, lay down on the carpet, and some who were cultivating, this is what we Arabs did, we were peasants."[38]

"Our main focus was on food, water, banquets, slaughtering of animals and you know what we were so busy at home and in a state of mess."[39]

"I swear to God they didn't know anything about politics and they didn't see or meet anybody, they would harvest the field and then they would go back home. They were not open and free like the women of today."[40]

"The women were just in despair, punching their faces with their hands, this was what they used to do, and this was what they were able to do. They would tear off their clothes and punch their faces with their hands. This was what we were able to do. We didn't dare carry weapons and go to fight! We couldn't."[41]

However, when the narrators become more at ease and were able to open their hearts and minds and put aside what they have inherited in terms of their values and explain what they meant, their positive role, which they were raised to deny, began to appear, reflecting not only their specific role but the role of rural women during that period. There were many narrations relating to exactly what role women played in the Palestinian revolt. Narrators mentioned more than one role for women, and often their political, social and economic roles got mixed up, and it became difficult to separate them from one another. However the research has tried to confine itself to those narrations which reflected the socio-political roles of women. Those narrations which addressed the socio-political roles of women amounted to 150 (128 by women and

Chapter 2: The Political Participation in the 1936 Revolt

18 by men), whereas the narrations that discussed the military role of women amounted to 75 (65 by women and 10 by men). As you would expect the number of narrations exceeded the number of narrators given that the narrators often brought up, in the same interview, many different roles that women played.

Despite the fact that the narrators did not give an accurate classification of the roles women played, the analysis of the results of the research clearly indicated these various roles. The political-social role was the most obvious among a small educated group of narrators especially those who were active in women's societies. It was important to broaden the concept of politics to include everything that is related to politics both directly and indirectly. It was necessary to abolish the separation of the private from the public and consider both kinds of activities in order to acknowledge and understand the contributions of women.

It wasn't possible to look at the social roles of women within the context of charitable social activity - which is political in content and aim - given that only 4 of the total narrations given actually talked about charitable social activity as being part of the socio-political role of women. Similarly of the total narrations, only one narrator talked about social-religious activities and one about women's social activities. This led us to confine our examination of the activities and interactions of women to two main roles: socio-political and military.

Whilst military activities cannot be separated from politics completely a separation between the socio-political role and the military role is made for the purposes of our research. The fact that some narrators claimed women had no involvement in military activity whilst others specifically mentioned women's military contributions[42], led us to review the kind of involvement some women had with arms, and examine the role of women in this area, which required classifying this as a military role.

The Socio-Political Role

We received many answers that can be classified as part of the socio-political role. According to these answers women played the following roles: they provided food, prompted or incited people to action, transmitted news, carried letters, hid and smuggled rebels, camouflaged and designed methods to enable men to escape from the hold of the

British army, in addition to throwing stones at soldiers and setting fires for the rebels. They also provided first aid for the injured and worked in the post-office in order to maintain the secrecy of phone calls. In addition to all of that women also established unions and societies and participated in political conferences.

The Role of Women in Providing Food

The role played by women in providing food for the rebels was a major one. This was made clear by the narrations as 58 of the narrators (50 female and 8 male) talked about this role in some detail. This role has been mentioned by recorded history, however it was not given much significance and its political and social dimensions have not been outlined. For example the inhabitants of Qaqoun village were recorded as having said that the participation of women was marginal.[43] Many history books relied on statements like this without inspecting or examining their historical reliability.

The narrator, **Kamal Abdul Rahim**, talked about a woman from Bal'a by the name of Um Irmaih, who is a reflection of what has been established in popular memory about the role of women during that historical period.

"She was with the rebels; they used to stay at her house. She would accompany them to the battlefronts and take them food and water; when there were battles in Bal'a at Al-Mintaar, many of the women living in Bal'a used to send food and water to the rebels. The battles would last hours at Al-Mintaar. Um Armih was their leader and the rebels in Bal'a used to go to her house to have a rest."[44]

The narrator **Rasmiyyeh Al-Barghouthi (Um Al-Abed)** also spoke about her participation in providing food for rebels:

"We were organized: we used to wake up early, wash, put on our clothes, go distribute some food, and then by ten in the morning we would participate in demonstrations. At night we would take food to the rebels."[45]

The narrator **Kamleh Shneik** talked about both her activity and that of Fatmeh Khaleel[1]: "I swear to God, I used to bake bread on the thin sheet iron (bread or baking tin), when the taboon was not available, they used to ask me to bake bread on the baking tin as they wanted to take food to the rebels who were in the western part of the village. I used to prepare the dough and then bake on the baking tin even when the dough was not yet ready (it had not yet fermented). The bread coming from the taboon would not be hot or ready or smoked enough but we just used to give them everything, all the bread. And my husband used to give the women eggs, halaweh (a type of sweets) and sardines and they would then go to deliver all the food to the rebels. I didn't go. Not only me but all the women in our neighborhood used to stay home and prepare food for the rebels. The families of Abu Jamal and Abu Hammoudeh used to prepare food and those who lived close to us would say let's get food from this family and that family and then everything they collected would be well wrapped and taken to the rebels by Fatmeh Khaleel."[46]

The narrator **Latifa Mahmoud Darbas** from Bal'a, Tulkarm, talked in great detail about the role of women: "We would take food and water to the rebels. They would eat lunch and then move from one mountain to the other and when the British soldiers would see us walking and ask us where we were going, we would answer that we were going to the place where charcoal was made and we would say that we were going there to put out the burning charcoal with the jars of water we were carrying on our heads. Then we would go to where the rebels were hiding and from there we would move from one mountain to the other carrying bundles which we used to hide weapons. We would carry them on our heads and take them to other parts of the mountain and give them to the rebels who would be waiting for us.

- What were these bundles?

- We would carry bundles of logs or firewood and we would hide weapons in between the wood. We would carry these bundles and then take them and move them to another place, this meant that we had to move with the rebels from one place to the other, from this mountain to that mountain; we were living in areas such as Um Al-Darj, on a

---

1. The first martyr who was mentioned by recorded or written history: Fatmeh Al-Khaleel Ghazal

Part 1: The Political Participation of Palestinian Women

temporary basis, where we used to graze flocks of sheep. I had a cousin whose name was Ragheb Darbas, he was the leader of the revolt in the north and they used to call him Abu Durra; we all, my sisters, women from our neighborhood and myself, we used to go and take food and water to him and the rebels.

- You and who?

- My sisters and women from the neighborhood.

- What were their names?

- One woman was Zahideh, my sister, another Safa', another Salha Al-Safouri and a fourth Rabi'a Ziadeh, they all used to go to the rebels and give them food.

- Where did you go, to the mountains?

- Yes we went to the mountains."[47]

The narrator **Bahjat Abu Gharbiyah** described the role of women with the following words:

"During the 1936 revolt, to which I was an eyewitness and a participant, in the cities there were attacks and counter-attacks, while in the mountains there were armed guerrillas; guerilla warfare and this kind of fighting was mainly in rural areas. In the village of Bal'a[1], for instance, I saw with my own eyes, especially after 10 or 11 at night, groups of women, some carrying bread, others carrying water and others carrying cheese. And they would all be shouting and asking the rebels whether any of them had not yet eaten dinner?"[48]

Despite the fact that such a role was well-known and recognized, some women tried to downplay or even deny it. For example the narrator **Fatmeh Al-Khateeb** tried to deny this role during her preliminary interview, leading the researcher to attempt to investigate the issue further in the second interview:

"- Ok, when the rebels were in the mountains, who was it that used to go and deliver food for them? You and who else?

- I would go to the mountain! But the men would send the food.

- You then would cook and provide food for them?

---

1. Bal'a is a Palestinian village in the district of Tulkarm

Chapter 2: The Political Participation in the 1936 Revolt

- Yes, we used to boil eggs, make the dough and then bake the bread, milk the cows and then heat the milk and send everything.

- Men would go up to the mountains then?

- Yes

- She told me that you used to go to a village by the name of Irribin.

- The olives and our land are in Irribin (Khirbat Irribin)

- You used to take food for the rebels in Irribin and on the way back what would you do?

- What?

- Tell me, when you used to take the food to the rebels in Irribin what did you exactly do? You already told me about the incident yesterday?

- Oh, yes we used to provide them with food and then we would leave, we would go and harvest the olives and there we found the rebels hiding between the olive trees. We had to leave of course because we couldn't stay there while men were around!"[49]

In the preliminary interview, the narrator had mentioned how they used to send the rebels food and in order not to arouse the suspicion of the British soldiers on the way back they would pretend that they were harvesting olives.

As well as providing food the narrators also described making some financial contributions to enable the rebels to buy weapons and ammunitions. Many narrators mentioned that they would not hesitate to sell their own jewelry in order to support and maintain the revolt. The narrator Fattoum Al-Ghurairi mentioned this:

" - Where did the rebels get weapons from during 1936? From where did they manage to get the money to buy weapons?

- They would get money from their families who would sell everything at their disposal in order to buy weapons.

- They would sell their jewelry or anything else they had to provide money?

- Women would sell their jewelry.

- How do you think the rebels managed to buy weapons?

Part 1: The Political Participation of Palestinian Women

- Did you sell anything?
- Of course I did!
- What did you sell?
- I sold the gold that I had, which we used to call "Kirdan" as well as rings and earrings, not like the ones that I am wearing now. I bought all of these from Beirut."[50]

With regards to urban women, the narrator **Wadee'a Qaddourah Khartabil** asserted that they used to help the rebels by collecting money from families. Such work required organized efforts, which in most cases was done by women's societies.

"In the 1936 revolt, we used to do all the necessary preparations to help men. Those who were politically active or who were involved in guerilla work (meaning the rebels as this was how they were classified during the 1936 revolt) would come to us in order to ask for our help. We used to help them financially and morally as well as helping their families by giving them money. We would collect money from families who were ready to make a donation. They were happy to donate what they could afford because they were certain that their donations were being spent on the national cause."[51]

Women's Role in Incitement

The role women played in inciting other people was a major one, coming second in importance only to the role they played in providing food for the rebels. Thirty-five narrators talked about this issue (thirty-two female narrators and three male narrators). The term incitement includes all those who played a role in motivating and encouraging people to act and in raising their political awareness. It also includes participation in demonstrations.

According to two of the narrators interviewed, **Anis Al-Sayegh** and **Ahmad Maw'ed**, Arab women's cries of joy (Zaghrouda) was known to be one of the more effective ways of motivating and inciting men to fight the British soldiers. It had a very positive impact on their mood and helped create a sense of deep solidarity in the resistance to British colonialism:

"The role of women was to show courage vis-à-vis guerilla action. A mother would trill cries of joy when her son died as a martyr and people would go to her house to congratulate her. In general, mothers never prevented their sons from participating in the resistance against British Mandate. On the contrary, they would at the very least agree to allow their sons to carry guns and fight British soldiers and then at the end of the day come back home. They would encourage or at least consent to what their sons were doing and in the event that they died as martyrs, they would consider their martyrdom an honor."[52]

"- After the end of a battle a woman would trill cries of joy and other women would go to her house to express their condolences. When they went to one woman she said 'You should congratulate me on my son's wedding' and then she added 'If I had another son I would ask him to join the rebels, you shouldn't express your condolences.'

- Does this mean that she only had one son?

- She didn't have any other sons, he was her only son. The woman said 'I told them if I had another son I would ask him to join the rebels, this was God's will, God gave me that son, you should congratulate me on his wedding day, you should not express words of sorrow.'

In reaction all the women in the village and in other areas trilled cries of joy. They would all express such joy and they wouldn't care anymore about what would happen to their sons or the sons of their neighbors or get concerned about those rebels who hadn't yet returned home."[53]

In many cases the women's cries of joy were also accompanied with songs. However, these were not sung only to incite men to fight the British but rather they were expressions of joy, especially after a victorious battle, reflecting the sense of happiness women had for victory and their hope that the rebels would win additional victories. The narrator **Latifa Al-Taher** elaborated on this point:

"We woke up in the morning and we clapped and sung and uttered trilling cries of joy and then everybody asked 'What's the matter?' The answer was that the rebels were victorious in Acre. They were able to force the British soldiers out of Acre and that would subsequently mean that the revolt was successful in that city."[54]

Women would sing and shout cries of joy in times of victory, but they would also sing songs of encouragement when they took the food to the rebels. Women therefore played multiple roles – encouragement and the provision of food and water - simultaneously.

Part 1: The Political Participation of Palestinian Women

"Palestinian women deserve to wear shoes made of gold. At the beginning of every battle you would find them walking alongside the rebels carrying jars on their heads to provide them with water whenever they needed it. They wouldn't leave the armed rebels alone. It was only the young, active and energetic girls like you, not old women like me, who used to accompany the fighters and carry water jars and provide them with food and water. There was a woman who was known as Khadra, she was from a family by the name of Alhajj Hasan, and she was one of those women who never missed a battle; she was present at every battle. When the Israelis occupied Al-Barwah, Palestinian armed rebels launched attacks against the Israelis and were able to recapture Al-Barwah. For Khadra Al-Sheikh Khaleel, who was also the sister of Abu As'ad, the incident was so special that she stood on the roof of the Mosque and began to celebrate by singing and proclaiming to everyone that the rebels had been successful in recapturing Al-Barwah."[55]

It should be noted here that as a cultural habit, singing and trilling cries of joy was common among rural rather than urban women. Urban women, especially those who were fortunate enough to get some education, played a role in politically inciting female students at schools by raising their awareness of political and social issues and through delivering politically charged speeches and talks. They were also active in organizing symposiums to raise awareness and in forming awareness committees under the umbrella of women's societies.

Despite the fact that there were not many narrations on this issue, it was important to note the role played by women in inciting and encouraging people to participate in political activities because it is a role which has not been fully acknowledged. Recorded history has not made note of this activity and therefore oral historians should highlight this role when it is mentioned in the narrations.

With regards to their contribution to political awareness, **Issam Hamdi Al-Huseini** and **Izdihar Al-Shurafa** talked about their role in indirectly raising the awareness of students:

"We used to use the opportunity of participating in some school activities, such as school symposiums, to bring up issues and ideas pertaining to British colonialism and other political matters."[56]

"So in reality various issues that would raise political awareness were brought up."[57]

Chapter 2: The Political Participation in the 1936 Revolt

According to the narrator **Widad Al-Ayyoubi** urban women played an active role in encouraging and inspiring women to be politically active.

"The Women's Union would organize various symposiums to which prominent figures from Jerusalem and other places would be invited to talk about matters pertaining to the political situation in Palestine. At that time we didn't have any strong political organization to allow us to do anything serious. Activities were instead channeled through the youth groups and organizations, most commonly through the arrangement of symposiums."[58]

As the narrator **Wadee'a Qaddourah Khartabil** discussed, urban women, through their participation in women's societies, played a role in establishing committees that were active in raising the awareness of women in rural areas:

"We formed awareness committees and we would go to the villages and talk about various political issues that would help raise the awareness of villagers about Palestine. We tried to figure out how we could help the villagers understand what was going on in our homeland and at the same time maintain a good relationship with the people in the district of Tulkarm, with the rebels and the women's union as well. In this way we were able to work and be active alongside the rebels.

- Which villages did you go to?

- We went to Thinnaba, to Taibeh, to Bal'a, to many villages."[59]

Political incitement was directly connected to demonstrations. A political speech, which was usually delivered by an active and energetic girl or woman for the purpose of encouraging people to be active, would come as the culmination to a popular demonstration.

Samiha Khaleel spoke to her interviewer about a speech that she delivered at the Mosque:

"It was the first time that I had ever participated in a demonstration. Young men used to gather at the Mosque, but they wouldn't go outside for security reasons so our gathering was inside the Mosque and I gave a very short speech. I had to shout while I was giving the speech because of the noise - I swear to God nobody was able to hear what I had to say - but I was very happy that night, thinking about how I had been able to serve my nation by speaking out against the Balfour Declaration and against the selling of land. I also gave a talk in 1936."[60]

Part 1: The Political Participation of Palestinian Women

Maymanah Ezzedin Al-Qassam also talked about a speech that she gave at Al-Istiqlal Mosque[1], which has been confirmed by other narrators:

"They say that I delivered a speech but I don't know! I don't remember. They told me that I gave a speech at the Mosque, at which mosque? I can't remember the name. In Haifa? Al-Istiqlal? I don't know anything! I loved my people and my nation; but I don't remember what I said!"[61]

But when the researcher asked the narrator whether she participated in the demonstrations, the answer was positive:

"- You did participate in the demonstrations? Don't you remember?

- I participated, I participated"

The narrator **Khadra Al-Sari** talked about the speech that was delivered by Maymanah at Al-Istiqlal Mosque, indicating that such an unusual event remained in the memory of Maymanah's contemporaries:

"I don't know her name, the daughter of Ezzedin Al-Qassam. According to what my husband relayed to me the daughter of Ezzedin Al-Qassam was giving a speech at the mosque to an audience made up mostly of veiled women, when she pulled a revolver out of her purse and said with a voice full of passion 'I shall kill those who refuse to revenge the killing of my father'. This was what my late husband told me, and in fact on the same night Ahmad Nayef and another girl who was close to Al-Qassam's family revenged the killing of Ezzedin."[62]

The narrator **Issam Hamdi Al-Huseini** talked about a demonstration that was led by Rabab Al-Huseini from Gaza who gave a very passionate and enthusiastic speech at both the great mosque and the church.

"I remember when I was still a student my parents used to always talk about the demonstrations and rebellions that were taking place in different parts of Palestine. In fact my sister Rabab even participated in one demonstration and it was the only demonstration that ever took place in Gaza. My mother made an Arab flag for her which she carried. Then she went to the great mosque and gave a very inciting and enthusiastic speech urging and encouraging people to fight. At the end of her speech she threw the flag to where the crowds were gathering

---

1. The narrator was trying to deny her role, not because she didn't remember it, but because of her reluctance to reveal any information

and said 'I am giving you this flag, go fight and start a Jihad against the British'. Some of the Palestinian youth that were present at the mosque carried the flag and went marching in a demonstration that culminated in the killing, by the British soldiers, of one young man from Gaza. She then went to the church and delivered a similar speech. In reaction to Rabab's political activity, the British authorities summoned her father as they considered him to be responsible for his daughter's actions. Her father was however able to convince them that he had nothing to do with his daughter's political involvement."[63]

The narrators **Haroun Hashem Rasheed** and **Abdul-Qader Yaseen** further talked about the leadership role of Rabab Al-Huseini which clearly demonstrates how her political activity remained alive in the memory of the narrators:

"At the end of Rabab's speech, people gathered outside the great mosque and began to march in a demonstration which included both Muslim and Christian clergymen. They all marched towards Omar Al-Mukhtar Street, heading eastward towards where the British government buildings were located at that time, buildings which have now been replaced by Al-Zahra School and the Post Office. While the demonstrators were marching, the far end of the street was blocked with barbed wires and the British soldiers were standing there ready to fire. At that moment one of the British soldiers threatened to fire at any person who would dare march one step further. The demonstration stopped immediately; however a young energetic girl by the name of Rabab, who being carried on the shoulders of the demonstrators and holding the Palestinian Flag aloft, began to yell, urging the crowd to continue marching. That moment was so inflammatory that it incited a young man from Al-Sha'ban family to step forward and stand in between the soldiers and the crowd. The soldiers fired at him and he died a martyr. As a result the demonstrators got more aggressive and the situation deteriorated leading to more deaths. The British soldiers then imposed a curfew to control the crowd. What is important to note here is that the demonstration was led by a woman whose name was Rabab Al-Husseni. This further demonstrates that women were present all the time, participating in all kinds of political activities."[64]

"There was someone whose name was Rabab Al-Huseini who participated and led a demonstration in 1936 in Gaza. This was rather odd given that Gaza was more conservative than any other Palestinian

Part 1: The Political Participation of Palestinian Women

city. It was really strange to witness a demonstration led by a young energetic girl like Rabab! Perhaps she was more able to do that because her father was a prominent leftist thinker and because Rabab herself was highly aware and politically motivated which made it more normal for her to be at the forefront of the demonstration."[65]

Urban women were able to remember the names of those women who led and organized demonstrations as these women used to go to schools and ask the students to participate in various political activities and occasions. The narrators **Samira Khoury** and **Amneh Al-Wenni** confirmed this saying:

"That was what made us enthusiastic about political participation; when these young women used to come to our schools and ask us to leave and join the demonstrations. Amongst the women who used to come to schools was someone whose name was "Saba Al-Fahoum". She was older than us; I don't really know how old she was but I think she was in the 9th or 10th grade while I was, if I remember correctly, in the 2nd or 3rd grade. I was born in 1929 which means that I was probably only seven years old in 1936, I am not sure what age I was exactly, all I know is that I was in the 2nd or 3rd grade and girls who were in the 10th or 11th grade used to come to our classes and we used to consider them almost like our mothers, although they were teenagers, just teenagers. They would come and talk to us and after that we would want to go and participate in a demonstration. That woman Saba Al-Fahoum and another whose name was Masarra Kan'an and Imzayyen Khaleel Rashed, who I believe has died, in addition to Georgette Bishara; they would all come to us and we used to say out loud "Palestine, Palestine, freedom, freedom to Palestine" and then sing national songs, oh the songs! To be honest with you I have forgotten the songs but if Georgette Bishara and I try hard, we should be able to remember some of those songs, because she and others used to repeat them all the time. They used to teach us these songs and we would sing them in the demonstrations."[66]

"What else do I want to tell you?! When we were living at Al-Hijjawi's family house, a woman called Suheir came, she was the wife of 'Abdallah Al-Rimawi and she was leading a demonstration of forty women.

- Suheir or Suhaila?
- Suhaila (Abu Reesheh) yes you're right. She came with forty young

girls, all of them going on a demonstration. I left my children behind and I joined them, we went all the way to where my house was and then back again to where the demonstration started.

The important issue here was that she led the demonstration, carrying the flag all the way to the furthest point of our town. Then on our way back, while I was walking behind her, I asked her and the others whether they all would like to come to my house and drink tea?"[67]

The narrator **Samira Khoury** talked about demonstrations that were organized by some of the women's movements but which were feminist rather than political in nature and stressed demands like the need for women to stop wearing the veil. Such demonstrations have not been recorded in the history books that cover that period of time. This feminist awareness was particularly present amongst those women who were politically active, pointing to the connection between national and social liberation.

"We used to hear about demonstrations that were organized specifically to highlight women's struggle for social liberation and my mother was amongst those women who used to participate in these demonstrations. During the Palestinian revolt they used to wear the veil, however there were some moments during the thirties when women voiced their rejection of the veil and asserted their right to go out without it. Women had to struggle for their social liberation and they held demonstrations, I cannot remember which year exactly, but they did express their refusal to wear the veil. My mother used to wear the veil and one day they organized a demonstration and at the end of it they took off the veil. We also used to hear about demonstrations that were organized against colonialism and other issues, for instance in Jaffa and Nazareth there were demonstrations organized by Adele Qanaze' and Mateel Mghannam on women's rights issues."[68]

There were relatively few narratives about demonstrations by rural women with only two focusing specifically on the role of women in demonstrations. The narrator **Jamila Badran** from Dayr Al-Ghosoun Village, Tulkarm, talked about the role women played in demonstrations surrounding specific political events or when there were some injuries or deaths amongst the rebels and they were brought to the village to be treated or buried:

"When the rebels were brought to the village either injured or dead

Part 1: The Political Participation of Palestinian Women

how could anyone expect people to be silent? Why?! Aren't these our brothers and children?! If one of the injured or dead rebels was not her brother, he would be her son and if not her son he would be her cousin."[69]

Afifeh Hijaz from 'Anabta, Tulkarm talked about a woman leader from 'Anabta, who participated in the revolt and played an important role in organizing demonstrations:

"Ruqayya, the daughter of Sheikh Mamoud Abdul Rahim (who was well known for his courage) was a revolutionary during the revolt. She was always with the rebels, hiding in caves and in the mountains, in addition to her role in leading demonstrations and urging women to participate in political activities. We women used to meet and gather in the mosque and she would come to the mosque looking for us but she wouldn't dare say anything. In fact, nobody would dare say anything! She would come to the mosque to hide and she would find many of her relatives there who would ask her not to go back home. They were all afraid of being imprisoned and afraid of informers. So nobody would dare utter a word that might endanger his/her life. Ruqayya was in fact a very courageous woman; she would act and behave as if she were a man."[70]

Rural women participated in demonstrations specifically to honor the martyrs and the political activists, not necessarily to express their objection against the British as was the case with urban women. This can be seen clearly in the narration of **Jamila Badran**:

"When women heard about the death of their fathers or their sons they would become extremely sad and they would leave their houses and we would march behind them. They would walk in the streets shouting and expressing words of sorrow and when any young man from Al-Mintaar -between Bal'a and Bait Amrein - was injured or killed, they would say that the Jews were the cause of his death or of his injuries. When the British brought the dead or injured rebels to our neighborhood their families would come out and we women, regardless of our age, would follow them expressing our sorrow and our solidarity."[71]

With regards to the issue of political pamphlets, we were not able to get enough information about them from the interviews. We concluded from the narrations that women didn't give much attention or significance to such an issue. During that historical period the writing and distribution of pamphlets was part of the political activism of men, however the narrator **Amneh Al-Wenni** acknowledged that she was involved in hiding these political pamphlets and in her discussion of this matter she said:

"During the six months strike, I was about 12 years old or maybe a bit more. My husband's friends used to come to our house and bring pamphlets but I wasn't aware what these were exactly. They would just ask me to hide them somewhere safe in the house. Once, the British soldiers came to search our house at night and I was confused, I didn't know what to do or where to hide these pamphlets. I asked myself several times where should I hide them? In the end I simply dropped them in the well which was situated in the middle of the house so that they wouldn't discover who was behind the writing of the pamphlets. After that the British would come every other day searching the house and looking for anything that might give them a link to any political activity."[72]

The oral narratives clearly indicate that the carrying and dissemination of information for the rebels was an important role that was played by both rural and urban women; it was a crucial political role of real importance to the Palestinian revolt and the rebels. An example of such activity was when urban women used to inform rural women about the movements of the British soldiers and the rural women would in turn pass such information on to the rebels. Four female narrators and one male narrator talked about this specific role. Additionally, rural women had their own direct source of information from the rebels when providing food or smuggling weapons to them. The narrators **Ahmad Al-'Isawi** and **Khadra Mustafa Al-Sari** from Haifa and **Farha Al-Barghouthi** from Kobar, Ramallah discussed this issue:

"There was a sort of political relationship between urban and rural women in the different cities of Palestine but British intelligence forces made this a bit difficult. Women in urban areas were especially effective at passing information to rural women when they would meet each other in the cities. Rural women would in turn pass such information to the rebels. Whatever information this or that woman from rural areas was able to get from women in the cities, especially given that the British army's camps were stationed in the cities and all of their movements and activities were carried out there, they would simply pass on to the rebels. In addition, rural women would go up to the mountains carrying weapons and food to the rebels and they would pass news from one area to the other."[73]

"Men were not able to go to the city. I used to provide them with all the information that I was able to get from different sources."[74]

"When the area of Al-Nabi Musa was under siege one of us (we were both married then) would pass a piece of information to the other. Despite the siege we were able to find a way to go from one area to another using secret routes, and people used to pass on information that Al-Nabi Saleh was under siege and that the British were in this area or that area, or in Beit Rima."[75]

A different method was used with regards to the transmission of messages between the rebels. In one of the interviews **Widad Al-'Arouri** clearly described the role of women in transmitting messages between the rebels. She confirmed that women not only constituted a source of contact between the rebels but also played the role an intelligence officer would usually play but in the service of the revolt of course.

The narration of **Ahmad Al-'Isawi** further confirmed that both rural and urban women participated in such activities in a very effective way:

"My mother was a source of contact between the rebels. Whenever the rebels needed to send a message from 'Arura to Ramallah, my mother would travel from 'Arura to Um Al-Safa and Birzeit, and then go to Ramallah carrying the message they wanted her to transmit. My mother was illiterate and she used to pass on messages orally. The messages were usually about the rebels' transportation routes, the locations of weapons and other related matters. My mother was therefore a source of contact between the various rebel groups."[76]

"She was what they would usually call a spy; the British occupiers were mostly in the cities and there, some of the rural women, who were as decent and as active as you are, would make contact with those housewives living in the cities who many people would usually visit. Rural women would therefore travel to the cities wearing village dresses and when they arrived in the cities, they would change their dresses. The urban women would make the rural women feel at home and they would stay in the house talking about political issues and I am sure you know how much women start gabbling when they meet. The rural women would pass on whatever new messages they had. Then the six or seven women present at the house would hold a meeting and make a plan of how two them would try to catch a person who they suspected was a collaborator. One would open the door and the other would catch the collaborator. When you have such smart women what could the occupiers do?! These women would carry out the plan and of course they had the support of the rest of the group of women. Such initiatives on the part of both rural and urban women led to the discovery of many collaborators especially those who were active in rural areas. Women therefore played the role of intelligence officers as well as providing food and water to the rebels. So in general they had very effective role in the revolt of 1936."[77]

Women did not only hide and transmit messages but they were also active in hiding the rebels and helping transport them from one place to another as they did with a leader from Kufr 'Aboush by the name of Salim. Women helped him disguise himself by wearing one of their dresses and because of that the area where they were hiding him came under siege for eight days, this event was confirmed by the narrator **Ma'zouzeh Qasem** from Beit Reema, Ramallah:

"They helped Salim wear one of their dresses and with the assistance and cooperation of other women they were able to travel through 'Aboud to Kobar where he was finally able to find his way back home."[78]

The narrator **Kamleh shneik** from Qalqilya also talked about similar incidents of women hiding men, in particular those who came to the Mosque in the village.[79] Furthermore urban women also played an important role in hiding and smuggling some of the rebels. Tens of narrators talked about incidents of this kind. The narrator **Fatima Al-Darhali,** for instance, talked about the role her mother played in rescuing one of the rebels:

"One day one of the rebels came to our house requesting help. My mother let him in and gave him a pair of pajamas to wear. She hid him somewhere in our house and was able to convince the British soldiers that he had managed to escape through one of the windows."[80]

Urban women were like mobile warning systems protecting the rebels from the British. They would watch the roads, hide the rebels from the British soldiers and help them escape. Three women talked about such a role. The narrator **Jamila Sabbah,** from Qafin, Tulkarm, said:

Part 1: The Political Participation of Palestinian Women

"Oh, we used to hide them (the rebels) in the caves and keep an eye on them and when there was news that the British soldiers were coming towards the location of the caves, we would immediately warn them to withdraw."[81]

"I was a child then. The British soldiers used to go to the mountains while the rebels would go to the Mintaar. The soldiers would go to the mountains looking for the convoy of armed rebels arriving from Nablus and armed clashes would take place. Women and men from the village would act quickly by taking the injured rebels to the caves and some used to travel on horses to Tulkarm in order to bring doctors to treat the injured in Nablus. I used to stand at the opening of the cave which was covered with bundles of straw and when the soldiers arrived asking about the whereabouts of the rebels I would give them wrong directions sending them instead to places where they would find no rebels. The doctors on horses would then arrive to treat and look after the injured."[82]

Another narrator, **Ahmad Al-'Isawi**, talked about the role played by a woman from 'Anata, whose name was Jamila Abdul Jawad, in watching the roads and keeping a close eye on the movements of soldiers. She was very fast at alarming the rebels once she discovered that the soldiers were approaching the area where they were hiding and her actions in fact helped save many rebels from being caught by the soldiers:

"The woman from 'Anata was very talented. Cars used to travel to two towns; Mikhmas and 'Anata, and the cars which went to 'Anata had to take a roundabout route. Jamila was always cautious and she would ask the women there to watch the roads. We used to live in the eastern part of 'Anata and when the British soldiers came from the western part of the town to attack us Jamila would immediately go to where we were hiding giving the necessary alarms to those rebels who were staying in 'Anata to move to other parts of the town. Jamila would use all kinds of statements and words which were understood by the people living there, covertly informing them that the British soldiers were on their way to the town. If it were not for Jamila, many rebels including myself would have been caught by the soldiers."[83]

As well as protecting of rebels by hiding and smuggling them and by monitoring the roads and movements of the soldiers the role of women

Chapter 2: The Political Participation in the 1936 Revolt

also included obstructing the movement of soldiers by throwing nails onto the roads. In some instances they would engage in clashes with the soldiers as they tried to rescue rebels and they would throw stones at convoys of soldiers. Two female narrators and one male talked about this role.

The narrator **Amneh Al-Shinnawi** described how women used to throw nails on the roads to obstruct the movements of the soldiers:

"Our house was a refuge for many women, I apologize but I don't know their names. My uncle was a carpenter and as a result he used to have large quantities of nails. Women would come to our house, they would take what they could carry and they would then go and throw them on the roads where the British tanks were expected to be passing. These activities helped in obstructing the movements of the soldiers as, in most cases, they caused punctures in the wheels of the tanks.

- How many times did they manage to do that?

- Many times, in fact such activities were done continuously."[84]

Another narrator by the name of **Khadra Al-Sari**, talked about some women, especially very young girls, hitting soldiers with their hands in an attempt to rescue the rebels. It should be noted here that in contrast, during the first Palestinian uprising of 1987, it was the older women rather than the young that would clash with the Israeli soldiers.

Rafeeqa Hamada made reference to these events in her narration:

"Women would hit the soldiers while they were holding the rebels in an attempt to help them run away, and of course the soldiers did not dare shoot at them. One of my relatives, may God have mercy on him, was called Mohammad Tawfiq, and his son, who was a member of one of the popular councils, was called Ahmad (Abu Kamel). Mohammad Tawfiq, who was one of my cousins, lost four or five members of his family. When he was captured by the soldiers, and badly beaten, the women reacted in a similar way and began to hit the soldiers, trying to help the men run away from them. In fact we managed to rescue five or six men. Only young rather than old women used to participate in such actions."[85]

On the other hand **Su'ad Tawfeeq Abu So'ud** talked about the role of young girls in throwing stones at the soldiers (similar to the role played by women during the Palestinian uprising of 1987):

"In the demonstrations of 1936, we used to throw stones at the soldiers and the soldiers would start shooting at us but we were not scared. All the high school girls participated in stone throwing."[86]

In her interview, the narrator **Samira Abu Ghazaleh** confirmed the role that young girls played in throwing stones at the vehicles that were carrying Jewish immigrants from Jaffa to Jerusalem:

"Whenever I heard about those very young Palestinian children during the uprising of 1987, what immediately came to my mind were those days when I was still a high school student in the town of Ramla. We used to leave school and hide behind a rock in order to throw stones at those vehicles travelling from Jerusalem to Jaffa. The incidents of the uprising have brought back those memories. The uprising has in fact brought many back many memories of our actions; actions which we were punished for. But in any case we were at least able to express ourselves."[87]

The narrator **Ahmad Maw'ed** was a witness to the role women played in fighting and hitting the soldiers in protection of their houses and children:

"With regards to women I saw with my own eyes how women, my mother amongst them, used to hit soldiers with sticks whenever they tried to enter people's houses after declaring a siege on the town. My mother for instance used to carry a stick and she would use it to hit the British soldiers and prevent them from entering the house. Another woman whose name was Amina Mustafa, also from our town of Safouria, used to hit the soldiers with her hands. In some cases some of these soldiers would run away."[88]

The narrator **Rafeeqa Hamada** talked about women who were involved in fighting and hitting soldiers who had killed a number of rebels in Kweikat:

"Once, when I was still young, I was standing near my house when the soldiers came in the late afternoon. Meanwhile, someone from a village by the name of Sa'sa' was travelling through Acre on a donkey and when he got near the cemetery in Kweikat he was shot dead by soldiers. In fact at that incident the soldiers shot a total of nine people including my uncle (from my mother's side). The women reacted angrily and began to hit the soldiers as they shouted and mourned the dead. I began

Chapter 2: The Political Participation in the 1936 Revolt

to run and suddenly I saw two dead men in front of my house. I was the only young girl who participated in hitting the soldiers with my bare hands. They wouldn't dare shoot at us. But they went from house to house searching and moving men, old men and women from one place to another leaving nobody in their house."[89]

The narrator **Ali Musa Abu Yousef** also talked in his interview about a woman, Um Reem Abed Rabo from Hebron, who hit the commander of the British campaign in Hebron.[90]

What can clearly be seen from the narrator's statements is the spontaneous participation of women in clashes with the British soldiers, trying to help the rebels and resistance fighters run away.

We thought it necessary to inquire further about the extent to which narrations about the throwing of stones at the soldiers and Jewish immigrants were accurate as we wanted to ensure that such narrations were not getting mixed up in any way with memories of the role of women in the 1987 Palestinian Intifada. The worry we had was about the possibility of different narrations from the distant and very distant past getting mixed up during the interviews.

However, when we examined statements made by the writer Hala Al-Sakakini in her memoirs it confirmed what the narrators Samira Abu Ghazaleh and Su'ad Tawfeeq Abu So'ud said in their interviews about the role women played in throwing stones at the British soldiers. The only difference was that Hala discussed the special role of urban women in throwing stones at buses carrying Jewish immigrants as well as their role in throwing large nails on the roads to obstruct the movements of British tanks.[91]

In addition to helping the rebels in their clashes with the British army, prior to the eruption of the armed revolution of 1936, women also played an important role in the preparation of the torches which rebels used to help them burn the wells in Jewish towns. Only the narrator **Kamal Abdul Rahim** talked about such role. He was from Tulkarm and was the son of the leader of the Palestinian rebellion of 1936; the martyr Abdul Rahim Alhajj Ahmad. Kamal talked in his interview about the role of his aunt Halima (the mother of Ashraf Fadda) as well as other women whose names he did not mention.

"So many revolutionary incidents took place then. Women participated

Part 1: The Political Participation of Palestinian Women

in clashes with the soldiers and burned the Jewish wells that were situated west of Tulkarm with torches. Men and women used to go in groups carrying torches to burn the wells and other things that belonged to the Jews. The armed revolt of 1936 initially started at Al-Sayed mountain in Tulkarm when a group of men from there, including my father, began to shoot at British military convoys. Halima, together with other enthusiastic women, played a role in inciting and encouraging the rebels to shoot at the British army."[92]

The role of Palestinian women in inciting and encouraging people to resist the British Mandate continued during the six-month strike of 1936. Some narrators discussed the role women played in encouraging shopkeepers to close their shops and maintain the strike. As the narrator **Khazneh Al-Khateeb** confirmed, women would go from one place to another sticking inciting flyers on the doors of shops urging shopkeepers to close their shops and encouraging people to maintain the strike.

"- Like other women, I used to stick inciting flyers and publications on walls and the doors of shops.

- Did you stick publications on walls and doors?

- Yes

- You used to do this yourself?

- Yes, we would do it at night and we would watch out for people coming. Then if the rebels came we would give the flyers to them and then leave. It was very late at night; three o'clock in the morning.

- What time was it when you used to give the rebels the flyers? Three in the morning, really?! (..)

- Yes three in the morning, and they would stay up all night, the British government didn't suspect them. They would stay there all the time and they were a part of the Black Palm group."[93].

Maymanah Al-Qassam also confirmed women's involvement in incitement activities:

"- We would force all shopkeepers whose shops were open to close them.

- So you used to participate?

- Yes, but I wasn't on my own.

- But you used to do things
- Maybe I did!
- Were there women or men with you?
- Mostly women."[94]

The narrator **Arab Abdulhadi** mentioned in her interview a story about a nine-year old girl who stood next to the shop of cloth merchant urging him to close his shop:

"An interesting story was relayed to me by my mother Tarab Abdulhadi[1]. In Jaffa a man opened his cloth shop during the strike. A nine-year old girl came and stood next to his shop all day. At the end of the day the man asked the girl 'What do you want, you have been here since the morning? Would you like to buy a piece of cloth, or do you want anything else?' The girl said no and then in an enthusiastic tone she told him 'I need a piece of honor'. He answered 'What do you mean by a piece of honor?' And she said, 'the whole town is on strike, why aren't you on strike?' "[95]

Despite the fact that this story was relayed to the narrator by her mother, it is given weight by the fact that it very much corresponds with other stories discussing the role of Palestinian women in strikes and other related activities.

According to some narrators there was an outbreak of demonstrations in different towns during the strike. The narrator **Su'ad Tawfeeq Abu So'ud** talked about the demonstrations she and other girls enthusiastically participated in during that period. She confirmed that the girls were in the front rows of the demonstrations whilst the boys were behind them:

"Every day there was a demonstration. Our mothers used to make a Palestinian flag for us and you would see us carrying the flag and walking with the boys in Al-Moukhtar Street. We were only in sixth grade and we would march from one street to the other chanting national anthems."[96]

The narrator **Bahjat Abu Gharbiyah** talked about the very distinct role that rural women played during the sixth-month strike. During that

---

1. Tarab Abdulhadi was a Palestinian political activist who was involved in establishing women societies and unions

Part 1: The Political Participation of Palestinian Women

period rural women used rocks to close the roads that were used by the British army particularly when battles or clashes occurred between the soldiers and the rebels:

"Participation in the strike of 1936 was both spontaneous and broad, but the question is how? For example, there was a town here and another there and in between there was a road for cars. It was on such road that we could monitor the movements of the British army. So when a battle took place, it would be a result of an ambush. The inhabitants of the village or town on one side of the road and those from the town on the other side would go to the main road and fill it with rocks over a distance of one kilometer. Women, children and men would rush to the main road and would start filling it with stones and rocks. It used to take the British army three to four days to clear the road again or else they would force the inhabitants to clear the road themselves. During the strike there was broad participation on the part of women in obstructing the movements of the army through creating barriers of stones."[97]

With regards to the collective role of Palestinian women during the six-month strike, which was declared on the 19th of April 1936, we asked the narrators who had a good memory of that period to talk about their memories and to describe how they managed to cope with the situation at that time. We tried to learn from these conversations about the various roles that women played during the strike. A group of female narrators which included **Khadra Al-Sari** from Beir Al-Maksour, **Latifa Mahmoud Saleh Dirbas** from Bal'a, **Jamila Ahmad Sabbah** from Qafeen and **Shams Al-Titi** from Halhoul said the following:

"We used to hear about the strike. Our freedom of movement was restricted so we tried to manage with what we had available in our house. We used to decide what we would eat that day and the next day then we would make the dough and bake the bread. We would eat what was available - cheese, milk etc. - so we managed. Of course back then it was very difficult to travel to the city unlike today."[98]

"The shops were closed and it was prohibited to buy or sell anything. We used to go during the night to the shops to buy what we needed. The shops would open for a short period of time and then they would close again. At times the bakeries were banned from opening their shops

Chapter 2: The Political Participation in the 1936 Revolt

during the day and the night so we had to bake at home using a metal baking tin. With regards to vegetables, such as tomatoes, cucumbers, courgettes and the like, these were available from our gardens. What do you think people used to eat at that time? They would boil rice, make lentil soup and also cook a burgul (crushed wheat) meal."[99]

"Oh, I swear to God my dear, during one of those years we were completely out of flour, so we had to collect what we had available - ervil, lentil and barley - and grind it. Then we used to go and bake the dough made out of this mixture at the bakery in our town. Children would be crying out with hunger so we used to feed them this. With regards to the older people, they managed with difficulty to eat barley, lentil and ervil and we had to grind these three and feed our children with the mixture most of the times. As you might expect the British emptied the shops of almost everything, they threw out the entire contents of the shops in our town."[100]

"Do you think we were affected by the strike? On the contrary, our gardens were full of everything we needed. We used to plant, sow and harvest our land. We didn't care if the British stayed for a hundred years, we had everything we needed. We had our cows, sheep, etc. so we didn't care. Corn, barley and many other food products were very cheap to buy. We had hundreds of kilos of corn, barley, and lentil. We used to plant Egyptian cucumber, zucchini, onions, okra and many other vegetables and fruits on our land and we would use collected rain water to water our plants in the fields."[101]

With regards to urban women they dealt with the strike in a different way and tended to also describe the situation in a different way. This could be clearly seen in the statements made by the narrators **Su'ad Qarman** from Haifa, **Sa'adeh Al-Kilani** from Nablus and **Doumia Al-Sakakini** and **Salma Al-Huseini** from Jerusalem.

"My family left for Beirut during the strike, they went to Lebanon because during that time nobody was able to work and maintain a regular job. My father was a merchant; a wholesaler. The men stayed in town, in their shops - they used to sleep in one room and they would eat whatever was available at the restaurant - but we had to go to a central area in Haifa. We had friends at that time from Al-Deik family who were our partners in a cigarette company. However, as the area we went to was situated between a Jewish town and an Arab town near the border, our friends thought that it was a bit dangerous for us to stay there so they asked us to come and stay with them in a building near the central court. Later on I remember that we went to Beirut for a year whilst my father and mother stayed behind in the town. There was no stability at all during that period."[102]

"We managed to survive through the six-month strike. We used to bake our own bread and produce our own dairy products (milk and the like). Every family used to have everything it needed for the whole year. At that time Palestinian families would store a year's supply of food products.

- So what did people use to do when they ran out of food or dairy products?

- Neighbors would usually help if a family ran out of food."[103]

"During the six-month strike there was no transportation. We were living in Baq'a then and at that time my father was an employee at the Directorate of Education there. He had to walk all the way to work and then walk back home at the end of the day as there was no transportation. Also during the strike we stopped going to the Jewish neighborhoods. In fact we stopped any kind of dealings with the Jews; we wouldn't buy anything from them. By the time the strike ended, the war had started and during the war all kinds of movements stopped of course as people were busy monitoring the developments of the war."[104]

"During the six-month strike schools and shops were closed. Life in general came to a halt in Jerusalem, in fact all over Palestine, in Jaffa, at the harbor and everywhere. We stayed at home (...) Wajiha, Abdul-Qader's wife, opened her house in 1936 to the Palestinian fighters. She took care of the martyr Abdul-Qader Al-Huseini. A lot of the time Palestinian fighters would go to her house to eat; we used to call them fighters then. She also helped in smuggling weapons. There were some battles at that time and in the battle of Bani Na'im her husband was injured and Abdul-Qader's cousin Ali Hussein Salim Al-Huseini died as a martyr. Wajiha took care of the women too; she took care of Abdul-Qader and the rebels in 1936 in Lebanon, in Syria, in Baghdad. Wajiha, yes the mother of Faisal Al-Huseini, Musa, Ghazi and Haifa. The role of this woman was not properly accounted for in Palestinian history books and nobody knows what she did after her husband died as a martyr.

Chapter 2: The Political Participation in the 1936 Revolt

During the strike of 1936 many students were not able to go to school and unfortunately that did have a negative impact on them. It should be stressed here that people gave a lot to the struggle for Palestine. A whole generation of students in 1936 was not able to obtain a proper education. Furthermore many students could not pursue their studies in the aftermath of the rebellion either due to the fact that the British colonial government then prevented those who participated in the strike from going back to the grade he/she had been in. Most had to repeat their class or grade. Some decided to enroll in the same class again so that they could pursue their studies later on but others, especially boys, left school for good. The strike of 1936 demonstrated how much the Palestinian people were willing to give and sacrifice for Palestine. I mean today the world hears and knows about the sacrifices of the Palestinians, but in 1936 nobody would have heard about these sacrifices. At least now the world knows that there exists a Palestinian people; this is all I really want to say.

At that time we had what we needed to survive. We had meat, we had fruit and vegetables and women from the villages used to go from one house to another giving out vegetables and fruit to those who were in need. They would sometimes provide clothes too if anybody needed them. That was how people managed.

Of course, the Women's Union and the Arab Women Society in Jerusalem had the means to help those arrested by the colonial government, and do you think the mandate government left any family alone?! They had to arrest a few of each family's members. In one night they arrested my father, my uncle and three of my brothers. Maybe talking about these issues is not important but I just want to show how bad the situation was at that time. I remember when a Jewish student found the wallet of the President of the Hebrew university Dr. Mackenzie who lived close to our neighborhood and had a rented house there. The Jewish girl took a taxi and brought the wallet and went up to his house leaving the taxi driver waiting behind, apparently she was hoping that the President would reward her. In the meantime one of the Palestinian fighters passed by, and when he discovered that the driver was Jewish he killed him and then ran away through a doorway very near our house. The Jews heard about the incident and they came to our neighborhood and began to search every house. They destroyed everything in our houses, they threw out all the food products we had; lentil, rice and sugar etc. They ruined

Part 1: The Political Participation of Palestinian Women

virtually everything and then left. At that time, during the 1936 strike, the British soldiers would also come to people's houses every week or so and tell the inhabitants to leave so that they could do the necessary search. They would declare a curfew on the various neighborhoods and start searching houses, destroying everything they found in their way. I remember that they used to go to the Old City in Jerusalem, to Wadi Al-Jouz, Al-Sheikh Jarrah and Herods Gate, more than neighborhoods like Qattamon, Baq'a and such like.[1] We had to stay in our houses for days without bread or anything else. I remember that once we had to go for a whole week eating only very basic Palestinian dishes like Maslou'a, Mujaddara and Fasoulia (beans). These were things we had available at home in addition to olives, white cheese and labneh (dairy product), so we had to eat what was available until the curfew was lifted. There were collaborators then too but not as much as today. They used to help the British arrest Palestinian activists until our houses in Jerusalem were virtually emptied of their occupants; only women, children and very old men were left behind."[105]

"I believe that most Palestinian towns were in a bad financial situation in 1936. Everybody was suffering financially. So when the six-month strike was declared, Palestinian women had to do everything they could to cope with the new situation. They had to cut down on their daily expenditures and spend half of what they used to spend before. During the strike there emerged a sense of social solidarity among families, neighbors and relatives and also among the various neighborhoods in Jerusalem. Neighbors would share things like bread, food, milk and other basic necessities. People would run out of these necessities from time to time and they therefore had to rely on each other to meet their needs. As I said before, during the strike life was difficult. Schools were closed and people were out of work. In consequence Palestinians would focus on doing something patriotic for their country and the only context within which national activities could be channeled at that time was through the existing youth and men's societies. Women didn't have a specific or distinct national role to play at the time; they had to focus on coping with the daily needs of their families. Thankfully the charitable societies that were present at the time also managed to continue with their humanitarian work supporting those families that were in particularly dire need."[106]

---

1. All of these are neighborhoods in Jerusalem

Chapter 2: The Political Participation in the 1936 Revolt

It is clear from the narrations that unlike urban women, rural women were not very heavily affected by the strike. They had most of the things they needed available at home. They would make dough, bake bread and plant and grow vegetables such as zucchini, okra, parsley, Egyptian cucumber, and radish. They would also raise chickens and other kinds of birds, milk the sheep, sow the fields with seed and cultivate the produce. Unlike urban women, who couldn't leave the house, rural women continued to work at home and in the fields and so the life of rural women during the strike was not that different from their life beforehand.

Urban women on the other hand were heavily affected by the strike. There was a period of deep instability and turbulence which forced some merchants to take their families and move to other countries like Lebanon, as was mentioned in the statement made by the narrator Su'ad Qarman. With regards to most other families, in order for them to survive they had to produce their own bread, milk and other dairy products. They also stored many of the food products they would use throughout different parts of the year. Families developed a sense of solidarity amongst themselves which helped them to endure the difficulties they encountered during the strike and carry on with their lives. As mentioned before there was no transportation during the strike so people had to walk to their places of work and then back home again at the end of the day.

The narrators extensively described the 1936 strike and the various roles that Palestinian women played during that period. In their discussion and description of the situation they mentioned many of the problems that Palestinian people faced as a result of the strike. They talked about the deteriorating economic situation that Palestinians had to deal with and the considerable difficulties that students faced because of the interruption to their education, especially those who participated in the strike. In general all the narrators made reference to the great sacrifices they had to make in abiding by the strike. They also made reference to the active role of Palestinian women in supporting the rebellion and in taking care of the rebels and giving them all the support they could offer. This could be clearly seen in the role played by Wajiha Al-Huseini who opened her house for the rebels and did everything she could to ensure the success of their military activities. What was clear from this too was how the strike made women more aware of the role of media.

Nobody at that time had heard about the Palestinian question so the strike played an important role in bringing the attention of the world to the plight of the Palestinians. In addition the narrators highlighted the role of women's societies during the strike such as the one played by the Women's Union and the Arab Women Society in Jerusalem in helping detainees, as well as the aid and relief work that these societies were able to provide to those Palestinian families who were most in need. The narrations also brought up something that has not been accounted for in recorded history which was the role women played in inciting and encouraging people to participate in demonstrations during the strike. According to the narrators women would carry the Palestinian flag, give inflammatory speeches and pressure shopkeepers to abide by the strike and close their shops. Finally we also learnt that women were involved in distributing political pamphlets and sticking flyers on walls and on the doors of shops during the night.

However, on the other hand, contrary to the many narrations which talked about the active role of women in the strike, there was a narration, given by Madiha Al-Batta, which revealed that many young girls and women refused to participate in the strike, a phenomenon which has also not been recorded in written history. A narration like this raises all kinds of questions and it needs further investigation, or even an independent research project, as it points to the refusal of a part of Palestinian society to abide by the popular consensus prevailing at that time. What is more surprising is that the narrator talked with admiration about the director of the school who prevented the students from participating in the strike:

"In 1936 the strike was declared. Schools were therefore closed and teachers were out of work. However the director of our school in Khan Younes, Bahader Al-Souwwan, who was a very capable woman, refused to allow us to abide by the strike. So our school remained open until July 1936 and then we went for our summer break."[107]

The Medical Role

The medical role played by Palestinian women in the 1930s was restricted to providing first-aid to the sick and injured. As a result many societies organized various sessions for women to give them proper first-aid training and enable them to care for the wounded.

Chapter 2: The Political Participation in t

In general the narrations didn't mention anything about
role of women, according to four narrations, was strictl
to providing first-aid services to the wounded rather than do...
professional nursing work.

The narrator **Ulga Al-Aswad** asserted that women were given training sessions in first-aid:

"We used to go to the Coptic club of the Greek Orthodox community where we received first-aid training. The club was located in a street near the church."[108]

The narrator **Mahira Al-Dajani** also confirmed that she received first-aid training:

"We were young at the time, so they wouldn't rely on us. We therefore had to attend training workshops in first-aid in case they needed us in an emergency in the future. So if, for instance, a student was injured for one reason or the other, I would be in the position, as her teacher, to provide first-aid for her; I would have the courage and the skill to offer help. Had I not attended such training sessions I wouldn't have been in a position to offer help to anybody. So that was what we used to do, in addition of course to participating in demonstrations and helping with charitable work."[109]

The narrator **Bahjat Abu Gharbiyah** also described the role of women in providing first-aid:

"Even in the middle of the night the girls were ready to provide first-aid for the wounded and do other things such as fetching water whilst the fighting was taking place in 1936."[110]

Widad Al-'Aruri talked about the difficulties encountered in transporting the wounded to hospitals and also about the role her mother, who was a midwife, played in helping the injured:

"They were not able to take the wounded to hospital because they were afraid that they would be caught by the British soldiers. Instead they used to hide them in the caves nearby. My mother used to put medicine and other medical items into a basket and then fill it with vegetables. She would then go to the caves to assist the wounded. I know my mother was a midwife; she was recognized as a legal midwife in appreciation of her continuous work in providing first-aid for the wounded."[111]

It was evident from the responses of the narrators that the medical role of women was slightly limited due to the fact that women at that time didn't have the necessary medical skills that would enable them to save the lives of the severely wounded. This was clear from the rather short answers given by narrators in response to questions about their medical role. When the narrator **Khazneh Al-Khateeb** was asked about the kind of medical treatments she would offer to the wounded, her response led the researcher to conclude that the role of women didn't go beyond providing first-aid for the wounded. They had to wait for the doctor to arrive as only he could give the wounded the medical treatments that would help save their lives:

"Did you use to provide the necessary medical treatments for the wounded?

- Of course not, I had to wait until the doctor arrived

- Did you use to bring the doctor from his house?

- Our brothers the rebels would do that

- Would they bring the doctor to your house?

-Yes, he would come barefoot. However some of the injured who had a bullet somewhere in their body sometimes had to wait until the next day."[112]

The Role of Women in Postal Work

One role that was brought to light by the narrations was the participation of women in postal work. The aim of their work was to ensure that telephone conversations between the Palestinian committees remained secret. The narrator **Alice Elias Nawrasi** talked about this role:

"Arab girls only used to work as teachers. They would rarely work as employees in companies or places such as the post office as that was not socially accepted. There was a post office in Jaffa and most of the employees there were Jewish. There were only four or five Arab girls working there back then. One of the directors, whose name was Malvina Al-Nims, was an Arab; the rest were Jews. When the Palestinian revolt of 1936 began, the Jewish girls used to wiretap the conversations between the various Palestinian committees. As a result the Arab girls who were working there tried to get rid of the Jewish girls and began to look for other Arab girls who would be willing to work at the post office. They went to schools looking for suitable girls, but of course they would only employ us after talking to our families and convincing them how important it was for us to take on such jobs. It was obvious to us that the reason why they employed us was political; they didn't want Jewish girls to continue wiretapping conversations between Palestinians. That was at the beginning of the revolt."[113]

The Establishment of Societies and Unions

In their narrations the narrators didn't only discuss the role of rural women in the 1930s, but also the role of urban women, who were particularly active in establishing societies and unions. These societies and unions played a direct social and political role in the lives of Palestinians in 1930s, for example the narrator **Wafiyyeh Al-Khayri** talked in her narration about the Arab Women Society:

"I remember that there was the Arab Women Society in Jerusalem which was established prior to 1948 by Rabiha Shihabi, Shahinda Al-Disdar, 'Iffat Abdulhadi and Samha Al-Taji who was my cousin and the daughter of Dr. Hamdi Al-Taji. These women had relationships with women who were living abroad such as Huda Hanem Sha'rawi and others. Sha'rawi was known to be a prominent leader in the Arab world and in fact she visited Jerusalem in 1948. The founders of the Arab Women Society visited Egypt and participated in demonstrations there, and there was also Soumayya Al-Khalidi who participated in demonstrations in Jerusalem against the occupation."[114]

The narrator **Ulga Al-Aswad** spoke about the social role of women, which was often channeled through women's societies. These societies held courses that taught women sewing and embroidery and classes aimed at combating illiteracy amongst women. In addition they offered first-aid training courses which were, in one way or another, linked to political activities:

"There was some activity but I was very young then so I wasn't really fully aware of what exactly was going on at that time. I know that there was the Islamic or 'al-Fatat' Society which - amongst other things - sought to teach girls the Arabic language. Um 'Isam Al-Houri here in Beirut, she was in charge of that society. The Al-Houri family was of

Part 1: The Political Participation of Palestinian Women

course from Haifa before that. There was another woman, whose name I cannot remember now, who was active in this society. The society was very active and its founders used to organize training courses in first-aid. Girls also used to learn sewing and embroidery and there were courses that aimed at combating illiteracy. I was at school then but I used to go to the center on Thursday and Friday afternoon. They offered courses in Arabic for those girls who couldn't read or write. I used to take courses in sewing and embroidery and I was really good at sewing. Our school was also run by the Al-Fatat society and so in the morning we would take lessons but in the afternoon, especially on Thursdays and Fridays, we used to have training sessions in first-aid. The society was located in the Islamic neighborhood on Stanton Street or in the Western neighborhood, I am not exactly sure."[115]

The narrator **Widad Al-Ayyoubi** talked about the Arab Women Society in Jerusalem which played a role in establishing the Women's Union. Her narration helps us not only in writing the history of the society and its leaders but also in understanding the relationship between its social and political work:

"I was still a student in elementary school however I remember that in Jerusalem there were female social activities that were organized by women's societies. The Arab Women Society for instance was established by then and it was directed by Shahnad Al-Dizdar with the help of Zahiyyeh Al-Nashashibi, Fatima Al-Nashsashibi and Zulaikha Al-Shihabi. There was a large women's social gathering which lasted for seven years from 1929 to 1936 and it led in 1936 to the formation of The Society of Women Union in Jerusalem. The society emerged from the Arab Women's Society in order to intensify the social and revolutionary work. Every society has its own objectives. I remember very well - although I was still very young then - that The Society of Women Union was indirectly involved in organizing political activities. For instance the society did a lot of fundraising work by organizing various exhibitions and other related activities. All the funds collected were given to the rebels to help them buy weapons and other things. The rebels of course emanated from youth organizations and other politically oriented societies and activities which existed in different parts of Palestine and in Jerusalem."[116]

Another narrator, by the name of **Daoud 'Eirikat**, talked about the activities and role of societies in Jerusalem. His narration is of great assistance in writing the history of the activities and work of these societies. He also mentioned the names of a number of people who were active - but not leaders - in these societies who we didn't know about before:

"In Jerusalem there was a society which I remember very well; it was directed by Zulaikha Al-Shihabi. She was active in this society for a long time and was assisted by a group of women including my mother, my aunt and many others. It is difficult for me to determine the exact numbers because I don't have the documents but there was certainly not many of them. My mother's name is 'Aisha Alhajj Khaleel Al-Makki, she is from Herod's Gate, Jerusalem and my aunt's name is Ruqayya Alhajj Khaleel Al-Makki. My aunt had a small sewing factory and she made many financial contributions to the rebels in addition to her fundraising activities. Both of them were very active in fundraising, in organizing political activities and in participating in the many protests and demonstrations led by the men. They participated in most of the activities despite the fact that they were small in number."[117]

The narrator **Samiha Khaleel** also talked about a women's society: "There was a society; a Women's society. The president was Wadee'a Qaddourah Khartabil who was Lebanese. My mother and other women were active in this society and they used to help people."[118]

The narrator **Wadee'a Qaddourah Khartabil** described a society which she established in Tulkarm. The information she provided taught us a great deal about the society's structure, activities and method of work as well as the factors that led to its establishment:

"I established a branch of the Palestinian Arab Women's Union; the headquarters was in Jerusalem, but it had branches in other Palestinian cities too and I established the branch in Tulkarm and worked in it all my life. When I went to Tulkarm I was asked to work under the name of the Women's Charitable Society, but later I changed its name to the Palestinian Women's Union. We had so many meetings and we developed all sorts of plans to help people. In our work we did a lot to help children; we provided financial aid to needy families and established a school - "a kindergarten" - for children. So when the Palestinian revolt began we were ready to help women in all sorts of ways. Through my leadership of this society I succeeded in making a contribution to the Palestinian revolt. We established committees that used to go out to the

Part 1: The Political Participation of Palestinian Women

villages. Their aim was to raise the political awareness of women with regards to the revolt and other related matters and also to help them in coping with their daily lives. We maintained good relations with the people in Tulkarm and also with the rebels. It was in fact through such activities that our involvement and connection with the rebels developed and was channeled."[119]

It is important to note that urban women, due to their level of education and their participation in societies and organizations, talked more than rural women about the social-political role of women in addition to their role in demonstrations and in transmitting and hiding letters during the 1930s.

The narrator **Salma Al-Huseini** talked about the role of The Women's Union and the Society of Arab Women in Jerusalem during the 1930s. Her discussion revealed the role of a number of women whose participation in Palestinian revolutionary politics during this period was somehow neglected by recorded history:

"They used to help the detainees arrested by the mandate government. The British had arrested all the men by then; they didn't leave anybody behind in peace in their homes. In one night, they arrested my father and three men from our family. In 1936 Wajiha Abdul Qader made her house available and open to Palestinian fighters. She was the one who protected and looked after Abdul Qader. Fighters used to come to her house to eat and have a rest. She looked after both women and rebels. She protected and looked after Abdul Qader and the rebels in 1936. She looked after them in Lebanon, Damascus and Baghdad. Yes Wajiha, the mother of Faisal Al-Huseini, Musa, Ghazi and Haifa did all that but unfortunately she was neglected by recorded history! Nobody knows what this woman did for Palestine! After her husband died as a martyr she did everything to educate her children and to deepen their nationalist sense of belonging to Palestine. She did everything she could for her children until she died."[120]

With regards to rural women, their role in supporting the detainees was more spontaneous. The narrator **Ali Musa Abu Yousef** spoke with admiration about the social and political role of rural women:

Chapter 2: The Political Participation in the 1936 Revolt

"I wasn't there when Britain occupied Palestine. When Al-Tel[1] was established, women used to create all kinds of problems for the soldiers. They used to fight them, hit them and be hit in return of course. In any case many old and young men were detained and sent to Al-Tel. The conditions there put the lives of many prisoners at risk especially given that many were left without water to drink. As there were no embassies in any city other than Jerusalem, some politically active women went there to meet with consuls and discuss with them the conditions of prisoners at Al-Tel. They went to all the embassies in Jerusalem. Some reacted positively to their requests and others were extremely negative, for example the American Embassy which refused to even let them in. Ever since the 1930s, even before America's position was clear to us Palestinians, we always believed that America was the "head of the snake", i.e. the real cause of our problems. Later on medical experts from England arrived and visited Al-Tel. Other doctors also checked the prisoners and one doctor - I cannot recall whether they were German or Russian - insisted that if these prisoners continue to live under the conditions prevailing at Al-Tel they would all die. So the role of women was crucial in this incident; their active role in rallying the support and intervention of foreign embassies and doctors helped save the lives of those prisoners."[121]

The Participation of Palestinian Women in Conferences

Although the history books have recorded the participation of urban Palestinian women in the Arab political conferences which were held in support of the Palestinian question in the 1930s, these records are not complete. In our study we have used oral history to learn more about these conferences and discover and explore the aspects of women's participation that have not been accounted for in recorded history.

It was evident to us from the narrators' discussions of the Arab conferences during this period that there was some confusion regarding the history of these conferences, especially those which were held in the beginning of the 1930s. Narrators, both male and female, did not remember the participation of women in these conferences; however, they remembered very well the Conference of Eastern Women for the

---

1. These are large detaining centers and prisons which were named Al-Tel. At the time many detained rebels suffered dearly from thirst. Twelve martyrs died there

Part 1: The Political Participation of Palestinian Women

Defense of Palestine which was held in Cairo between the 15th and 17th of November 1938. In total 27 narrators (22 female and 5 male) remembered the events of that conference.

In answering the question of whether they remembered anything about the conferences that were held in the beginning of the 1930s (in Beirut in April 1930 and in Damascus and Baghdad in 1932) the narrators **Salma Al-Huseini** and **Yusra Al-Barbari** gave confusing answers which clearly reflected their inability to properly remember the events of these conferences:

"Mrs. Zliekha and representatives of the women's union attended that conference which was held in solidarity with Palestine. I believe that it was Huda Sha'rawi who organized these conferences and they all went to Beirut to attend it in support of Palestine and the Palestinian question."[122]

"I read about it but I am not sure whether I read anything about the other conferences; however, I remember the conference in Cairo because I was there at the time studying at the university and I participated in it."[123]

With regards to questions about the conference that was held in Cairo in 1938, we saw a large degree of certainty and confidence in the narrators' answers. Furthermore there were numerous statements in the narrations which reflected certainty about the participation of women in the conference. Some of them, for instance **Maymanah Ezzedin Al-Qassam**, participated in sessions of the conference and others were witnesses to the active participation of Palestinian women in the various sessions. What helped the narrators to remember the conferences was the availability of books and pictures which recorded the history of that important event and the role of Palestinian and Arab women in it. This was in contrast to discussions on other historical events when it was found that having documents about the events didn't always help the narrators to remember them better. However, some narrators held the attitude that these documents were enough to provide all the necessary information about the conferences, as the narrators **Abdul-Qader Yaseen** and **Salma Al-Huseini** stressed:

"I've heard about the first one in 1938.

- Tell us about it?

Chapter 2: The Political Participation in the 1936 Revolt

- No, there is a book about it, here look at it."[124]

"There are pictures of those from the women's union who participated in Cairo. If I remember exactly where I can find the women's union book - maybe I'll find it somewhere here - I will give it to you, just bear with me, I will look for it and will give it to you."[125]

Some of the women who were present at the time of the conference still didn't remember it, as was clear from the narration of **Yusra Al-Barbari**, or in the case of others they were able to remember the general events but without any detailed information, for example in the narrations of **Subhi Ghousheh** and **Isam Abdulhadi**:

"With regards to the conference organized by Huda Sha'rawi, I read about it and I also heard about it from the radio but I didn't participate in it and I don't remember who the participants were!"[126]

"This information that I am sharing with you, it should give you a general idea about the conference but it is not in any way detailed because I cannot really remember."[127]

"Both the first and second conferences were about Palestine, the whole Arab movement was behind Palestine. Both the conferences were headed by Huda Sha'rawi and a special fund was established for the purpose of buying land. However, I don't know whether anything was done with this fund or whether any land was purchased."[128]

Some narrators referred to historical documents and pictures in order to talk in greater detail about aspects of the conference. This was the case with the narrators **Zuheir Al-Shawish** and **Fuad Ibrahim Abbas**:

"As I already told you, the movement began in 1936 after the death of the martyr Ezzedin Al-Qassam. Here is the picture; I will give you a copy. In this picture you can see the Palestinian women's delegation to the conference that was held in Cairo in 1938. You can see, among those who were sitting on the chairs: Nabiha Naser, Subhieh Raid Al-Tamimi, the wife of Ameen Al-Tamimi (they didn't know her name or perhaps they didn't want to mention her name), Nafeeseh Mohammad Ali Allouba, (she was an Egyptian), Mateel Mghareb (he means Mateel Mghanam), Sathej Nassar, Maryam Hashem and Bahira Al-Athmeh (from Syria). Those who you can see sitting on the floor are: Wahida Al-Khalidi, Salma Rajai Al-Huseini, Fatima Al-Nashashibi, Zulaikha Al-Shihabi, Zahiyyeh Al-Nashashibi, Samiha Al-Khalidi and Mary Kheil.

Finally those who are standing up are: the wife of George Salah, Badra Kan'an, Arnasteen Al-Ghori, Rayya Al-Qasem, Eiva Habib Al-Masri (Egyptian), the wife of Shukri Deeb and Tarab 'Awni 'Abdulhadi."[129]

"What was noticeable in this conference was that the Palestinian delegation was the largest; it was made up of 24 women. The Egyptian delegation was made up of 13 women, while Iran had one delegate and Iraq had 4. Some of the decisions that were taken and the recommendations that were made were considered to be of great significance:

- Europe, especially the alliance states, should be held fully responsible for what Palestinians are going through due to the fact that they were the main cause of the problem.

- Arab kings and princes should endeavor to find a solution to the Palestinian problem.

- A tribute should be made to Palestinian fighters.

- Jews should be stripped of their weapons like Arabs are. (The British used to collect and confiscate weapons from Arabs and give them in secret to the Jews).

- Support for the Palestinian struggle should be provided as follows: the Red Crescent should establish a medical unit to fully attend to the needs of injured Palestinians. In addition the Egyptian ministry of education and all religious institutes should provide free education to the sons and daughters of Palestinian martyrs.

The conference was held during the period 15-18 October 1938."[130]

The statement made by **Maymanah Ezzedin Al-Qassam** about the conference was a particularly important one. She not only represented Haifa in the conference but also delivered a speech on behalf of the Palestinian delegation. She mentioned that she received three invitations to the conference: one from King Farouk, another from Palestinian deportees and a third from Huda Hanem Sha'rawi. She talked about her acceptance of the invitation from Huda Sha'rawi and the reasons why she specifically decided to accept Huda's invitation and reject the other two. Despite the fact that historical sources have documented the conference's proceedings, oral history, in addition to confirming the events and proceedings of the conference and the speeches that were delivered, is particularly useful as it raises political issues from the point of view of women, issues that have not been accounted for in

Chapter 2: The Political Participation in the 1936 Revolt

historical sources. Reading between the lines of **Maymanah Ezzedin Al-Qassam's** statement we get an indication of the accusations that were directed towards some Palestinian women regarding their behavior during the conference and we learn that some of these accusations were publicized in newspapers. We can see from her statement how the political atmosphere that was prevailing at the time when she delivered her emotional and highly political and revolutionary speech, helped not only in allowing Palestinian women to attend the conference but also in putting an end to rumors about the behavior of some of the women. It is important to note here that Maymanah was helped by the writer and politician Akram Zuaiter, who was known to be an accomplished public speaker. Mr. Zuaiter helped her in writing the speech that she delivered at the conference. After a number of questions were addressed to her by the researcher, the narrator Maymanah revealed many important details about the conference:

"O.K. you mentioned a very important issue to do with the conference; so you received an invitation and then you travelled to Cairo, do you remember any details about what went on with regards to the conference?

- I attended the conference as I was chosen as the representative of Haifa.

- Firstly, where did you get the invitation from?

- The women's societies that decided to attend the conference insisted that I should attend. They found somebody to accompany me and they discussed the issue with my mother. My mother said she would refuse to send me so then they informed her that somebody would accompany me, i.e., somebody would travel with me (..)

-Who was the person who travelled with you? Was it Sathej Nassar?

-Yes that's correct she was the one, god bless you how did you know? The women's societies attended the conference and I was one of the attendees (..)

- So you were nominated to attend the conference?

- When I arrived in Cairo, I was very well received. In fact when I was still in Palestine I received three invitations.

- From whom?

Part 1: The Political Participation of Palestinian Women

- I chose to go to the conference, don't you worry about the other invitations!

(Everybody urged her to talk saying 'we want to know', 'you did mention something about this' and 'you should tell us'; they tried to assure her that it was normal to talk about such things and there wouldn't be any problems for her as a result of disclosing the information.)

- We want to know who thought so highly of you? Who invited you?

- I was visited by a delegation from King Farouk and a delegation from Huda Sha'rawi.

- You mean an invitation, you were invited by them?

- They wanted me to be their guest; the Palestinian deportees also invited me, I received three invitations. I was young then and I was confused. So I said to myself if I accept the King's invitation, or the deportees, people would suspect my motives. So I decided to accept Huda's invitation.

- Huda, so you accepted Huda Sha'rawi's invitation?

- Yes, I was her guest (...)

- So you went there to attend the conference? Who were you representing then?

- I was representing the city of Haifa.

- Or perhaps you were representing one of the societies?

- No, I represented Haifa.

- So you represented Haifa, who else was present in the Palestinian delegation?

- Who?

- Who was there with you in the delegation, do you remember?

- Many from Jerusalem.

- Do you remember any names?

- I remember that 'Abdul-Qader Al-Huseini's wife was one of the delegates, in addition to the directors of the women's societies, you know them (..)

Chapter 2: The Political Participation in the 1936 Revolt

- No, remind me of them.
- I don't remember their names.
- So how many Palestinian delegates were at the conference, do you know? (..)
- There were a lot of us, we numbered forty women.
- Forty women.
- Jordanian women were part of the delegation too.
- So a large delegation.
- You told us that the wives of the Presidents of Lebanon and Syria were at the conference?
- Oh, I cannot remember their names, but yes the wives of the Presidents of Lebanon and Syria. I don't remember their names exactly and so I don't want to sound as if I am lying and give you the wrong names.
- So who delivered the speech on behalf of the Palestinian women? I mean who delivered the speech from the Palestinian delegation?
- Which speech?
- In the conference wasn't there a woman who was asked to deliver the speech on behalf of Palestinian women? Was it you who gave the speech for instance?
- Well I wasn't alone, I wasn't the only one; there were forty women there, some from the most prominent Palestinian families.
- Okay. So all of them would have been very knowledgeable and well-known? Who were their fathers, their grandfathers and their mothers, etc.?
- People did not appreciate and respect each other, some were jealous, so they spread some rumors about other women. May God have mercy on his soul, the man who died, what was his name
- You mean Akram Zuaiter?
- Yes, Akram Zuaiter said to me whilst we were at the zoo 'There has been some talk about some of the women who came to Egypt to attend the conference. What's the solution, what should we do?' I told him

-73-

Part 1: The Political Participation of Palestinian Women

'Whatever you suggest!' So he said we should write a speech that I could deliver, and we would show the whole world what Palestinian women can do and how respectful and intelligent they are.

- Yes, of course

- Akram was a well-known writer of course and he was far more knowledgeable than me. He wrote the speech but I did contribute a bit and I was the one who delivered it. It was published in books (..)

- Do you remember anything from the speech?

- I remember the first few sentences of it.

- Go on then, try to remember and say it.

- *Ladies and Gentlemen (..) Do you know who I am?*

It was very difficult for me to talk, I was mad, I was angry; I wanted to give them an idea about myself and people like me. I said 'Do you know who I am?' and they all nodded.

I am the daughter of the one who knocked on the door of freedom with his bare bloodstained hands, and there, in the land of Palestine, is my resting place. (She spoke in a careful, punctuated tone).

(..) This is what I recall (..)

- What was the reaction of people towards your speech?

- They stopped talking about the women in the delegation and after a few days the newspapers stopped writing and slandering.

- What was the slander?

- You know, Akram, God bless his soul, told me that they might talk.

- About the women who participated in the conference?

- They talked about some members (..) not everybody. They talked about some; actually about most of us. My speech had some value because after it people were deterred and they came to their senses."[131]

It is clear from the narrators' answers that there are many hidden secrets surrounding the participation of women in political activities during this historical period. It appears that those women who participated risked leaving their reputation exposed to rumors and slander. It is also clear that the political speech that Maymanah delivered was very effective in putting an end to the rumors and malicious talk that surrounded these women.

When the narrators were asked about their opinions with regards to the effectiveness of holding such conferences, the replies were mixed. Of the sixteen narrators who answered the question, thirteen women and one man (87.5%) endorsed the effectiveness of the conferences while two narrators (12.5%) said they were not effective. However, it should be noted here that all the women who believed in the effectiveness of holding or attending conferences came from the class of educated citizens who participated in such conferences for the sake of serving the Palestinian cause.

The narrator **Munawwar Salah** discussed the effect that these conferences had on women's ability to achieve a higher level of freedom. She said "I do not deny the right of any woman to struggle for the cause and dignity of women. What Mrs. Huda Hanem Sha'rawi did was not in vain; rather it supported both Egyptian women and Arab women in general. Recall the situation of Egyptian women and men during monarchy; at that time even men did not have their own freedom, and neither did women. Both of them were subjugated. Sha'rawi's call for the freedom of women and for raising their political awareness is a contribution that history should record. What history recorded about her achievement does not do her justice; history should honor her even more because the condition of women was miserable then. Egyptian women in general were not educated at that time. There were only a very small number of women who were educated, who were able to hold a pencil, and who were able to go to school. However, the number of educated women was large compared to other countries, and thus a sense of responsibility to contribute to the empowerment of women in Egypt emerged within every educated woman.

These pioneering women were courageous and very politically aware. More and more women developed a better level of understanding and a desire to sacrifice and work for Egypt. Some of the attendees had a very high level of education such as a doctorate degree either in education, medicine or in other sciences. From this point onwards, Huda Sha'rawi was not a single women struggling alone; she had a group of people working with her and she was more able to serve the cause because she had so many friends and followers."[132]

Part 1: The Political Participation of Palestinian Women

In similar manner **Wadee'a Qaddourah Khartabil** described the way that these conferences brought women together and encouraged them to support each other and grow in strength and power. She said "Yes, this conference brought us closer to each other. There were many agreements that strengthened a common sense of ourselves and our goals. We had to come to an agreement to work together for our homeland because we only have one enemy; the Zionist enemy."[133]

On the other hand, some of the narrators were very skeptical with regards to the objectives of the conferences, especially those which did not deal solely with the question of Palestine. For example the narrator **Fatima Al-Budairi** said:

"The feminist conferences were good, but they were not solely serving the question of Palestine. They were global, international and national, and this meant that these conferences had wider objectives rather than purely Palestinian-based goals, especially given the fact that nobody actually cares about Palestine. These conferences failed to represent the real face of Palestine. There was a lot of media coverage of the conferences and there were many Jews attending; not only Israeli representatives but also the majority of the attendees were Jews."[134]

However, the narrator **Haroun Hashem Rasheed** confirmed the significance of the Conference of 1938. Due to the large women's delegation that participated in this conference, Rasheed inferred that there was a great degree of political awareness amongst women during this early period. He said "The conference was large, and it was widely covered by the media especially because it was headed by Huda Sha'rawi and Sha'rawi had a reputation all over the region. What was evident was that Palestinian women were the primary participants. I do not recall the names of any Palestinian women who attended and participated but such wide participation proves that Palestinian women had a high degree of political awareness at that level."[135]

The narrator Maymanah Al-Qassam, a participant in that conference, said that she considered the the conference to be an act of charity. She also linked the conference to the political struggle in general:

"- Do you think that these conferences had any impact or value?

- They must. They must have.

- Do you think that the participation of a large women's delegation was effective?

- It was very effective. Nobody really criticized them. There was a bit of that, but not so much. But it had a great effect because all of the participants were (..)

- Do you think that it is a form of struggle? I mean the participation of women in these kinds of conferences?

- Every act of charity is a struggle. Every act of charity is a struggle."[136]

It should be noted that two women leaders, both of whom worked in the field of politics for a very long time, organizing and attending conferences, not only on the Arab level but on the international level as well, surprisingly said that they did not see any point in holding such conferences. **Samira Abu Ghazaleh** said "At that time, (wondering) what was the point of our conferences? We were holding these conferences but you might wonder what the aim was? Firstly they were a wake-up call for women, and secondly they were a chance to hear the demands of women. But all the demands were the same as the demands we are making now. There was no difference in the demands: cessation of immigration, cessation of selling lands, and funding Jerusalem…etc. We are still repeating ourselves."[137]

Similarly **Yusra Al-Barbari**, when asked about her recollections of the 1938 conference, said:

"– It was the same as the rest of conferences. They come out with recommendations that were not implemented.

- Was it different from the conferences prior to it?

- No, it was not, and no conference after it would actually be any different as long as we did not actually implement the recommendations."[138]

In the judgments of these narrators it is clear that they are seeing the past in light of the present. The narrators could not judge the past in reference to the convictions they held during those days when they eagerly participated not only by attending the many conferences but also by organizing and preparing for them. Rather they saw the significance and impact of the past in the context of the dark present, and thus their judgment of the past was cut off from its context.

In conclusion, the majority of narrators saw great value in attending women conferences as was clear in their testimonies. In such conferences, they saw firsthand political action in its direct form, as well as participating in events that indirectly gave woman more social freedom, as described in the testimony of Maymanah 'Ezzedin Al-Qassam.

The Military Role

With regards to the military role, **Yusra Al-Barbari** was the only narrator who directly pointed to a link between the social and political struggle of women and the military struggle. She said "I do not deny the role of Palestinian women in the military struggle alongside men. Palestinian women have been struggling since the conspiracy of the Balfour Declaration and the Sykes- Picot Agreement; since the British occupation (Mandate) of Palestine and Jordan and the French occupation of Syria and Lebanon. Palestinian women took on the responsibility of providing provisions and military weapons to the rebels in their mountains and caves. They also took on the responsibility of passing on commands and instructions outside of the cities and they lead the secret resistance. How can we accuse them of ignorance and failure after more than thirty, perhaps more than fifty, years of struggle? How can we accuse them of being enslaved women, who do not have the freedom to talk and to work inside the Palestinian family, after all this time and all these decades of them struggling socially, militarily, and politically?"[139] Other narrators also described how Palestinian woman were involved in the military struggle in various ways including cleaning weapons, moving and hiding them, as well as learning how to use the weapons and participating in using them alongside the men.

Hiding Weapons

Hiding weapons was the most frequently mentioned military role in the testimonies; twenty-six narrators (23 women and 3 men) described women doing this in their narratives. For example it was discussed by the narrator **Khadra Mustafa Al-Sari**, who had previously said that women's primary role was assistance with farming.

"- Tell us about the women at that time.

- About women? In the cities, they formed the Black Palm group. The

Chapter 2: The Political Participation in the 1936 Revolt

girls would carry baskets - this is in Haifa - women and girls would take the food and water and head towards the mountains.

(The researcher then tried to gather more information about the women of the Black Palm group in Haifa and their work)

- What did they do exactly?
- They walked with the Black Palm group.
- Do they fight with them or just walk alongside them?
- No, they knew what was going on. They were connected to them (the young men), for example the men would tell them 'we will shoot at a certain place'.
- Do they go to shoot with them?
- No, they walked alongside them, ready to help. When anything happened, the men would drop their pistols and these women would pick them up, put them in the baskets, and cover them with vegetables."[140]

When the researcher asked her about women and political work, the narrator **Shams Al-Titi** initially limited the role of women to preparing food and drink, however after further discussion she revealed that "Hamida Abu Rayyah used to fill the baskets with weapons and carry the baskets away. The military soldiers were standing at the door. She would pass by, fill the basket with weapons and carry the weapons away; she did this during the British mandate."[141]

Although she played down the political role of the woman, the narrator Hamida Abu Rayyah was herself an example of such participation, according to both her testimony and the testimonies of other women. She explained her work in detail, saying: "There was a rug in our house that could be hung like this and when my father arrived home from being with the rebels I used to wrap it around the gun and cover it with a Hatta (a traditional cloth that is worn on the head). Then I would go down to the lower cave (Al-Tahta) and bury it."[142]

In her testimony Hamida Abu Rayyah also described another similar incident. She said "Um Subhi's name is Amina; Amina Al-Barham. One day, she knocked on the door. I asked her what the matter was and she said the village had been besieged. She asked if Abu Muhammad was there and I confirmed that he was, and then she told me to 'get arranged'. I couldn't make up my mind what to do. The gun was over there and the pistol was over there, what should I do with them? Then, as soon as we stood up, the old woman, his mother, went to dig a hole in the taboon (a very small room of yellow mud where the traditional Palestinian fireplace was) to bury them. She buried them along with his uniform."[143]

It is interesting to note that the relationship the women had with the weapons was quite intimate; they didn't seem to be scared or horrified by them. We can see this particularly clearly in the testimony of the narrator **Amneh Alwinni**, who used to continually carry weapons on a belt around her waist in order to hide them from the British soldiers. In her testimony she said "Every few days, they would break into the house. He (her husband) had a pistol and when I heard them knocking I would tie the pistol around my waist and put on my Dishdasha (a loose home dress). I hid the pistol three or four times in this way."[144]

Rural Palestinian woman recognized the significance of arms and understood early-on the connection between these weapons and the achievement of a free and honorable life. Their understanding of this connection made them want to hide the weapons and protect them with their own bodies and the bodies of their children; the most precious things they would ever have. The narrators **Jamila Badran** (from Dair Al-Ghsoun) and **Fatima Al-Khatib** (from Ain Bait Al-Ma') talked about the ways in which they used to protect their husbands' ammunition:

"They were searching for weapons so I took my husband's weapon and I tied it to my belt like this (she pointed to her waist.) I have a sister-in-law who once left her own little girl at home. All of them went to that building. All of the inhabitants of this village went to the same building, except me, I stayed at home. Then I found this little girl screaming because her mother had left her alone and had gone out. They would go out and leave their children due to the harassment of the soldiers. I took the girl and I hid my gold in a cloth that was attached to me like this (she pointed at her waist). I attached the gold and went out with the girl towards the east. As I walked in the street, I was completely amazed by the enormous number of soldiers. I saw how they were prepared with their arms and weapons. Then I realized 'Oh my God! I forgot the pistol!' so I went back to get it for my husband. It was a pistol that he brought from Jaffa and he was very fond of it. I found it in the closet where he used to hang it when he went out with the rifle so I took it and hid it under my velvet dress with a belt around it. Then I took the little girl and headed east."[145]

"- Hajjeh, tell me, how did you help the rebels in the past?

- When the British soldiers declared a siege on the village the rebels would give us their weapons and I used to hide some in my chest. We would hide the other weapons in the hearth; we used to dig the hearth and cover the weapons with waste. Sometimes we would hide the weapons inside sacks too.

- What were these sacks?

- Inside the wheat sacks. We put them inside the wheat. There were some sacks which were as high as this buffet (she pointed at the buffet), so we pushed the weapons inside the wheat, covered them with some more wheat and sprinkled some water on top.

- So you used to hide weapons?

- Yes, we hid the weapons.

- What else did you do Hajjeh?

- We used to hide the weapons between the brooms in the backyard and in our chests. Then we used to leave the house in which these weapons were hidden."[146]

The narrator **Ahmad Maw'ed** also talked about a clever trick his mother used to hide his father's weapon. He said "One day, there was an accident and the British soldiers were approaching our house from the Western side. Our house was made of beautiful traditional stone, with high ceilings, two doors and two entrances. As the soldiers approached, my father, who had been holding his pistol and ammunition, put the pistol in my mother's Harj; you know the very long traditional village dress. Just as he has put it in her Harj, they entered and she went out through the second door. Of course they saw her, but they did not talk to her and I was just a small child following his mother around. We had a backyard to the eastern side of the house where we used to plant potatoes, marrows and other plants. It was very big and very wide. They entered the vault and started to search the cupboards and closets inside of the house. One of them had noticed that the way my mother had gone was not normal and that she had hidden something on her and so he ran behind her! Although she was illiterate she was very smart. She went to the place where we used to store potatoes and she dug beneath it. Then she buried the pistol in the hole and she took some potatoes and put them in her Harj. One of the British soldiers - the soldier who had noticed her leaving and followed her - came and stood next to her while she was working. As she started to get the potatoes out and put them in her Harj. He asked her 'You, what are you doing?' She replied 'I take from this' and showed him some of the potatoes she was carrying, then she said 'In order to feed him' and pointed at me standing next to her. She repeated 'In order to feed the boy'. He asked 'Just that?' and she said 'Just that'."[147]

Some narrators also talked about urban women hiding weapons too; for example in the testimonies of the two narrators **Khadija Hedayah** and **Um Kayed**: "When the British soldiers used to search our houses in the old town, we would throw the rebels pistols in the well."[148]

"I will tell you about the incident when a British soldier was killed in the area between Bab Al-'Amoud (Damascus Gate) and the valley. The rebel was still in the area and they said that the British soldiers had besieged the town. Coincidently there was a woman walking in the area at the time, so in order to escape detection the rebel discreetly gave her the pistol. She took it and hid it under the veil she was wearing. Then when the British soldiers checked him, they did not find anything on him. The woman continued walking very slowly so that he could follow her and when he reached her house, she gave him back the pistol."[149]

Taking Care of Weapons

The village women also took care of weapons in the same way they took care of their family. In addition to hiding weapons, they would wash, clean, lubricate and prepare them, so that when their husbands came and took them they would be ready to be used. Six women mentioned Palestinian village women doing such things.

Um Kayed, for example, narrated an incident which reveals how much responsibility women had for the weapons. She said "The gun was lying on the mattress with the pistol next to it. I wrapped the blanket around the gun and I ran downstairs wondering frantically

Chapter 2: The Political Participation in the 1936 Revolt

where to go? There was an attic in my aunt's house that was full of waste, so I dug and dug and I buried the gun inside the waste, then I piled stones up against the door of the attic. But there was still the question of what to do with the pistol? I could hide it on myself next to my stomach but if it went off, I would be shot (..) Nevertheless I put the pistol on my belt and got dressed. Then I picked up some dough and left the house. I swear it was still dawn and as I walked from the door of our house to Dar Al-Shabah stove I was completely surrounded by dogs lurking around me and watching me. The British soldiers were behind me in the street but as I entered the stove, they left (..) Where did they go? They went to Dar Al-Shabah; the house from which the rebels distributed weapons. They started to hit the door, then they smashed it in and entered (..) But everything was well prepared and they found nothing. There was no trace of weapons and all the young men were at work. They left without finding anything. My husband told me later that when he heard the British soldiers had come to the village with their police dogs he thought that we were going to lose the gun as well as the house. He had to stay outside of the village whilst the soldiers were there but he was worried and wanted to go back. His companions told him 'If your wife is clever, she will arrange everything. Do you want to be killed? Can you not see the siege? The tanks are planted around the town. Where will you go? Just sit there and calm down.' As soon as the siege ended he came to me and asked what happened? I said 'It's none of your business, everything is arranged'. He said 'Do you mean nothing has happened?' and I replied 'Thanks to God! Nothing has happened' and gave him the pistol. He said 'Oh crazy woman, it is not locked' and I said: 'No, I did not dismantle the magazine'. He used to give me the pistol when he arrived home and would tell me to clean it. I would prepare some hot water and then clean it with some rope, cloth and cotton. I would make sure it was cleaned, lubricated, loaded, and hung up. So when he needed it again it was ready to be used and he could just take it and go out."[150]

The narrator **Zahida Ahmad Mustafa** said something very similar in her testimony: "My husband would bring weapons to the house. When the bullet was stuck, we would remove it. If the men needed to eat, we would feed them, and if they wanted to drink, we let them drink, so that they did not need to go out."[151]

The narrator **Samiha Khaleel**, spoke in her testimony about a village woman from 'Attil who used to take care of weapons. She said "Yes, there was a woman with them. Her cousin was Abdullah Al-As'ad. He was a revolutionary leader. She used to go to them in order to clean their weapons exactly as they wanted. A woman from 'Attil was with them."[152]

The Transportation of Weapons

Transporting weapons was the second most mentioned activity that women undertook during this time. It was mentioned in twenty-two narrations; seventeen from women and five from men. **Huda Amer, Najeyyah Barham, Zakiyeh Hulaileh** and **Sa'dah Dakar** all talked about the role of village women in transporting weapons to rebels;

"They used to clean the weapons and load them with bullets. Then they would transport the weapons."[153]

"They cooked, they baked, and they attended to everything that needed to be attended to. When the rebels needed weapons, these women used to put the weapons in their children's cradles and go out pretending that they were carrying their children. Their children's cradles were filled with weapons."[154]

"A strong woman would come carrying bullets and bombs. She would crawl on her belly and build a bunker. This is what we used to do."[155]
"We were still young then, but we were aware of everything. I was completely aware of every little thing. Sabha Al-Ali, for instance, used to carry weapons and walk with the rebels. They called her 'Bent Bnout' (this means unmarried but here it indicates her strength) because she used to carry weapons and walk with a millstone on her head. In front of her and behind her, young men used to clap their hands as she walked. She was a very strong woman to be able to carry that stone and walk. As soon as the British soldiers got distracted she would throw down the stone and deliver weapons to Abu Jeldah and Abu Hasaballah in Salamah (a village near Jaffa)."[156]

Similarly, Salma Al-Husseini talked about a woman by the name of Wajiha Al-Husseini (from Jerusalem) who used to help her husband and other rebels by transporting weapons to them.[157]

Chapter 2: The Political Participation in the 1936 Revolt

Training to Use Weapons

There were seven narratives which indicated that women were actually trained to use weapons, as well as looking after and transporting them. For example, **Zakiyeh Hulaileh** talked about how she was trained to use some types of weapons: "I was trained to use the Sten and the Tamgen (British gun machines). I was also trained to use the bomb which was about this size (she clenched her fist tightly) which you immediately throw at your target. Today, I am not capable of doing so. I am not capable of using the Sten gun: I am not able to do so. My brother Abu Ali tried to teach me how to use it. Nevertheless, it immediately falls from my hands. On the other hand, I am very professional at using the Tamgen and other big gun machines. I don't know exactly how many bullets they take but they shoot great numbers of them, sprinkling the bullets the same way water drops would sprinkle from a spray. 'To, to, to' that was the sound of shooting. Yes, I learnt how to use it (..) (she laughed)."[158]

-"You mean that you used to shoot?

- Yes, my brother taught me. He took a course and then he taught me.

- Where did you train?

- I trained at home."[159]

"He used to teach me to use the Sten. I used to shoot using the Sten. Yes, the Sten; that tough iron machine. I am not like the women these days! Yes, he trained me to use it. He used to place a stone in front of me and tell me to shoot it. I used to say 'Oh, you poor miserable thing, you think I can shoot?' And he would answer 'Just do it!' This is what was happening to us in the village. We used to help the men. The clever woman, the woman who takes care of herself, should clean the gun and load and prepare it for her husband. She should help her husband to sleep and make a cup of tea for him. When he stays at home, she should take care of him. This is what we could do to help in the village."[160]

A number of narrations brought to light how the men involved in the revolution were interested in training their daughters and wives to use weapons. The narrator **Nadeyyah Omar Hamed** reveals, throughout her narration, the reason behind her father's interest in training her. She used to go out with him at night and he was relying on her to do various tasks and to be able to move quickly and lightly. This meant that she had to be well trained in using weapons as well as different sports. In her testimony she said "Yes, at night he used to teach me how to shoot using a gun. He would place the gun on my shoulder and say hold the rifle tightly, lean your body and your weight to the front, so I bent my body forwards and shot while he was supporting my back from behind, God bless his soul. My father wanted to train me to use weapons. He also liked to teach me how to box. He used to say 'Come on, now, let's box' and he even used to say to my cousins 'Whoever defeats Nadeyyah will get to marry her'. Nobody of my own age was capable of defeating me. He trained me to shoot and to run. He said to me once 'Come on, I want to see who would win in a race, me or you. I swear nobody has ever defeated me so how could you win my little daughter?' And he would say 'I count on you in every way'. I swear he always used to say 'I count on you my daughter'."[161]

When the researcher asked the narrator **Haijar Mustafa Muhammad Dhafer** about her knowledge of weapons, she replied as follows:

"- Would you know whether a weapon is in a good condition or not?

- Yes, I would know. When I dismantle the mechanism of the weapon, I open it. If it is full (of bullets), then it needs two magazines."[162]

Similarly when a researcher asked **Karimah Ismail Barham** about her sister handling weapons her answer indicated a detailed knowledge of how to use such weapons:

" - What was your sister doing?

- One day, when we were young, I saw her holding a gun; she dismantled it, cleaned it, attached the magazine, adjusted it and then put the cloth down. I took the cloth to make a dress for my toy and she immediately said 'No, sister. We need this for the gun'. So, yes, they used to help."[163]

When the researcher asked the narrator **Hamida Abu Rayyah** about her weapons training, her father's role in training her became very clear:

"- Have you ever held a weapon or been trained to use one?

- Yes, my father trained me.

-You were being trained?

- Yes, yes.

Chapter 2: The Political Participation in the 1936 Revolt

- Did you hold the training at night?
- Yes, yes. I will tell you more about this because I forgot to mention it previously. One day, my father said to me 'My daughter, the rebels are at Mansouret Al-Salahat. Tell your mother to cook chicken and Musakhan. Then bring some water and the food to Mansouret Al-Salahat. Do you know where Mansouret Al-Salahat is? It is on the Bait Jebrin route.' I said 'You mean I should go near Zaitet Wedyan?' and he said 'They call it, in the village, the Murder of Shihada'. I said 'Father, the Murder of Shihada! I do not dare to enter there. The martyrs will reveal themselves to me. I'm afraid I will die from fear'. He slapped both his palms on either side of my face and said 'Let me tell you this: your father is Ahmad Abu Rayyah, how could you be afraid? You will bring the food!' I agreed that I would and he instructed me to take his gun. He said 'My daughter, I gave your mother a pocket of money which is hidden in her chest' (as though this is a secret message for her). My mother prepared the food and gave it to me on a large griddle along with a goatskin of water. I carried the goatskin on my shoulder and the griddle on my head. Whilst I was walking, near the Murder of Shihada area, a dark thing approached me and I shouted out in fear 'Is this the place where Shihada was murdered?' The stranger grabbed me and I started to scream. Then I started to make sounds to calm myself down. I was not trying to be a heroine. I said 'I will shoot you, stand up before me'. Then whilst I was preparing my gun and saying that I would shoot him, the stranger said 'I am your father, my daughter, I am your father. May God bestow happiness upon you. May the breast that fed you be praised; I am your father'. I answered 'No, you are not my father. Prove it or I will shoot you dead'. He said 'The pocket of money is hidden in your mother's chest. The proof is that the pocket of money is hidden in your mother's chest'. Then my father took the food, water, and the gun, and told me to go home."[164]

Bearing Arms and Participating in Battles

Both women and men remembered the names of women who not only hid, cleaned and transported weapons but also took up arms and participated in battles. There were thirteen narrations that described this role; 11 told by women and 2 from men. The narrator **Afifeh Hijaz** from 'Anabta, for example, talked about her neighbor Amina Al-Sheikh Ahmad taking up arms. She said "I did not have a weapon and I did not

Part 1: The Political Participation of Palestinian Women

know how to shoot but my neighbor Amina Al-Sheikh Ahmad, may God bless her as she was a good woman, used to bear arms alongside her husband. I used to ask her 'O poor woman, how?' and she answered 'What is wrong with that? I shoot'.

- Did her husband allow her carry a weapon?

- Actually, the two of them used to go together, helping each other."[165]

A number of narrators also witnessed the participation of women in battle for themselves. **Fattoum Al-Ghurairi, Ta'ah Awad** and **Najeyyah Barham** said the following;

"In the 1936 Revolt, in some villages like Al-Taiba near Tulkarm, there were women who held guns and fought. They participated fully; I genuinely mean a woman alongside her husband, him holding one gun and her holding another."[166]

"The courageous woman used to carry weapons, and the women that were more fearful did not. I told you that I carried weapons myself and fired them twice. Women also came to help with food and drink or to spray water on whoever fell down and give them assistance. I mean they participated alongside the rebels."[167]

"- So she held weapons?

- Of course, she used weapons. This woman used to go to the caves and sleep there.

- Ruqayya, the daughter of Sheikh Omar?

- Ruqayya, the daughter of Sheikh Mahmoud Abdul Rahim. Sheikh Mahmoud was the lion of all lions."[168]

- "Yes, she used to shoot at the British soldiers. Her brother also used to shoot at them, so she fought alongside him."[169]

In contrast to the women who played down the significance of their work in the revolution, there was a small group of women who praised their own contribution and considered their job to be participation in the revolution. However, certain characteristics were very common amongst both parties including strength, determination, and high self-confidence.

When the researcher asked the narrator **Khazneh Al-Khatib** - who is from Haifa but lives in Al-Yarmouk Camp in Syria - about her work during that period, she confidently summarized the role of women in the thirties as she saw and experienced it:

"I told you, I had the injured and the martyrs (staying at her place). I had the weapons here too."[170]

Furthermore when Khazneh Al-Khatib was asked in the questionnaire about her job, she answered: 'Revolutionary' and Haijar Mustafa answered the question in a similar way, saying: "During the days of the revolution, our job was 'Weapons'."[171]

Karimah Ismail Barham's description of her mother transporting weapons to the rebels in the mountains at night clearly shows admiration of her mother's strength and determination. Barham said: "At night, they would go out. I swear my mother, God bless her soul, was a gang leader. She was very courageous and smart. She would take the weapons and cover them with grass and straw."[172]

When **Khazneh Hassan Al-Khatib** was asked about carrying and shooting weapons, and getting trained to use them during that period, she responded, "Sheikh Ezzedin Al-Qassam trained me and my children. I was covered and had my pistol at my waist. I fought until we left."[173]

Chapter Three

The Impact of the Failure of the 1936 Revolt on Palestinian Women

The Impact of the Failure of the 1936 Revolt

After bringing to light the multiple roles that women played during the 1936 Revolt, it became necessary to investigate the effect of the eventual failure of the Revolt upon these women.

26 narrators (22 males and 4 females) responded to a question about the impact of the collapse of the Revolt on Palestinian women. 35 percent of these narrators (9 females) claimed that the collapse of the revolt had a positive effect on Palestinian women, whilst 31% (6 females and 2 males) believed the effect was negative. Of the remaining narrators 19% (3 females and 2 males) thought that the collapse of the revolt did not affect Palestinian women and 15% (4 females) said they were not able to determine what effect it had on these women. When we inquired further about the way in which the end of the revolt had a positive impact on women, we found that the replies we received were just general enthusiastic responses, lacking in detail and seemingly reflecting assumptions of what the situation should be from a woman's point of view.

The narrators **Fatima Al-Darhali** and **Subhi Ghousheh** saw the end of the Revolt as having no impact on women: "No, it didn't have any impact. Revolts have never affected women. I mean they could meet at any time, and women continued their activities because they were supported by the men. The Palestinian men were liberal and sympathetic and they used to support women."[174]

"Actually Palestinian women, as I said before, continued with their primary work such as teaching their children at home. In 1939 many

Part 1: The Political Participation of Palestinian Women

people died as martyrs or were arrested. However, women kept on with their activities and in fact probably increased them. There was a lot of solidarity; those women whose husbands were martyred or arrested did not give up, on the contrary, they kept going and continued looking after their children. So I don't think that women failed to do their duties. Some might have suffered a setback on the elite level, but this does not apply to the grassroots level."[175]

The following narrators expressed a similar opinion: **Ali Musa Abu Yousef**, **Suad Abu So'ud** and **Haroun Hashem Rasheed**.

"No, it didn't affect them negatively, but rather, encouraged them."[176]

"Well, in 1939, women here worked within the Women Union. My mother and Mrs. Issam Hamdi Al-Huseini, were members of it and their activities were not affected; they kept working. The Union has always been, and will remain, active. Today, the Union includes Yusra Al-Barbari and others, and they are still in action."[177]

"The famous statement by the Arab Kings and Presidents in 1936 supposedly put an end to the strike. We agreed with the British on whatever (…) But it was the Arab regimes that agreed to stop the strike, not us. Once we discovered that no real changes had been brought about by the agreement we immediately resumed the strike and the Revolt continued until 1939; the year that World War II broke out. World War II stopped the Revolt. Initially we just received lip service, then the White Paper was issued, so the Revolt stopped. But neither men nor women really stopped after 1939. I testify that neither men nor women stopped. They were not taken in by all those things."[178]

We can also notice more realistic answers – both in form and content - which talk about positive factors such as helping distressed and affected families, individually and collectively, through establishing societies and unions affiliated to Arab unions, as explained by the narrators **Afaf Al-Idreesi** and **Isam Abdulhadi**.

"The thing that I remember most is my mother's charitable contributions. Although she was old she was a good sewer and she usually gave things, such as handmade clothes, to poor families. I also remember her providing some food to people when there was conflict. Until her death, she remained active and patriotic."[179]

Chapter 3: The Impact of the Failure of the 1936 Revolt on Palestinian Women

"The women started to combine their efforts and realize their potential. Later, after 1936, they established the unions that became the symbol of women's action. Then the Women's Union itself came into being. A significant role in forming the General Arab Women Union and its local branches was played by Huda Sha'rawi. The Palestinian branch was the most important (...) given that all Arab women aimed to serve the Palestinian cause. Sha'rawi organized the first conference and then a second one which sought to further the aim of buying back lost land from the enemy; an action that represents a landmark in the history of the women's struggle. After that she started forming the different branches. As I told you earlier, Huda Sha'rawi first visited Jerusalem to attend a huge meeting - which included representatives from all the cities, villages and camps in Palestine - in order to establish women's unions, and it was through this that the women's unions came into existence."[180]

We can see from the narrations that the 'negative impact' of the failure of the revolt on women is actually the same as the 'positive' one; the difference lies in the perspective of the narrators. Those who see the effects of the failure of the revolt as negative focus on the suffering of the Palestinians at that time. They also speak about the establishment of societies and unions, yet they identify a point of weakness in them emanating from the failure of the Revolt. This point is revealed by the narrators **Virginia Tarazy**, **Salma Al-Huseini** and **Widad Al-Ayyoubi**:

"Because, you know, in 1939, the British were so cruel that they did not spare anyone from imprisonment, beating and humiliation."[181]

"The societies continued to exist, but they languished due to the outbreak of WWII and eventually they stopped. Everyone was imprisoned and the Revolt came to an end. Hajj Ameen Al-Huseini fled the country and Al-Qassam died a martyr. The communities survived three years of war, then in 1948 all the Palestinians were expelled and suffered severely."[182]

"I think it was a strike to the heart (...) to feel like the 1939 Revolt was not an important event. We expected something but were surprised with something else. In 1939 we felt that the British Mandate authority, government and people were supporting Zionism and working in league with the Zionist gangs, providing them with funds, military support, training etc. As I said before, the activity of Palestinian women was limited up until then; their action was restricted to indirect political activity. They were not able to go out and hold a large public demonstration and any small assemblies were dispersed quickly. The British police would not allow them to march. However, Palestinian women played a role in supporting their sons, husband and brothers. They did not sit down and say 'No, son! Stay at home'. Instead, they used to urge them on, telling them that this country is theirs, so they should take part in the activities in support of it."[183]

We received a particularly interesting and important testimony from the historian and narrator **Abdul-Qader Yaseen** who described how the general situation in the late 1930s actually became conducive to liberal social attitudes; however he claims that Palestinian women did not take advantage of this development due to a lack of educated women:

"The collapse of the 1936 Revolt had the following results: firstly large swathes of the bourgeois class started losing their revolutionary spirit and began to consider the clash with the British colonialists a fruitless endeavor. Then there arose a tendency for these people to compromise, particularly when the Mandate authorities permitted Arab Palestinian industries to operate. This measure was not intended to benefit those industries, but rather to meet the needs of the British forces deployed in Palestine during WWII (39-45), especially when German submarines kept sinking the ships which the British used to carry supplies to their forces all over the world. Consequently the British began promoting national industries in each of its colonies in order to cover the needs of the British forces deployed in them. This encouraged the tendency of large segments of the Palestinian bourgeoisie to cooperate with the British. Industries grew at a fast pace and as a result, the working class expanded and the local bourgeoisie became stronger. These two factors created a breeding ground (...) for socially liberal thinking. However, women did not benefit from this change in atmosphere due to the lack of educated women. As people know, it was men who summoned the women to support them in the fight against colonialism and Zionism, and he who summons you can send you home whenever he wants. This is what happened in Palestine."[184]

Abdul-Qader Yaseen's statement invites many questions concerning the socially liberal thinking that accompanied women's political thoughts of liberation at the time. The findings of our research show that such

Chapter 3: The Impact of the Failure of the 1936 Revolt on Palestinian Women

thinking was espoused by small educated groups of women[1] in the 1930s. The research also further investigates the growth of this thinking during later periods.

We find a different answer from the narrator **Samiha Khaleel** who claimed that the collapse of the revolt did not have any effect on women as neither they, nor the men, were actually aware that the revolt had collapsed. This explains why four female narrators said that they had no idea about the impact of the end of the revolt on women.

"- Nobody admitted the failure of the Revolt. Everybody knew that the British were against us and helped the Jews by confiscating land and killing young men.

- I mean the Palestinians themselves did not admit the collapse, and the result was (…)

- We never heard anything about the end of the revolt because there was no media."[185]

---

1. Please refer to p. 43 of the research that talks about the women's anti-hijab demonstration in the 1930s . Also refer to the testimony of Samira Khouri/ Nazareth/ Archive

Chapter Four

Women in People's Collective Memory

Whereas written history has generally overlooked and omitted the names of women who were involved in politics in the 1930s, oral history is full of their names.

In the Narrators' Memories

When the male narrators were asked to answer specific questions about women who were active in politics in the 1930s, their memory did not serve them well. In fact, whilst they emphasized the contribution of women they could not mention the name of a single woman active at that time. However, they were more able to remember the names of women from later periods. For example, the narrator **Subhi Ghousheh** spoke about the active participation of village women in the Revolt, and although he couldn't give us the full name of any women he was able to remember their family names.

"- The women used to take part in national action by smuggling in weapons from outside the wall, especially those wearing the Milaya (outer garment) who used to put the weapons (grenades and guns) under their clothes. There were many stories about these women.

- Can you name any of them?

- Actually they used to say *X's* mother or *Y's* mother, for example, from the Dkeidek family. It was said that village women usually hid weapons inside the parsley containers and brought them into Jerusalem for the rebels. We also learned about many village women who used to transport weapons, as well as food and news, to the rebels' locations."

The narrators sometimes mentioned women nicknames such as Um Al-Mu'mineen (the mother of believers) who was mentioned by the

Part 1: The Political Participation of Palestinian Women

narrator **Bahjat Abu Gharbiyah** although he didn't remember her real name. When the researcher asked him about women's involvement in military activities he gave an affirmative answer, but when she asked him to give specific names he was not able to. However, he did keep emphasizing the active involvement of women in military activities:

"- Did women take part in military activities?

- They did in a way (..) I mean a woman and her husband (..) he carried a gun, and she carried a gun.

- Can you mention any specific names?

- No, I can't.

- OK, but you witnessed examples of the involvement you mentioned?

- Yes, I saw with my own eyes a woman who was called Um Al-Mu'mineen (the mother of believers), one from Arab Al-Sawahreh and another from Bal'a. I also witnessed the demonstration in Jerusalem when the protestors and the police clashed.

-You mean that you witnessed a clash between women and the police?

- Yes, the police."[186]

The narrator **Kamal Abdul Rahim** also mentioned the nickname (Um Rmeih) of a woman who was involved in a leadership capacity.[1] When the researcher inquired further about this woman in her successive questions, the narrator's memory was stirred and the name residing in its depths rose to the surface to assume its deserved place in oral history.

This can also be seen when we listen to the testimony of the narrator **Ali Musa Abu Yousef** in which he mentioned, upon the insistence of the researcher, the names of a number of women:

"- I want you to tell me about your memories concerning the engagement of women in national public action in the past.

- On the political level, or in general?

- First, tell me about their role in national public action, but it's OK to also talk about other matters such as education and social activities etc.

---

1. To review the relevant paragraph, please refer to the narrator Kamal Abdul Rahim's testimony/ Archive

Chapter 4: Women in People's Collective Memory

- How much did women help men then? Do you mean this?

- Yes.

- Since the beginning of my life, women have always stood side by side with their husbands; her hand with his in the field. However, at the beginning of the British occupation (Mandate), before I was born, the Tel[1] was established, so women rushed to Jerusalem because it was the only city with consulates and embassies. They went to the embassies and whilst some of them felt sympathy for these women and responded to their appeals, others simply dismissed them, as was the case with the American embassy, which has been the head of the snake since the beginning. Back then it was the woman who went to those embassies and they played a major role in saving many detainees.

- Can you elaborate on the issue of the Tel, and explain exactly what role women played and, if possible, mention the names of some of those who went to Jerusalem and took part in these events? What happened exactly at the Tel?

- The detainees meant everything to these women and they were getting close to death. Each woman, who had a father, son or husband behind bars, would not sleep on the ground, but instead lean on the stone walls around the so-called Tel, which was given this name because it was located in a hilly area.

- Wasn't the area called the Tel?

- No, this wasn't the name of a certain place. It was the label applied to a number of large detention centers and prisons. They really went there, as I said, but we didn't know many of them.

- Can you mention any names?

- Only a few.

- Who were they?

- One was called Aisha Anani, the wife of Abdul-Qader Mahmoud who was in jail, and Um Reem Abed Rabbuh who I saw with my own eyes throwing dust and hitting the chief of police. There was Halima Reemash from Jerusalem, and Hamdeh Al-Arja and Maryam Abdul-Fattah Imran (..) but my knowledge of women activities is not very

---

1. Refers to Large prisons and detention centers

Part 1: The Political Participation of Palestinian Women

deep. Those were the women, as far as I can remember, who went to Jerusalem and visited the embassies.

- Now, are you saying that these were the only women who went to Jerusalem, or were there others with them?

- There were many others with them.

- OK, approximately how many?

- I can tell you that there were more than 20, but I don't know them.

- Alright.

- I don't know them.

- Well, who do you think was the strongest one? I mean the one who lead or directed them?

- It was Aisha because she had literate relatives there and they showed her the way.

- Is Aisha Anani alive?

- No, she's dead.

- None of those women are alive?

- No, they're all dead."[187]

When a researcher asked the narrator **Ahmad Al-'Isawi** about the names of women he could remember, he tried to evade the question despite the fact that he actually knew the names of many women who had participated in politics at that time.

"- Do you remember any names?

- Oh, my daughter! There are too many names but I can't identify any."

The researcher was not satisfied with this brief answer and kept asking questions that might uncover the names of unknown women who played active political roles:

"- Do you know any prominent names? I mean very active women?

- In fact, I know one from my town called Manseyya."

The researcher was still not contented with this one name and instead continued trying to get more information that could be a valuable addition to recorded history.

"- Manseyya what?

- She was from Beit Hanina. Her daughter is still alive. Another one was called Latifa Al-Salman and there was also Hasna Al-Qattouna. She had two sisters who still live in my town.

- Do you remember any other names from the past?

- I remember one.

- From your town?

- My town? No! From Mukhmas - Fatima Al-Mikhmasiyyeh."

The researcher again pursued her questioning in order to try to understand what made this woman so important to the narrator, who had previously declined to give any names. Her questions refreshed his memory and he started to recall many other names as well.

"- What was it that she used to do?

- When the British warplanes attacked the rebels at Mukhmas, four of them were killed. Fatima Al-Mikhmasiyyeh gathered a number of women and they stood up to the British soldiers and prevented them from taking the bodies of the dead. They put the bodies in a well, and then later they took them out and buried them. I remember a woman from 'Anata called Jamila Abduljawwad, she was nicknamed 'the mother of rebels', and there was another one from the Oudeh family who saved many people (Interviewer: at this point Mohammad, who helped me to arrange this meeting, intervened and asked: Ni'ma or Fatima?) Fatima Oudeh. There were also some women from Al-Tur.

- What did the one from 'Anata, Jamila Abduljawwad, do?

- She was really clever. Cars used to come to the distant villages of Mukhmas and 'Anata by the same road, and then those coming to 'Anata would take the bypass. When the rebels were in 'Anata, a group of women, who usually stayed at home, were ordered by Jamila to keep an eye on the road, which they did. We were living in the eastern part of 'Anata when the soldiers attacked the town from the west. Jamila made her way through the soldiers and got to the town center, where she began screaming 'Those who can hear my voice praise your prophet Mohammad. Whoever has seen or done a bad thing, may God deprive him of children and may he suffer the lack of children'. This alarmed the surrounding people and they began to notice the soldiers. If not for the alarm, the soldiers would have killed or done very bad things to us because they raided the town very suddenly."[188]

The narrator **Ahmad Al-Zaben** mentioned the names of several women in his preliminary interview, however in the recorded interview, when the researcher asked him for the names of the women who helped the rebels, he was initially only able to give one name;

"I know about seven or eight women. In my village, Al-Teera, although young women were not allowed to walk around or sit with men, the old women were helpful.

- Do you remember any of the women who used to transport weapons and help the rebels in 1936?

- Shamseh Al-Hasna from Al-Teera. She used to sell milk in Haifa so she usually carried the milk and walked around. She would get a gun and carry it from one place to another all the time calling "Milk! Milk!" Then when it was time, she would hand it to a specified individual who, in turn, would shoot the targeted person and hand the gun back so she could hide it under her clothes (...) then, she usually went on calling "Milk! (...) Milk" while people were running away.

- Do you remember any women other than Shamseh Al-Hasna?

- No, I don't remember any except Shamseh Al-Hasna, the milk seller."

However, the researcher did not give up on this line of inquiry and continued asking both direct and indirect questions:

- Were there many women involved in the 1936 Revolt?

- They were too many to remember. They used to jump onto anyone that the police were searching for and cover them with the milaya to help them escape. Every woman in Haifa, be they Muslim or Christian, used to help the 1936 Revolt.

- Now I want to ask you about the women who were disciples of Al-Qassam. What happened to them after the martyrdom of Al-Qassam? Did their group remain active?

- They continued to act in secret until the 1936 Revolt. The members contacted each other and collected money. Those who had gold usually gave it to the rebels, as did a bride from my town.

- What was her name?

- It was Maryam Husein from the Ammouri's. She gave her gold to the rebels."[189]

When we examine the narrators' reports of the actions of their next of kin - reports which naturally have high credibility - it is interesting to note that whilst they talk about their mothers and aunts, they do not mention their names unless specifically asked to. This is clear in the testimonies of the narrators **Ahmad Maw'ed** and **Dawud Eraikat**.

"- Speaking of women, I saw with my own eyes that when the British soldiers encircled the town and broke into the houses, which they did often, women would stand up against them. Take my mother, for example, she used to hit the British soldiers with a stick to prevent them from entering the house. Another woman called Amina Mustafa from my village, Safforia, hit the British soldiers right before my eyes.

- What is your mother's name?

- Zahra Hasan Maw'ed."[190]

"The women's struggle in Palestine started very early. They contributed to political and social activities and before 1948 a number of women's organizations working in many different fields emerged in Palestine. One of them, which I remember well, was in Jerusalem and was chaired by Mrs Zulaikha Al-Shihabi. She spent her whole life doing this kind of work, as a leader assisted by *dozens* of women. I remember both my mother and aunt took part in this society, but I can't be sure of the extent of their participation due to the lack of documents.

- Don't you remember the name of that society?

- It was the Women's Society. After that it became larger and a branch was opened in Jericho. It performed many activities. Mrs Zulaikha was a real leader. People used to compare her with Huda Hanem Sharaawi.

- Would you tell us your mother's name?

- It's Aisha Alhajj Khaleel Al-Makki, from Bab Al-Sahira Jerusalem.

- And your aunt's name?

- It's Ruqayya Alhajj Khaleel Al-Makki. She owned a sewing workshop

Part 1: The Political Participation of Palestinian Women

and was very active. They used to raise funds, organize meetings, protests and demonstrations, and take part in all the battles together with the men. Although there were not a great number of them, their participation was significant."[191]

The narrator, **Zuheir Al-Shawish**, explained why the names of women were intentionally overlooked, pointing to the fact that referring to a woman by her name was disliked and shameful. This may partly account for the way recorded history has overlooked women who were involved in public activities in the 30s as 'mentioning a woman's name was shameful'.

"- Many Palestinian women moved across the northern part of Palestine to Al-Maidan for fear of the British forces, because if it was known that there was a gun in a certain house, whether it had been used or not, the British police used to come and arrest the whole family. They would arrest the woman first to force her to tell them where the gun was hidden. They would usually take her to jail where she might get tortured and abused, but she never told them where the gun was.

- Did this happen often? I mean, did you hear of it?

- As a child, I often heard about these things from the women in my family. That's because an 11 or 12 year old boy was not allowed to see other women as the situation is now. In the past, we didn't see them, but we usually heard what they were doing from our parents. For example, we often heard how a woman had hidden a gun or a rifle; how she had left her house, how she dropped it in the water well, how she retrieved it and so on. So, women were men's partners and shouldered half the responsibility for the Jihad. This all took place and we heard about it. Then, when the women had to escape, they used to cross the borders which were guarded by the British police and their Palestinian collaborators, not to mention the Zionists. A woman would usually leave her village and travel to a distant one on the Syrian border, before going on to Syria. This journey often took 5 - 10 days, sometimes on a donkey or sometimes on a camel. After that, the woman would find a car to carry her from place to place, but at that time cars often got overcrowded. Then, she would arrive in Damascus and from there head south to Al-Maidan and eventually she would find some people she knew. The entire journey would be crowded and difficult. Wasn't this Jihad?! For God's sake, what is Jihad then?! Killing?! Opening fire?! She opened fire.

Chapter 4: Women in People's Collective Memory

People didn't use to say, for example, 'Fatima Mahmoud Said did this or that', because mentioning a woman's name was shameful. You asked me the names of my wife and daughters and I told you them because I'm old enough and times have changed. Maybe, if I had been asked the same question in 1936, I would not have told you my mother's name. Not because I was uncivilized, but because that was the situation then."[192]

The narrator, **Anis Al-Sayegh** talked about the involvement of both rural and urban women in the Revolt. However he was only able to mention the names of urban educated women such as Sathej Nassar, Zulaikha Al-Shihabi, Matil Maghnam and Tarab Abdulhadi (whose first name he could not actually remember since some women were primarily referred to as "the wife of" their politically active husbands.

"I know a lot of stories about the contribution of women, but these only relate to the villages. Inside cities, I don't think there was the same degree of encouragement and enthusiasm, except in literate circles. In cities like Jaffa, Jerusalem, Acre and Haifa, where women's societies came into existence, there were quite a few literate women who contributed to establishing societies, writing books and articles and attending conferences. Back then the women in each city would usually elect one woman from amongst themselves to attend conferences. Some of them used to write wonderful articles and books such as Sathej Nassar in Haifa, the prominent figure Zulaikha Al-Shihabi and Matil Maghnam in Jerusalem, and the wife of Awni Abdulhadi (..) I can't remember her first name (Tarab). All of them were related to national figures and activists; either as wives, daughters or sisters. They all were descendants of elite families."[193]

In Women's Memories

The female narrators had retained within their memories the names of many women who were active in the 1930s. It was noticeable that urban women were more able to remember the names of other urban women who were active:

The narrator **Samira Khouri**, for example, recalled the names of women involved in leading demonstrations: Saba Al-Fahoum, Masarra Canaan, Jurjeit Bshara. Mateel Maghnam, Adele Qanaze', Mazeen Rashed, as

Part 1: The Political Participation of Palestinian Women

well as her mother whose name she didn't mention.[1]

Similarly, the female narrator **Issam Hamdi Al-Huseini** and the male narrator **Haroun Hashem Rasheed** both mentioned the name of Rabab Al-Huseini whose name is associated with leading a famous demonstration in the city of Gaza.[2]

The narrator **Amena Al-Winni** also mentioned the name of Suhaila Al-Rimawi in connection with leading demonstrations in the same period.[3]

Furthermore, the narrator **Awatef Abdulhadi** mentioned the name of her sister Tawadud Abdulhadi in addition to the name of Nader Al-Aref's mother when talking about the participation of Palestinian woman in the political action and leading demonstrations in the Jenin area.[4]

The narrator **Salma Al-Huseini**, mentioned the names of Wajeeha Al-Huseini, Zulaikha Al-Shihabi, Zahia Al-Nashashibi, Khadija Al-Huseini, Aisha Al-Huseini, Rabab Abdulhadi and Hiba Al-Jazzar as women who were actively involved in women's societies and unions. In addition, she emphasised Wajeeha Al-Huseini's significant role in sheltering the rebels and smuggling weapons.[5]

In addition the narrator **Samiha Khaleel** talked about the significant role played by Wadee'a Qaddourah Khartabil in Tulkarm[6] and the narrator **Ulga Al-Aswad** talked about a the role of Um Isam Al-Houri in Haifa.[7] Finally the narrator **Zakeyya Khaled** also spoke about the

---

1. To review the relevant paragraph, please refer to the testimony of Samira Khouri/ Archive

2. To review the relevant paragraph, please refer to the testimonies of Issam Hamdi Al-Huseini and Haroun Hashem Rasheed/ Archive

3. To review the relevant paragraph, please refer to the testimony of Amna Al-Wenni/ Archive

4. To review the relevant paragraph, please refer to the testimony of Awatef Abdulhadi/ Archive

5. To review the relevant paragraph, please refer to the testimony of Salma Al-Huseini/ Archive

6. To review the relevant paragraph, please refer to the testimony of Samiha Khaleel/ Archive

7. To review the relevant paragraph, please refer to the testimony of Ulga Al-Aswad/ Archive

Chapter 4: Women in People's Collective Memory

special role her mother, Jamila Ma'touk played, together with other women, in transferring weapons to the rebels.[1]

Some prominent names of urban women were mentioned repeatedly, especially those who played an important role in women societies and unions, for example Shahanda Al-Dazdar, Zahia en-Nashashibi, Fatima Al-Nashashibi, Badreyya Al-Huseini, Salma Al-Huseini, Nuzha Darweesh, Fatima Abu-Su'od, Zulaikha Al-Shihabi and Wadee'a Qaddourah Khartabil. This emphasized the significant role of societies and unions in publicizing the names of some women who performed public activities in that early time:

"I remember well that in Jerusalem there were a number of women's assemblies that started with the Arab Women Society headed by the late Shahanda Al-Dazdar, along with her companions Zahia en-Nashashibi, Fatima Al-Nashashibi and Zulaikha Al-Shihabi. It was a huge women's assembly that was active from 1929 to 1936. In 1936 it gave birth to the Arab Women Union Society. This new society was formed with the purpose of enhancing the social and revolutionary activities, and because it was thought that each society should have its particular objectives. Although I was just a little girl then, I can clearly recall that the Women Union Society was involved in indirect political action, e.g. raising funds and organizing exhibitions. All the money collected was given to the rebels to buy weapons and other necessities. The rebels were groups of young men spread all over Palestine including Jerusalem."[194]

In contrast when they talked about rural women, the urban narrators did not mention specific names, although they did acknowledge their significant role.

"It was the rural women who struggled and participated in the revolt more that urban women. I knew a woman from Ein Karem who used to carry a gun. Regrettably, she died.

- What was her name?
- I wish I could remember it.
- What did she usually do with the gun?
- She fought like the men did, along with her husband.

---

1. To review the relevant paragraph, please refer to the testimony of Zakeyya Khaled / Archive

- *Third party*: In Ein Karem?
- In Ein Karem."[195]

"There was a woman from Al-Falouja. I don't remember her name, but most likely it was Um Ali or something similar! She was 60 years old. My father, may Allah have mercy upon him, used to tell us about her. He often said that he had never seen such a great woman. Although she was from Al-Falouja, she used to carry her weapon and travel along the road to Acre, then onwards to some unknown destination."[196]

In the same way that the urban narrators didn't give the names of rural women, the rural women interviewed didn't mention the names of urban women who participated in the revolt. However, they did give the names of female relatives and next of kin whose struggle they witnessed close-up. We can see this in the testimony of **Widad Al-'Arouri**:

"My mother was very smart. She was illiterate but she had a bag in which she kept all the documentation for her properties. She was one of 52 shareholders in the house which had once been the residence of the High Commissioner. When we sometimes asked her to give us a paper from the Turkish era, she would not allow us to touch the bag. Instead, she herself would always open it and say 'this paper is for this piece of land, this to prove our share in the electricity company and this to guarantee our share in Palestine Railways Company'. I mean, she was so clever to recognize papers and memorize a whole letter. Also if a statement was issued, she would put it in her basket, cover it with food and leave the place.

- Did she accompany the women who went to the High Commissioner and gave him a paper?

- To be honest, I don't know whether she ever went with her aunt and those other women.

- Who was her aunt?

- She was Ahmad Jaber's mother. She was called Khazneh Qasem Murrar, mother of the Mujahed Ahmad Khazneh, a disciple of Abdul-Qader Al-Huseini.

- Did her aunt go with the others to Abdul-Qader Al-Huseini?

- Yes, she did, and she went to the High Commissioner and gave him a letter appealing for him not to execute her only son.

Chapter 4: Women in People's Collective Memory

- What did she do when the British executed him?

- My great-aunt did not bury his body at her home, nor in her village, Beit Attar.[1] Instead, she buried him in a nearby village and planted tomato seedlings on his grave. This was what we were told. I recall that whenever my great-aunt Khazneh entered Bab Al-Amud (Damascus Gate), where there was a café named Za'tara, men would stand up, seat her among them and order her a narghile and a cup of coffee because she was a mother of a martyr, and a fellow rebel too. She suppressed her grief as she buried her son lest the site of grave be discovered. Then she planted about a dunum (1/4 acre) around his grave with tomato seedlings and kept watering them every day to grow the plants and hide the grave.

- When she sat in the café, was there any political meaning to this?

- I think she used to sit with the Palestinian rebels in Jerusalem. At that time, women wearing hijab (traditional Muslim body garment) used to enter Bab Al-Amud with their canes and rosaries. Whether they were entering or exiting, they had to pass by that café. So, when my great-aunt happened to be passing by the café called Za'tara, men would stand up, hold her hands and help her climb the stairs. Then they usually seated her on a chair among them and ordered her a cup of coffee and a narghile. She used to sit only among the important men (...)."[197]

The narrator **Latifa Al-Taher** named a woman called Khadra Alhajj Husein who she said took part in battles alongside men: "There was a woman called Khadra from Alhajj Husein's family who did not miss a single battle."[198]

For her part, the narrator **Fatima Al-Khatib** connected the name of Khadra Alhajj Ali with courage and leadership side by side with men:

"- Now, Hajjeh I want you to tell me about your cousin Khadra Alhajj Ali. Okay?

- Okay, my cousin.

- So she was with the rebels, what was it that she used to do?

---

1. The narrator most likely means Beit Attab, one of the Destroyed Villages within Jerusalem district

Part 1: The Political Participation of Palestinian Women

- When they decided to kill a traitor, they would assassinate him in the centre of Haifa, not in rural areas. She used to knock on my window and I would ask 'who is it?' She would reply 'It's me, unlock the door so that if someone sees me on my way back I can drop into your house'. Then I would unlock the door and start pacing to and fro while the door was closed but unlocked.

- You mean you were waiting and watching for her?

- Yes, she used to leave for two hours or so, and then come back after they had finished their work.

- What kind of work was it?

- Killing traitors.

- So they would shoot the traitors and then Khadra would come back and hide in your house?

- Yes, when she came back she used to say 'Okay, now lock the door and go to sleep'. I would keep the door unlocked so that she could drop in and have a rest before anybody saw her.

- Rest and spend the night with you?

- No, on her way to work. My house has a separate gate.

- Was there anything else Khadra used to do?

- I knew everything she did, but sometimes she didn't come by because occasionally she went off with her brother and his companions and acted as a leader side by side with them.

- Her brother was a rebel leader, so she would usually keep them company?

- Yes.

- And go with them to the mountains?

- Yes, she would."[199]

For her part, the narrator **Afifeh Hijaz** mentioned the name of Ruqayya, the daughter of Sheikh Mahmoud, who she claimed was very courageous and used to carry weapons:

"She was from our village. All her family were rebels and her father, who was a revolutionary, was killed. Ruqayya acted publicly and fearlessly. She often incited people to rebel, she encouraged the men and went with them and slept in the caves. She was much older than me, Ruqayya, the daughter of Sheikh Mahmoud Abdul Rahim, the most courageous man."[200]

Finally the narrator **Shams Al-Titi** mentioned in her testimony the name of Hamida Abu Rayyah[1] connecting her with smuggling weapons for the rebels.

In the Memory of both Male and Female Narrators

The woman who occupied a remarkable position in the memories of both men and women was Halima Mohammad Alhajj Mohammad. In addition to being a sister of the 1936 Revolt leader Abdul Rahim Alhajj Mohammad, she had many personal traits that have ensured that she has been remembered throughout the generations. She used to make torches for the rebels to take to the orange orchards and burn what the Zionists had built there. Although she did not act on her own - Um Ashraf Fadda and many others usually worked with her - her powerful personality and leadership made her a prominent figure in discussions about the courageous activities that women performed in that era. For instance the narrator **Kamal Abdul Rahim Alhajj Mohammad**, nephew of Halima, said:

"- She used to carry weapons under her milaya and transport them to certain rebels after she had been hiding them.

- Where did she hide them? In her house?

- She used to hide them in places like the Khabia which was built of clay and had a hatch about this size (indicating a small opening with his hand). It was used to store wheat, barley and corn. When they wanted to take out the corn, they would lift the lid up. She used to put the weapons in there, where nobody would discover them."[201]

However when that same narrator, who was male, was asked about Halima's prominent role in leading groups, he refused to acknowledge her leadership, other than with regards to little things:

"- Mr. Kamal, I understand from your speech that Halima occupied a leadership position?

---

1. To review the relevant paragraph, please refer to the testimony of Shams Al-Titi/Archive

- Yes, she did.

- So everything was under her command?

- Concerning little things, yes. She was a woman who was always travelling. I told you she went to Damascus several times to meet Alhajj Ameen Al-Huseini. She also met Izzat Darwaza and many other personalities and she often went on her own.

- Why did she go?

- After her father died, she went to tell them that Abdul Rahim had died, and that they should keep on fighting and not stop because of his death. This is what she told us. She was strong; compared to other women of her time she had a very strong personality. She was respected, and even feared, by all."[202]

Alhajjeh Halima was also mentioned by female narrators, in particular her role in taking the body of her brother the leader Abdul Rahim Alhajj Mohammad, after he died as a martyr, to be buried in the village of Thinnaba; defying the decision of British authorities that banned his burial in his village.

"- Was it Alhajjeh Halima who said that the body should be exhumed and brought to the village?

- Yes, secretly at night, lest the British should find out.

- Didn't she go with them?

- No, she didn't. (Here his wife intervened saying that Alhajjeh Halima did go with the rebels to the village of Sanour (North Palestine) and that they dug up the grave and took his body."[203]

The testimony of **Alhajjeh Najeyyah Barham** supports the view of Kamal Abdul-Raheem's wife, emphasizing the fact that Alhajjeh Halima actually went to Sanour, arranged the matter with the rebels and brought the body back to bury it in the right place. She said:

"- His body was taken by the people of our village and his sister.

- His sister came and took him?

- His sister came down here and took him on his camel.

- She accompanied them to Sanour?

- She went with them on foot.

Chapter 4: Women in People's Collective Memory

- On foot?!
- Yes, (stressing) *On foot.*"[204]

The same narrator also emphasized the involvement of Alhajjeh Halima in armed struggle:

"Yea, she used to fire at the British forces. Both her and her brother used to open fire at them."[205]

Often when female narrators described a woman's involvement in using arms they would ascribe male characteristics to them, calling them 'manly'. This can be seen in the testimony of the narrators **Haijar Mustafa** and **Zahida Mustafa**:

"Yea, but Halima went with the delegation because she was manly."[206]

"Um Al-Rajeh spent her life as a great manly woman."[207]

In the collective memory of the narrators the martyr Fatima Khaleel Ghazal, whose name can also be found in recorded history, held a particularly prestigious position. The oral history collected from the narrators further highlights and enriches her life story.

Written history records the events of a battle against British troops that took place in Azzoun valley, during which Fatima Ghazal died as a martyr. The books give us a basic outline of the event and note that many rebels died as martyrs in that battle; amongst them an armed woman in military uniform. This led us to wonder exactly what happened in that battle. Where are the testimonies of eyewitnesses who can clarify the events, give us some details and enrich our knowledge? Then, when we listened to the testimony of **Alhajjeh Kamleh Abdul-Rahman Shneik** from Azzoun, it was as if an entire world came into existence. Her description of what happened allowed us to feel the richness and dynamism of history; hers is a testimony which deserves to be recorded, documented and analyzed:

Alhajjeh Kamleh spoke about Fatima Al-Khaleel as follows:

"Fatima Al-Khaleel! Alas! I was so sorry for her death! May Allah have mercy upon her. She was poor, but she used to wear white clothes like a pilgrim and she was always clean. She always looked neat in her cloak. She often went out to work and offer help. She would collect things from different houses, fill up her basket and then find out where the rebels were and catch up with them."[208]

Then she spoke about the event of Fatima Ghazal's martyrdom, and the battle between the British soldiers and the rebels in 1936 (in a sad tone):

"Her son was a rebel. She knew what time he and the rebels used to come to the village, so she usually collected some food such as bread, cooked eggs and yogurt from her friends and carried it to an olive grove where he used to sit. That time, as the rebels were on their way, a British warplane spotted them among the olive trees. In the meantime, Fatima filled her basket with a pot full of cooked food, bread and other foodstuffs and headed to the olive grove to feed the rebels.

As soon as she started walking away up a road at the edge of the village, she saw the soldiers descending towards Wad Al-Sham and trying to encircle the rebels. From her position on the mountain slope, she began shouting 'Go away! Go away! Go away!' (the narrator made a gesture with her hand). The plane attacked her and she fell down on the road before she could reach them. The rebels, for their part, opened fire over and over again at the plane and then started to flee. The plane fired back at them and they fled and managed to reach Jabal Al-Khirba (Soufin, the highest area in Qalqilya). Fatima lay there still. The whole village escaped and when they returned, they found her body thrown in a field. The body of a man called Abu Ahmad Al-Anani was also found in another field, and so were the bodies of Abu Al-Hamshari and Ahmad Al-Qaddoumi."[209]

Chapter Five

Social Changes Accompanying the Political Struggle of Women

In the thirties, women suffered from severe social inequality. Some narrators talked about this inequality in terms of imposed clothing and exhausting work, especially in the case of rural women. These women usually endured heavy work both indoors and outdoors, those under 30 years old were banned from talking to men - preventing them from offering help to the rebels – and scarce attention was paid to their education; they were considered subordinate to men and often married very young. The narrators **Izdihar Al-Shurafa** and **Ahmad Al-'Isawi** talked about this inequality and the suffering of women at that time:

"Despite the fact that all women wore the hijab - the barefacedness we see today was absent – there was inequality."[210]

"Palestinian women suffered a lot. I recall that they had to do all the work; paid work was rare and they were mainly limited to agriculture. The men used to plow the land, thrash and reap the crops and so on, and the rest of work was to be done by the women. She had to take care of the children and prepare the food and, if she happened to have any leisure, her husband would demand that she help him dig and reap the crops. Women then were almost so will-less that in most cases they carried all the burdens of work on their own shoulders. For instance, when the water wells that the people of my village depended on for their water - we didn't have any springs - ran short of water, the woman would walk for 1- 2 hours to collect a tin of water, and so they got very tired."[211]

Both the narrators **Huda 'Amer** and **Rasmiyyeh Al-Barghouthi (Um Al-Abed)** talked about inequality in the form of the strong objections that women faced if they took off their burqa (face cover) and the way women who did this were compared to dancers and thought to deserve severe punishment.

Part 1: The Political Participation of Palestinian Women

"Everyone started wearing the hatta (headscarf). We used to wear the mandil (head cover) (..) Nobody was allowed to wear (..) just a bonnet. If a woman wore just bonnet she would be punished by people throwing burning acid in her face; they would call her a *dancer* and shout at her: 'the bonnet wearer is a dancer who deserves a bullet'. We used to wear black head covers and continued to do so until Alhajj said 'Take it off and put on a shawl' (..) A shawl?! Then, I felt like everybody was watching me because I wasn't used to it! There was no makeup in those days." [212]

"If a woman went out with only a bonnet on, they always said 'The bonnet wearer is out; the dancer who deserves a grenade and a bullet'. Then she would be hit or have burning acid thrown at her. She had to wear a milaya, a pleated skirt and a cover. Both young and old women who started wrapping themselves up completely were considered the best and those who didn't follow these orders were often publicly humiliated."[213]

The narrator **Widad Al-'Arouri** described the urban Jerusalemite women's clothing, which helps to create a detailed knowledge of urban women's clothing in the 30s:

"The clothing of urban Jerusalemite women was composed of a pleated skirt, a burnus (a sort of robe) and a burqu' made of two layers, sometimes the women would put it on and lower both of the layers if the cloth was too thin."[214]

Some narrators identified the position of women in society at that time. Women had a secondary position in the social hierarchy, both in society and at home. Unlike men, they were deprived of the right to work and their movement outdoors was restricted. This was made clear in the testimonies of **Anis Al-Sayegh**, **Alice Nawrasi** and **Ahmad Al-Zaben**:

"Compared with her husband or her brother(s), she was number two in society and at home as well. Therefore she had to accept what the men said."[215]

"Arab women didn't usually have a job other than as a teacher because women's work was considered shameful."[216]

"In our town, Al-Teera, women were forbidden to walk around or sit with men, excluding old women who were usually allowed to help the rebels. Most women - almost all of them - who used to show up were

Chapter 5: Social Changes Accompanying the Political Struggle of Women

over fifty years old because young women were too conservative to walk around or communicate with their relatives outside the home. They were conservative. Every old woman in our town used to treat rebels as their sons or brothers and provide them with food and water. We didn't have bathrooms then, so they used to heat the water and give it to the rebel to wash himself. When a rebel came to her house, she would receive him hospitably and feed him. However, those under 30 years never mixed with men, even a neighbour or a relative. Young women needed permission from their husbands or brothers. On the contrary, old women didn't need anyone's permission. In addition, the young were often more narrow-minded and conservative. In the village of Um Ezzeinat[1], even if a woman had a brother who had been absent in military service or elsewhere, she wasn't able to approach him to welcome him and shake hands, except within the home."[217]

Furthermore, according to the narrator **Sa'adeh Al-Kilani**, women were not asked for their opinion before their marriage was arranged:

"- At that time the people of Hebron were narrow-minded. They would not allow a girl to see her fiancé or vice versa.

- Did your brother or father ask you for your opinion on your fiancé?

- No, they didn't. They knew that his sister had recommended me to him, so my brother travelled to Jaffa and asked the traders about him because he himself was a trader. All of them commended him."[218]

In addition, early marriage for both young men and women was considered desirable as the narrator **Ahmad Al-Zaben** explained, and as we can see in the testimonies of the narrators **Fatheyya Al-Bahsh**, **Makram Al-Qasrawi** and **Zeinab Aqel**:

" I got married at 17. My wife was 14 years old. In the past, unlike nowadays, we used to marry early."[219]

"I was 14 when I got married. Too young! They forced me to marry. May Allah punish (...) I was only 14."[220]

"Due to my mother's illness, my father remarried. When I grew up, I realized that the reason for her illness was her early marriage. She was his second wife; the first wife had also married early but she couldn't endure the marriage and she died after nine months. Then my mother

---

1. A Palestinian village in Haifa district

came along as number two. She told us – may Allah have mercy upon her – that she was in the 3rd grade and too thin. I mean imagine a little girl in the 3rd grade marrying an 18 year old man! Of course her body couldn't stand this. Early marriage is very dangerous but they didn't realize this, so the second wife, my mother, got ill after she had given birth to me. Before me, she had a baby girl but she didn't know how to bring her up. Then, a quarrel took place while she was still in her post birth period (postpartum) and she went into shock. After that, she became very ill and stayed in bed for a whole year. Of course, my father wouldn't tolerate this and so he remarried."[221]

"We were in Deir Yassin[1]. My father had two wives and his father, my grandfather, had three wives. Each one had her own room but the front door was shared by all."[222]

Just as women were deprived of the right to choose their husband, they were also deprived of the right to an education. This is made clear in the testimony of the narrator **Latifa Al-Taher** in which she said that narrow-mindedness and fear of the girl's reputation was the reason girls were deprived of an education as there was a belief that education would enable her to write love letters to young men:

"- Girls didn't use to learn to write my dear! Few people knew a girl who was literate. If you asked anyone to let his/her girl receive an education, they would say "Why? To learn to write letters to boys?" Unlike nowadays, people were narrow-minded at that time. A fiancée could not speak to her fiancé and vice versa, nor walk with him, even to the front door! If he wanted to call on her, he used to sit with her family, and she would not sit with him even for a second. They never met, unlike these days when freedom is required. People in the past were better because the girl usually preserved her honor. Yes, it was better. A bride should not communicate with her groom before the wedding. That way, she keeps her honor. He doesn't speak to her, nor does she speak to him all the way up to the marriage. I was engaged for four years and not once did he said "Good morning" to me and nor would I have replied to his greeting although he was a real man."[223]

---

1. One of the destroyed Palestinian Villages which is located west of Jerusalem. On April 9, 1948, the Zionist terrorist groups, Irgun and Stern, attacked it and committed a massacre that claimed the lives of 250 people including children, women and elders. It was abandoned after that

Chapter 5: Social Changes Accompanying the Political Struggle of Women

This lack of education did not apply to women exclusively. In fact, Palestinian society paid little attention to education in general. This is evident in a number of narratives. The testimony of the narrator **Sheikh Zuheir Al-Shawish** sheds light on the view of education at that time:

"In our time nobody cared for academic education. Although we were an extended family including about 100 of boys of my generation - maybe five years older or younger - as far as I know only three of them from our neighborhood in Al-Maidan pursued their education, the rest left school at the age of 12/13, after they had learned just enough to differentiate between "from" and "to" and between X and Y, then they joined their families in their trade or business. My folks used to trade in sheep, horses, camels, cereals and agricultural products, etc. Our neighborhood schoolboys were mostly scattered amongst the different trades within a short time. This was one reason for the small number of pupils. The other was that after the French forces entered Syria in 1920, a number of schools were established but people boycotted them because they thought that they would turn students into disbelievers. Therefore we were unable to join the government-run schools. Back then there were many schools which were more or less like Katateeb (Qur'anic schools) and which were opened to preserve people's faith as well as to provide them with knowledge. They were simple schools, but, unlike the government schools which were free and offered books, notebooks, etc, they used to charge fees. However, motivated by their religious, patriotic, and nationalist feelings, people boycotted the government schools and as a result, very few continued to study at them."[224]

It is noteworthy that the Christians were often more interested in education than the Muslims, especially with regards to the education of women. This can be seen in a number of narratives, for example the testimony of the writer and historian **Anis Al-Sayegh** provides us with information about the social life and education of women, particularly Christian women, in Al-Bassah[1]:

---
1. The narrator says he knows a lot about the village of Al-Bassah even though he comes from Tiberias. That's because he used to spend 2-3 months of the summer there with his family

Part 1: The Political Participation of Palestinian Women

"- With regards to the social life in the village of Al-Bassah[1], you told me that the women there were different from the women in other Palestinian villages?

- Yes.

- Could you elaborate on this?

- Yes, the reasons were as follows; firstly, the majority of people were Christian and the Christian community is different from the Muslim community. Usually, in Palestine, as in all Arab countries, Christians are more liberal than Muslims in terms of mixing between the sexes. Secondly, the geographical location of Al-Bassah, on the northern border between Palestine and Lebanon influenced it culturally and socially. Life in Lebanon is more liberal than life in Palestine, and allows for a much wider range of mixing between sexes. Al-Bassah's contiguity to 27 Christian villages such as Ein Ebel and others, where mixing was allowed, had an influence on the people of this village."[225]

Anis Al-Sayegh also discussed the existence of a girl's school in Sidon which did afford some girls from Al-Bassah the opportunity to attain an education:

"- You mean that girls in Al-Bassah didn't receive as much education as boys did thanks to this school?

- Yes, but they weren't completely deprived of education because there was a good girls' school in Sidon. My school was also in Old Sidon, and had been established in the 19th century. Sidon is relatively near Al-Bassah so girls from Al-Bassah who couldn't complete their education at Al-Bassah school because it was government-run, usually went to Sidon. My mother graduated from Sidon school in about 1910, which means she had been at that school since the very beginning of the 20th century. She used to ride a horse to school, setting off on a journey passing through Ras an-Nakura and then Tyre, and finally arriving at Sidon. It was a boarding school, so she used to stay there, and then return to Al-Bassah at the end of the year. Since the very beginning of the 20th century there were some literate women; my mother was one of them. Indeed, the existence of that school in Sidon was a great advantage because, unlike now, there were no borders between

---

1. It's a small Palestine village located to the north of Acre, right before Ras an-Nakura

Chapter 5: Social Changes Accompanying the Political Struggle of Women

Palestine in the south and Lebanon in the north, whether economic, cultural or educational."[226]

It is also worth noting that, even at that time, some school girls were able to join national singing bands. The narrator **Fatheyya Al-Bahsh** talked about her membership, prior to her early marriage, in a folklore music band formed by Noah Ibrahim.

"- Well, tell me about that band. How did you join it?

- OK. He came to my school and requested to see the best girls who had pleasant voices and strong characters. Then we were taken to the Roman Church where we were asked to act out something.

- Do you remember which grade you were in then?

- Fourth.

- In fourth grade? You mean you were in your last year at school?

- Yes."[227]

There is no doubt that many social factors were responsible for hampering, to some degree, the political action of women. This was noted by the narrator **Fuad Abbas** when he discussed the activist Samira Abu-Ghazaleh and her appeal to the commander Hasan Salameh to train women in the use of weapons:

"During the 1936-1939 Revolt, Mrs. Samira Abu-Ghazaleh tried to make contact with the commander Sheikh Hasan Salameh to ask him to train, or rather help to train, some girls and women to use weapons so they could fight together with men in the battlefield. However, we must take into account that the initial stages of the women's awakening were hard due to the deep rooted customs and traditions that restricted women's full freedom. Indeed, there remained some social obstacles, no matter how much the national action was pushing towards freedom. She spoke with the Sheikh timidly and he, in turn, responded reluctantly and put off the fulfillment of her demand."[228]

However, women did keep trying to overcome the various social barriers that they faced. At times they succeeded, but at other times they did not. Some women overcame their treatment as the 'vulnerable sex' in that early period through their military activities which gave them the strength, courage and ability to defy the traditions of society and assume their own social position through their own efforts. The

Part 1: The Political Participation of Palestinian Women

narrator **Hamida Abu Rayyah** talked about this:

"I was like this; if a man followed me in the street, I would turn around and shout at him 'I'll shoot you'. and he always turned back and wouldn't dare follow me. I usually asked anyone who tried to follow me: 'Why are you following me?!' Neither a man nor a woman would dare follow me."[229]

Furthermore the requirements of the military and political situation urged some men to turn to their daughters and wives for help in spite of the low social rank of women at the time:

"My father never felt afraid. I used to accompany him if he went to Yasur, Yazur or Samuel. He loved me very much because I used to help him. I would stand on the roof and tell him 'Father, I can see some cars. Should I get dressed? Keep sleeping Mum and take your time'. I would say: 'Dad, The cars have come from Al-Falouja, should I get dressed? You must escape if necessary!' and he would usually say 'Okay daughter'."

Despite the fact that women were compelled to wear the hijab and any violators were threatened with the punishment of having their faces disfigured, a women's demonstration was arranged which called for the hijab to be removed and women's rights to be respected.[1]

Moreover, some women challenged the concept of "shame" particularly by taking up an occupation other than teaching: some of them broke with convention and worked in other jobs, for example Alice Nourasi who worked at the post office.[2]

The Changes in Customs and Traditions as reflected in the testimony of Fattoum Al-Ghurairi

In her testimony[3], the narrator **Fattoum Al-Ghurairi** identified some changes in customs and traditions that happened during this period.

---

1. To review the narrator's testimony, please refer to the interview with Samira Khouri / Nazareth / Archive
2. To review the narrator's testimony, please refer to the interview with Alice Nourasi / Jordan / Archive
3. To review the narrator's testimony, please refer narrator's archive / Al-Yarmouk Camp / Syria

Chapter 5: Social Changes Accompanying the Political Struggle of Women

We also saw this in the testimonies of other women too. In Fattoum's testimony, we can see evidence of women prevailing over customs and traditions as their involvement in political action had an effect on people's attitudes and society began to accept things that had not been accepted before. For example, we can note the increased acceptance of conversations between women and man if the purpose of the conversation was to offer help:

"- You used to talk to the rebels when they knocked at your door, and then you yourself used to give them food?

- Of course! Why not?!

- You used to go out and give it to the rebels?

- Of course I did.

- You would talk to him?

- Of course I would.

- I heard that the women of Safed would not talk to strange men.[1]

- We had to talk to them because our sons were with them. Why not talk to them? We usually gave them food, water and talked to them as well.

(Her niece: this means that they overcame customs and traditions)

Why not?! How could we give them food without talking to them?! We didn't talk to just anyone. We knew the good men and the bad men!"[230]

In her testimony, Fattoum also discussed women's freedom of movement when she talked about a group of women who travelled, upon the rebels' request, to meet Prince Abdullah to try to prevent the execution of a number of rebels from Acre:

"- Well, we drove to Tiberias and from there we went to Samakh by boat. Then we took the train and headed to King Abdullah.

- Where to?

- To Amman. We arrived there at night and no sooner had we gotten

---

1. In the first interview, she said the following about the women of Safed: If the door was knocked, the woman would stand behind it and never ask "Who is it?" as it might be a man and it was a shame if the man heard her voice

there than some damned guy wanted to take us to jail. We had no idea what was going on, and our sons kept asking him to take care of us while we were moving from place to place."[231]

We can also read in Fattoum's testimony a profound understanding of motherhood. She didn't have any children at a time when it was common to blame the woman for not bearing a child. It would have been normal for her husband to marry another woman. But on the contrary, he didn't, because he loved her, and despite pressure from his brother and his relatives to remarry, he didn't yield and he clung to her:

"- Why didn't you have any children?

- Act of God.

- Is it because of you or your husband?

- Nobody knows.

- Didn't you seek medical treatment?

- We didn't. There weren't any doctors and nobody cared.

- Well (..) didn't this affect your relationship with your husband?

- No.

- Did he try to remarry?

- No. He said to them 'Whatever she is, I'll keep her'. He quarreled with his brother because of me without my knowledge. Then, one day, I was told that he and his brother had fallen out, and I said to him 'Hell! Why? Why have you and Rasheed fallen out?' He said 'I do what I want! Stay away from me! What do you want from him?' and then I said to him: 'Hell! Today I'll invite him to dinner'.

- Didn't you feel like having children?

- Never. I didn't care. All the children of my relatives grew up in my home. Why did I need to have kids when there were always girls and boys around me?! Why worry about having kids?!"[232]

Chapter 5: Social Changes Accompanying the Political Struggle of Women

Conclusion

It is clear from this research that Palestinian women made a key contribution to political activities both before and during the 1936 Revolt in both the cities and countryside. Furthermore, the research shows that whilst the role of the urban woman was centered around political action, the role of rural woman was focused more on military action.

With regards to urban women, the oral history confirms what recorded history has stated about the presence of women in Palestinian political life, adding further information and detail to this record. However, with respect to rural woman, the oral history, through its gender analysis method, actually reveals women's active political and military role, and indicates that the military role was the most significant.

Through the method of oral history, the significant role played by women in the 1930s, before the 1936 Revolt, was revealed, particularly during the Al-Qassam Revolt, although it was established that they did not form an organized body called "the comrades of Al-Qassam".

With regards to the involvement of Palestinian women in the 1936 Revolt, it was shown that both urban and rural women played an important active role in politics. For example, they both helped the rebels by reporting on the movements of British soldiers; urban women would pass this information on to the rural women as soon as they learnt of it. The rural women, in turn, had direct sources among the rebels to whom they used to carry food and weapons. The narrators also talked about throwing rocks at the buses transporting British forces and scattering nails to pierce the tires of their cars.

Urban Palestinian women also played a significant role in creating and organizing women's unions and societies which enabled them to take part in Arab and International conferences and gave them an important political and social presence. Furthermore they organized and lead demonstrations, engaging – when necessary - with the British troops; for example the march in 1933 which was spoken about. They also played an important role in incitement which took the form of raising schoolgirls' awareness, delivering revolutionary speeches, holding sessions to raise awareness and inciting people to strike. Finally a social role was played by Palestinian women in the societies and unions where they taught sewing and embroidery, adult literacy, and first aid. This social role also involved organizing demonstrations calling

Part 1: The Political Participation of Palestinian Women

for feminist social demands, such as the freedom to remove the hijab; demonstrations which helped lay down a basis for the feminist trend in the women's movement.

Rural Palestinian women played political, social and military roles but the narrations indicated that the military role was the most dominant. Their involvement in politics was seen in incitement, food provision and active participation in the 1936 strike. In the military field, they transported weapons, hiding them and keeping them away from the view of the British soldiers, and they learnt how to use these weapons and took part in armed combat.

This research also attempts to answer questions related to the impact of the failure of the 1936 Revolt on women. The narrations indicated that the impact of the failure had both negative and positive aspects. On the negative side there was increased suffering for the Palestinian people, but on the positive side there was a highlighted need to establish societies and unions affiliated to Arab unions.

The research also observes the social changes which accompanied the woman's political struggle; changes which paved the way to strengthening the Palestinian women's movement. Despite the social barriers which restricted the freedom of Palestinian women, e.g., denial of education, work, and choice of spouse, as well as restriction of movement, they was able to assume - in a pioneering manner - a special position within their context. Their participation in military and political action equipped the women with daring, courage and resilience. All this emboldened them to defy some of the customs of society and conduct, at that early time, a women's demonstration calling for women's rights,

The distinctive position of Palestinian women in the thirties is highlighted in this research; a position that was buried deep in Palestinian popular memory. The research also adds to our knowledge the names of many women who have not been mentioned in the recorded history, despite their presence in the memory of many people who lived during that time.

This study tries to answer some of the questions posed at the start of the research project. The researcher hopes that it has taken a step towards answering these questions and that this work will encourage further studies aimed at unveiling the role of women in this rich era of the history of the Palestinian people.

References

1. Shihabi, Ibrahim Yahya. Lubia Village. Birzeit: Birzeit University - Center for the Study and Documentation of Palestinian society, 1994. (Series of destroyed Palestinian villages: 17).

2. Maghnam, Mateel. "The Historical Roots of the Struggle of Palestinian Women in the National Movement from the Mandate until the Year 1936". Samed Al-Iqtisadi. Amman, No. 62, 8th year 1986. pp.8-24.

3. Swedenberg, Ted. "Problems of Oral History: The 1936 Revolt in Palestine", Birzeit Review, No. 2, Winter 1985/6.

4. Tonkin, Elizabeth. Narrating our Pasts: The Social Construction of Oral History, Cambridge University Press, 1995.

5. Gluch, Sherna Berger & Daghne Patai (Ed), Women's Words: The Feminist Practice of Oral History, New York&London. Routledge, 1991.

6. Al-Saddeh, Huda. "How to Take Advantage of the Feminist Literature in Writing History" in the Palestinian Women and Memory. Prepared and edited by: Faiha Abdulhadi. Ramallah. Ministry of Planning and International Cooperation. 1999: p.168.

7. Anderson, K, S. Armitage, D. Jack, & J. Wittner, "Begginning Where we are: Feminist Methodology in Oral History", in Women's Words: the Feminist Practice of Oral History, p.103.

8. Minister, Kristina, "A Feminist Frame for the Oral History Interview" in Women's Words: the Feminist Practice of Oral History, p. 38.

9. Abd. p. 37

10. Abd. p. 37

11. Al-Dajani, Mu'taz & Jaber Sulaiman. "Dr. Rosemary Sayigh: Between Anthropology and Oral History" in Al-Jana (Beirut). No.3, August 1995. pp.17-22.

12. Fleischman, Ellen. Jerusalem Women's Organizations During the British Mandate (1920-1930). Passia, March 1995.

13. Najjar, Orayb Aref & kitty Warnock. Portraits of Palestinian women Introduction. Salt Lake City: University of Utah Press, 1992.

14. Abd. p. 126

15. Interview with Bahjat Abu Gharbiyah (1916)/ Jordan/ by researcher: Sana' Muharram on 20/8/98.

16. Interview with Suad Tawfeeq Abu So'ud (1925)/ Gaza/ by researcher Taghreed Abdulhadi on 3/ 1/ 99.

17. Interview with Haroun Hashem Rasheed (1927)/ Egypt/ by researcher Sabah Al-Khuffash on 28/ 9/ 98.

18. Interview with Sa'adeh Al-Kilani (1920)/ Jordan/ by researcher Maha Al-Tamimi on 9/1988.

19. Interview with Suad Tawfeeq Abu So'ud (1925)/ Gaza/ Abd.

20. Interview with Samira Abu Ghazaleh (1928)/ Egypt/ by researcher Hala Abu Mansour on 3/ 8/ 98.

21. Interview with Awatef Abdulhadi (1925)/ Jenin/ by researcher Sumayya Al-Safadi on 25/ 9/ 98.

22. Interview with Sa'adeh Al-Kilani/ Abd.

23. Interview with Isam Abdulhadi (1928)/ Jordan/ by researcher Sana' Muharram on 5/ 8/1988.

24. Interview with Ahmad Mahmoud Al-Zaben (1913)/ Al-Yarmouk Camp/ Syria/ by researcher Maha Al-Tamimi on 27/ 7/ 98.

25. Interview with Khadra Mustafa Al-Sari (1917)/ Haifa/ Beir Al-Maksour/ by researcher Muna Mahajneh on 5/ 9/98.

26. Interview with Samira Abu Ghazaleh/ Abd.

27. Interview with Adala Touqan (1913)/ Jenin/ by researcher Sumayya Al-Safadi on 11/ 8/ 98.

28. Interview with Ahmad Al-Zaben/ Syria/ Abd.

29. Interview with Haroun Hashem Rasheed/ Egypt/ Abd.

30. Interview with Khazneh Al-Khateeb (1917)/ Al-Yarmouk Camp/ Syria/ by researcher Buthaina Al-Kurdi on 28/ 8/ 98.

31. Interview with Ta'ah Awad (1930)/ Rafah/ Gaza/ by researcher Taghreed Abdulhadi on 2/2/99.

32. Interview with Khazneh Al-Khateeb/ Syria/ Abd.

33. Interview with Isam Abdulhadi/ Jordan/ Abd.

34. Interview with Sa'adeh Al-Kilani/ Syria/ Abd.

35. Interview with Haroun Hashem Rasheed/ Egypt/ Abd.

36. Shihabi, Ibrahim Yahya. Lubia Village/ Abd.

37. Anderson, Kathryn & Dana C. Jack. "Learning to listen: Interview Techniques and Anayses", in <u>Women's Words: The Feminist Practise of Oral History</u>. New York&London. Routledge, 1991.

38. Interview with Khadra Al-Sari/ Abd.

39. Interview with Shams Al-Titi (1919)/ Al-Arroub Camp/ Hebron/ by researcher Lamia' Shalaldeh on 8/11 / 98.

40. Interview with Hamida Abu Rayyah (1922)/ Al-Samu'/ Hebron/ by researcher Lamia' Shalaldeh on 20/ 11/ 98.

41. Interview Um Kayed/ Amman/ by researcher Sana' Muharram on 27/1/1999.

42. Al-Dajani, Ahmad Zaki. Our city of Jaffa and 1936 Revolt. Cairo: (D.N.), 1989.

43. Shihabi, Ibrahim Yahya. Lubia Village/ Abd.

44. Interview with Kamal Abdul-Raheem (1925)/ Thinnaba/ Tulkarm/ by researcher Nida' Abu Taha on 7/3/99.

45. Interview with Rasmiyyeh Al-Barghouthi (Um Al-Abed) (1926)/ Al-Bireh/ by researcher Rabab Tmish on 5/3/99.

46. Interview with Kamleh Shneik/ Azzoun/ Qalqeelya/ by researcher Sumayya Al-Safadi on 2/1/99.

47. Interview with Latifa Mahmoud Dirbas(1927)/ Bal'a/ Tulkarm/ by researcher Nida' Abu Taha on 27/9/98.

48. Interview with Bahjat Abu Gharbiyah/ Jordan/ Abd.

49. Interview with Fatima Husein Al-Khateeb (1912)/ Ein-Beitilma / by researcher: Nida' Abu Taha on 14/10/98.

50. Interview with Fattoum Al-Ghurairi (1916)/ Al-Yarmouk Camp/ Syria/ by researcher Buthaina Al-Kurdi on 23/8/98.

51. Interview with Wadee'a Qaddourah Khartabil (1915)/ Lebanon/ by researcher Suhair Al-Uzom on 11/9/98.

52. Interview with Anis Al-Sayegh (1931)/ Lebanon/ by researcher Suhair Al-Uzom on March, 99.

53. Interview with Ahmad Maw'ed (1923)/ Al-Yarmouk Camp / Syria/ by researcher Buthaina Al-Kurdi on 9/8/98.

54. Interview with Latifa Al-Taher (1914)/ Lebanon/ by researcher Suhair Al-Uzom on 11/12/98.

55. Same interview.

56. Interview with Issam Hamdi Al-Huseini (1919)/Gaza/ by researcher Iman Radwan on 31/8/99.

57. Interview with Izdihar Al-Shurafa (1930)/ Egypt/ by researchers Amaal Al-Agha & Hala Mansour on 7/10/99 & 22/4/2000.

58. Interview with Widad Al-Ayyoubi (1925)/ Jerusalem/ by researcher Sumayya Al-Safadi on 20/10/99.

59. Interview with Wadee'a Qaddourah Khartabil/ Abd.

60. Interview with Samiha Khaleel (1923)/Ramallah/ by researcher Hala Abu Hashhash on 15/12/98.

61. Interview with Maymana Al-Qassam (1911) /Jordan/ by researchers Ruqayya Al-Alami & Sana' Muharram on 14/9/98.

62. Interview with Khadra Al-Sari/ Beir Al-Maksour/ Abd.

63. Interview with Issam Hamdi Al-Huseini/Gaza/Abd.

64. Interview with Haroun Hashem Rasheed/ Egypt/ Abd.

65. Interview with Abdul-Qader Yaseen/ Egypt/ Abd.

66. Interview with Samira Khouri (1929)/ Nazareth/ by researcher Muna Mahajneh on 13/2/99.

67. Interview with Amneh Al-Wenni (1924)/ Cairo/ by researcher

Sabah Al-Khuffash on 8/11/98.

68. Interview with Samira Khouri / Nazareth/ Abd.
69. Interview with Jamila Badran (1924)/ Deir Lighsoon/ Tulkarm/ by researcher Sumayya Al-Safadi on 27/9/98.
70. Interview with Afifeh Hijaz (1921)/ Anabta/ Tulkarm/ by researcher Nida' Abu Taha on 13/9/98.
71. Interview with Jamila Badran / Deir Lighsoon / Abd.
72. Interview with Amneh Al-Wenni / Egypt/ Abd.
73. Interview with Ahmad Al-'Isawi (1909)/ Jerusalem/ by researcher Muna Mahajneh on 13/2/99.
74. Interview with Khadra Al-Sari/ Beir Al-Maksour / Abd.
75. Interview with Farha Al-Barghouthi/ Kouber/ Ramallah/ by researcher Hala Abu Hashhash on 20/4/99.
76. Interview with Widad Al-'Arouri (1941)/ Jordan/ by researcher Ruqayya Al-Alami on 1/9/99.
77. Interview with Ahmad Al-'Isawi / Jerusalem / Abd.
78. Interview with Ma'zouzeh Qasem (1923)/ Beit Reema/ Ramallah/ by researcher Na'ilah Oudeh on 13/10/98.
79. Interview with Kamleh Shneik/ Abd.
80. Interview with Fatima Al-Darhali (1928)/ Egypt/ by researcher: Hala Mansour on 3/10/98.
81. Interview with Jamila Sabbah (1920)/ Qiffeen/ Tulkarm/ by researcher Na'ilah Oudeh on 6/11/98.
82. Same interview.
83. Interview with Ahmad Al-'Isawi/ Jerusalem / Abd.
84. Interview with Amena Al-Shinnawi (1924)/ Syria/ by researcher Sabbah Al-Khuffash on 6/6/98.
85. Interview with Rafeeqa Hamada (1924)/ Lebanon/ by researcher Khadija Abdul 'Al on 5/7/99.
86. Interview with Suad Abu So'ud/ Gaza/ Abd.

87. Interview with Samira Abu Ghazaleh/ Abd.
88. Interview with Ahmad Maw'ed/ Syria/ Abd.
89. Interview with Rafeeqa Hamada/ Lebanon/ Abd.
90. Interview with Ali Musa Abu Yousef (1923)/ Halhoul/ Hebron/ by researcher Lamia' Shalalda on 12/12/99.
91. Sakakini, Hala. Jerusalem and I: A Personal Record. Jordan: Economic Press Co, 1987.
92. Interview with Kamal Abdul-Raheem (1925)/ Tulkarm/ by researcher Nida' Abu Taha on 7/3/99.
93. Interview with Khazneh Al-Khateeb/ Syria/ Abd.
94. Interview with Maymana Al-Qassam / Jordan/ Abd.
95. Interview with Arab Abdulhadi (1937)/ Egypt/ by researcher Sabah Al-Khuffash between 7/9 – 26/9/98.
96. Interview with Suad Abu So'ud/ Gaza/ Abd.
97. Interview with Bahjat Abu Gharbiyah/ Jordan/ Abd.
98. Interview with Khadra Al-Sari/ Beir Al-Maksour / Abd.
99. Interview with Latifa Mahmoud Dirbas(1927)/ Bal'a/ Tulkarm/ by researcher Nida' Abu Taha on 27/9/98.
100. Interview with Jamila Ahmad Sulaiman Sabbah(1920)/ Qiffeen/ Tulkarm/ by researcher Nida' Abu Taha on 6/11/98.
101. Interview with Shams Al-Titi/ Halhoul/ Abd.
102. Interview with Su'ad Qaraman (1927)/ Ibten/ Haifa/ by researcher Rabab Tamish on 15/10/98.
103. Interview with Sa'adeh Al-Kilani/ Syria/ Abd.
104. Interview with Doumia Al-Sakakini (1923)/ Jerusalem/ by researcher Muna Mahajneh on 3/7/99.
105. Interview with Salma Al-Huseini/ Jerusalem/ Abd.
106. Interview with Widad Al-Ayyoubi / Jerusalem/ Abd.
107. Interview with Madeeha Al-Battah (1924)/ Gaza/ by researcher Taghreed Abdulhadi on 5/2/99.

108. Interview with Ulga Al-Aswad (1934)/ Lebanon/ by researcher Khadija Abdul 'Al on 23/1/98.

109. Interview with Mahira Al-Dajani (1930)/ Jerusalem/ by researcher Muna Mahajneh on 30/1/99.

110. Interview with Bahjat Abu Gharbiyah/ Jordan/ Abd.

111. Interview with Widad Al-'Arouri/ Jordan/ Abd.

112. Interview with Khazneh Al-Khateeb/ Syria/ Abd.

113. Interview with Alice Elyas Nawrasi (1923)/ Amman/ by researcher Ruqayya Al-Alami on 10/4/99.

114. Interview with Wafiyyeh Al-Khayri / Ramallah/ by researcher Na'ila Oudeh on 8/9/98.

115. Interview with Ulga Al-Aswad/ Lebanon/ Abd.

116. Same interview.

117. Interview with Dawud 'Eraikat/ Jericho/ Abd.

118. Interview with Samiha Khaleel/ Ramallah/ Abd.

119. Interview with Wadee'a Qaddourah Khartabil / Lebanon/ Abd.

120. Interview with Salma Al-Huseini (1920)/ Jerusalem/ by researcher Muna Mahajneh on 6/11/98.

121. Interview with Ali Musa Abu Yousef/ Hebron/ Abd.

122. Interview with Salma Al-Huseini/ Jerusalem/ Abd.

123. Interview with Yusra Al-Barbari/ Gaza/ Abd.

124. Interview with Abdul-Qader Yaseen (1937)/ Egypt/ by researcher Hala Mansour on 14/8/98.

125. Interview with Salma Al-Huseini/ Jerusalem/ Abd.

126. Interview with Yusra Al-Barbari/ Gaza/ Abd.

127. Interview with Subhi Ghousheh / Jordan/ by researcher Ruqayya Al-Alami on 4/8/98.

128. Interview with Isam Abdulhadi / Jordan/ Abd.

129. Interview with Zuheir Al-Shawish (1925)/ Lebanon/ by researcher Suhair Al-Uzom on 6/3/99.

130. Interview with Fuad Ibrahim Abbas (1924)/ Egypt/ by researcher Amaal Al-Agha on 10/8/98.

131. Interview with Maymana Ezzedin Al-Qassam/ Jordan/ Abd.

132. Interview with Munawwar Dawud Husein Salah (1935)/ Jericho/ by researcher Nida' Abu Taha on 16/3/99.

133. Interview with Wadee'a Qaddourah Khartabil / Lebanon/ Abd.

134. Interview with Fatima Al-Budairi (1923)/ Jordan/ by researcher Ruqayya Al-Alami on 29/10/98.

135. Interview with Haroun Hashem Rasheed/ Egypt/ Abd.

136. Interview with Maymana Ezzedin Al-Qassam / Jordan/ Abd

137. Interview with Samira Abu Ghazaleh/ Egypt/ Abd.

138. Interview with Yusra Al-Barbari/ Gaza/ Abd.

139. Interview with Yusra Al-Barbari (1923)/ Gaza/ by researcher Iman Radwan on 21/9/98.

140. Interview with Khadra Mustafa Al-Sari/ Beir Al-Maksour / Abd.

141. Interview with Shams Al-Titi/ Halhoul/ Abd.

142. Interview with Hamida Abu Rayyah/ Al-Samu'/ Abd.

143. Interview with Karimah Ismail Barham (1924)/ Jordan/ by researcher Ruqayya Al-Alami on 30/6/99.

144. Interview with Amneh Al-Wenni / Egypt/ Abd.

145. Interview with Jamila Badran / Deir Lighsoon / Abd.

146. Interview with Fatima Al-Khateeb / Ein-Beitilma Camp/ Nablus/ Abd.

147. Interview with Ahmad Maw'ed/ Syria/ Abd.

148. Interview with Khadija Hedayah (1924)/ Cairo/ by researcher Amaal Al-Agha on 10/11/98.

149. Interview with Um Kayed/ Jordan/ Abd.

150. Same interview.

151. Interview with Zahida Ahmad Mustafa (1931)/ Rameen/ Tulkarm/ by researcher Nida' Abu Taha on 9/6/99.

152. Interview with Samiha Khaleel (1923)/ Al-Bireh/ by researcher Hala Abu Hashhash on 15/12/98.

153. Interview with Huda Amer (1996)/ Al-Yarmouk Camp/ Syria/ by researcher Maha Al-Tamimi on 26/7/98.

154. Interview with Najeyyah Barham (1924)/ Rameen/ Tulkarm/ by researcher Nida' Abu Taha on 9/6/99.

155. Interview with Zakiyeh Hulaileh (1916)/ Jericho/ by researcher Sumayya Al-Safadi on 4/3/99.

156. Interview with Sa'da Dakar (1914)/ Deir Al-Balah/ Gaza Strip/ by researcher Iman Radwan on 30/7/2000.

157. Interview with Salma Al-Huseini/ Jerusalem/ Abd.

158. Interview with Zakiyeh Hulaileh (1916)/ Jericho/ by researcher Sumayya Al-Safadi on 4/3/99.

159. Interview with Um Al-Abed Al-Barghouthi/ Ramallah/ Abd.

160. Interview with Um Kayed/ Jordan/ Abd.

161. Interview with Nadeyyah Omar Hamed (1930)/ Anza/ by researcher Sumayya Al-Safadi on 7/10/99.

162. Interview with Haijar Mustafa Mohammad Thafer (1914)/ Jordan/ by researcher Ruqayya Al-Alami on 30/6/99.

163. Same interview

164. Interview with Hamida Abu Rayyah/ Al-Samu'/ Abd.

165. Interview with Afifeh Hijaz/ Anabta/ Tulkarm/ Abd.

166. Interview with Fattoum Al-Ghurairi/ Syria/ Abd.

167. Interview with Ta'ah 'Awad (1930)/ Gaza/ by researcher Taghreed Abdulhadi on 2,3,6/2/99.

168. Same interview.

169. Interview with Najeyyah Barham/ Rameen/ Abd.

170. Interview with Khazneh Al-Khateeb/ Syria/ Abd.

171. Interview with Haijar Mustafa/ Jordan/ Abd.

172. Interview with Karimah Barham/ Rameen/ Abd.

173. Interview with Khazneh Al-Khateeb/ Syria/ Abd.
174. Interview with Fatima Al-Darhali (1928) / Egypt / by researcher Hala Mansour on 3/10/98.
175. Interview with Subhi Ghousheh / Jordan/ Abd.
176. Interview with Ali Musa Abu Yousef/ Hebron/ Abd.
177. Interview with Suad Tawfeeq Abu So'ud / Gaza/ Abd.
178. Interview with Haroun Hashem Rasheed / Egypt/ Abd.
179. Interview with Afaf Al-Idreesi (1928)/ Gaza/ by researcher Taghreed Abdulhadi on 9/8 – 17/8
& 23/8 –3/9/1998 .
180. Interview with Isam Abdulhadi/ Jordan/ Abd.
181. Interview with Virginia Tarazy (1930)/ Gaza/ by researcher: Iman Radwan on 18/6/99.
182. Interview with Salma Al-Husseni/ Jerusalem/ Abd.
183. Interview with Widad Al-Ayyoubi/ Jerusalem/ Abd.
184. Interview with Abdul-Qader Yaseen/ Egypt/ Abd.
185. Interview with Samiha Khaleel/ Ramallah/ Abd.
186. Interview with Bahjat Abu Gharbiyah/ Jordan/ Abd.
187. Interview with Ali Musa Abu Yousef/ Hebron/ Abd.
188. Interview with Ahmad Al-'Isawi/ Jerusalem/ Abd.
189. Interview with Ahmad Al-Zaben/ Syria/ Abd.
190. Interview with Ahmad Maw'ed/ Syria/ Abd.
191. Interview with Dawud 'Eraikat/ Jericho/ Abd.
192. Interview with Zuheir Al-Shawish/ Lebanon/ Abd.
193. Interview with Anis Al-Sayegh/Lebanon/Abd.
194. Interview with Widad Al-Ayyoubi/ Jerusalem/ Abd.
195. Interview with Alice Nawrasi/ Jordan/ Abd.
196. Interview with Suad Abu-So'ud/ Gaza/ Abd.

197. Interview with Widad Al-'Arouri/ jordan/ Abd.
198. Interview with Latifa Al-Taher/ Lebanon/ Abd.
199. Interview with Fatima Al-Khateeb/ Ein-Beitilma Camp/ Nablus/ Abd.
200. Interview with Afifeh Hijaz/ Anabta/ Abd.
201. Interview with Kamal Abdul-Raheem/ Tulkarm/ Abd.
202. Same interview.
203. Same interview.
204. Interview with Najeyyah Barham (1924)/ Rameen/ Tulkarm/ by researcher: Nida' Abu Taha on 9/6/99
205. Same interview.
206. Interview with Haijar Mustafa/ Rameen/ Tulkarm/ Abd.
207. Interview with Zahida Mustafa/ Rameen/ Abd.
208. Interview with Kamleh Abdul-Rahman Shneik/ Qalqeelya/ Abd.
209. Same interview.
210. Interview with Izdihar Al-Shurafa (1930)/ Egypt/ Abd.
211. Interview with Ahmad Al-'Isawi/ Jerusalem/ Abd.
212. Interview with Huda Amer/ Syria/ Abd.
213. Interview with Rasmiyyeh Barghouthi (Um Al-Abed)/ Ramallah/ Abd.
214. Interview with Widad Al-'Arouri/ Jordan/ Abd.
215. Interview with Anis Al-Sayegh/ Lebanon/ Abd.
216. Interview with Alice Nawrasi/ Jordan/ Abd.
217. Interview with Ahmad Al-Zaben/ Syria/ Abd.
218. Interview with Sa'adeh Al-Kilani/ Syria/ Abd.
219. Interview with Ahmad Al-Zaben/ Syria/ Abd.
220. Interview with Fatheyya Al-Bahsh (1926) / Lebanon/ by researcher Suhair Al-Uzom on Feb, 1999.
221. Interview with Makram Al-Qasrawi (1939)/ Hebron/ by researcher Lamia' Shalaldeh on 2,5/11/1998.

222. Interview with Zeinab Aqel (1924)/ Jerusalem/ by researcher Muna Mahajneh on 7/4/1999.
223. Interview with Latifa Al-Taher/ Lebanon/ Already mentioned.
224. Interview with Zuheir Al-Shawish/ Lebanonl Abd.
225. Interview with Anis Al-Sayegh/ Lebanon/ Already mentioned.
226. Same interview.
227. Interview with Fatheyya Al-Bahsh/ Lebanon/ Already mentioned.
228. Interview with Fuad Abbas/ Egypt/ Already mentioned.
229. Interview with Hamida Abu Rayyah/ Al-Samu'/ Already mentioned.
230. Interview with Fattoum Al-Ghurairi/ Al-Yarmouk Camp/ Syria/ Already mentioned.
231. Same interview.
232. Same interview.

PART TWO

Women's Oral Narratives

The Importance of this Part of the Book

This important part of the book exposes the reader, and interested researchers, to some of the historically authenticated documents that have been used in this research. It was not possible to include all the interviews; however the selected interviews were carefully chosen to represent the political era covered by the study.

When selecting the interviews we took into consideration several factors. The most important of these factors was the full representation of the different areas covered by the study: Palestine (North, South, Middle, Jerusalem and 1948 areas), in addition to the Palestinian Diasporas (Jordan, Syria, Lebanon and Egypt). Since the study focused on the importance of the role of women in the creation of the history of the 1930's period, the interviews were selected to reflect the conclusions that have been reached by the study. These interviews were of central importance in reaching these research conclusions, concentrating on the role of peasant women during the 1936 revolt.

Although the interviews focused on the 1930's period, we were keen to keep the full text of the interviews which also often included memories of other political periods that the narrators lived through and not only the period under study. In our opinion this will benefit future studies on the political contributions of Palestinian women in general as well as the 1930's in particular.

Symbols used in the interviews:

(-) Start of the interview: The Field Researcher's question or the Narrator's answer.

( ) Words between brackets: Clarification by the Field Researcher of the Narrator's intent, or description of the Narrator's emotions and body language e.g. weeping, convulsions, laughing, tapping on the floor …etc.

(..) Two dots between brackets indicate a short stoppage in the sentence.

(….) Four dots between brackets indicate a long stoppage in the narrator's speech.

Postal Stamp Issued during the Eastern Women's Conference in Cairo -1938

Name of Narrator	Maymanah Ezzedin Al-Qassam[1]

Date of Birth 1911
Recording location .... House of Narrator
Date of Recording 14/9/1998
Address of Narrator .... Amman - Jordan

Tape No. 3c
Tape Duration .... 90 Minutes
Field Researcher .... Sana' Muharram and Ruqayya Al-Alami

Researcher: Will you give us your full name please?

Narrator: Maymanah Ezzedin Abdulqader Al-Qassam.

- Place of birth?
- Jablah, Syria.
- Date of birth?
- In the newspaper they wrote 1911.
- Present place of residence?
- Amman, Jordan.
- Town of origin and district?
- The place where I lived when I was young? It was Jablah.
- The place where you were born?
- Jablah in Syria.
- Did you migrate in 1948 or did you stay?

---

1. Maymanah Al-Qassam passed away in Amman on: 28/6/2004

Part 2: Women's Narrations

- No, we came to Amman.
- What was your profession?
- Teacher, I am a retired teacher.
- What was the level of your education?
- I got my primary education at school (..) but the rest of my education was at home where I was taught by my late father; The Teachers' Institute gave me a conditional acceptance, but the conditions were rejected by my father.
- What were those conditions?
- I applied to the institution and my application was successful (..) but the institution made my enrollment conditional (..) the condition was that my father had to go to the institution to teach the girls (..) the Sheikh should go and teach in Jerusalem. He refused to accept that condition (..). When I taught Arabic in Jordan the pupils benefited. It wasn't just those pupils that I taught, I also taught illiterate women for eight years and gave special courses in schools; thank God I did all that I could.
- You were interested in teaching (..), I mean the father of the Sheikh had a Kuttab (school for young pupils) in Jablah, wasn't that so?
- Kuttab? You mean my grandfather (..)
- Yes, did the father of the Sheikh have a Kuttab? Did he have a school?
- Yes. I did not know my great grandfather; my ancestors originally came from Hejaz (the Arabian Peninsula). Al-Qassam performed a miracle, but I don't like to speak about it (..)

(The people present urged her to speak saying 'say it, it is very important').

- They will ask me where you got the information from!
- Don't worry (..) no-one will ask (..) you simply inherited the tale from the family (..) that is where you heard it from.
- When I was a child I heard (..) you know how houses in the past were built of wood and who knows what. In such cases the roof would not be tightly closed, therefore insects and snakes would come into the house through the roof. So, whenever there was a snake, they would call my grandfather, Abdulqader, (..) to solve the problem. He would say to

the snake 'come down you evil one' and the snake would fall down and split into two halves; that is how we acquired the name Qassam.

- This information is very important; it is important to know how the name came about! Aunt Maymanah, could you take us back to the days when you were a little girl and tell us what you remember best?

- As far as I am concerned I do not remember how I learned to read and write. However, I know that I knew the whole Quran by heart by the age of six (..)

- Mashallah! (praise to Allah)

- We celebrated the occasion and invited people to hear me recite chapters from the Qur'an. Most of the people present doubted that I was only six years old and so my father invited them to test me. Some men did and I passed without any mistakes, praise to Allah.

- Do you mean your father was not against educating girls? How many girls were there in your family?

- We were three girls.

- Three girls? Was he in favour of your education?

- He educated me, but not my sisters though.

- Was that because you were closer to him?

- Perhaps.

- I mean of all your sisters, were you the closest to your father?

- I don't know! (..) He taught me everything I knew and he taught me Arabic and grammar; I can show you now (smiling).

- Do you remember your mother?

- Yes, I remember my mother.

- Do you remember the role she played in helping your father; did he tell her about his work and secrets?

- My mother was wealthy and all her money was spent on good causes for the sake of Allah (..).

- You mean she gave him money?

- Yes, she never kept her money for herself.

- Did she give him the money to use for the cause of Jihad?
- The money was spent on good causes and what pleased Allah.

(Maymanah tried to avoid the question and not give direct answers).

- My mother was always very charitable: when she died in Syria they referred to her as the martyr (emphasis by the speaker) Aminah Al-Na'nou'. She cared for the young and for orphans (..) our house was (..).
- So did she just help him with money, or did she participate with him in his work, for example military operations?
- No, she also participated in the work he asked her to do. He would bring an orphan for her to raise, a patient to nurse; she always stood by him.
- Where would he bring the patient from? Do you mean the wounded?
- They used to find children at the Mosque's gate. My father would bring them for her to raise and care for.
- We know that he was amongst the first people who did clandestine work. Did he speak to your mother about his work, or the secret cells he organized?
- No, no.
- Did she try (to find out) though?

(Shaking her head to mean no).

- He did not share his secrets with you either, but you could deduce things by yourself?
- No, I was too young for that.
- You were young but sometimes even a child (..)
- On certain occasions, when he gave lessons at the mosque, we would tell him that we heard his teachings and that they were good. He would only give us directions with regards to religious and domestic matters, and those were a great asset.
- Do you mean he started his social involvement simultaneously with the struggle? Did his religious teachings involve raising people's awareness?

- It was more about raising awareness than religious teaching because people already knew they had to do their prayers and fast; it was more about awareness.

- Was it political awareness? He used to talk to people about politics?

- The British High Commissioner was once asked what was causing the revolt in Palestine. He replied 'It is being caused by an elderly man'.

- But he was young when he died!

- He was fifty three years old; when he spoke to people he melted their brains. That was how the British High Commissioner described Sheikh Ezzedin Al-Qassam.

- You told me he didn't share with your mother any of his work, but did he consult her about matters related to his work?

- I really don't know, but she was very intelligent.

- When you grew up and started becoming more aware of things around you, did you feel your father had sought out a particular path in life? How did you feel as a child in the house?

- The first thing I became aware of was how much he cared for our upbringing. He cared most about our table-manners. He would set the table and put empty dishes on it. Each plate had a piece of paper with the name of a given food - chicken, minced meat, or beans – written on it, then he would invite us to the table. He concentrated on me because I was his eldest (..) when we sat at the table, he would say 'Of course Maymanah likes chicken so she stretches her hand out and begins'. Then I would say to him 'No, I don't do that; I take from my plate' and I would say 'the Prophet (peace be upon him) said to eat that which is right in front of you'.

- He was a modernized preacher (..) modernized (..) (A lady in the room commented that 'his teaching method was most beautiful'.

- Yes.

- That was a civilized way of teaching you how to take your food.

- He studied at the revered Azhar. When he completed the Kuttab my grandfather sent him to Egypt, to Al-Azhar, where he spent twelve years

Part 2: Women's Narrations

without returning home once. He came back when he had completed his education.

- At Al-Azhar in Cairo?

- Yes, and Mohammad Abdu was one of his teachers (..)

- You said your house in Haifa was always open to people and that many people visited the house daily. Who were those visitors? Were there women visitors coming to hear a preaching or get directions from the Sheikh?

- There was something like that, but very little (..)

- You said there were many visitors. Who were they?

- He did not have any male children. He had one but he died. The room was filled with people and food and drinks, but I didn't know them. They are all dead now.

- Do you remember the names of any of them?

- Sheikh Mohammad Hanifa, and my cousins, Zhafer and Abdulmalek Al-Qassam (..)

- Do you remember any of the women?

- We did not have women in the house (..)

- Didn't women ever come to see him; not even the wives of his cousins?

- We were in Haifa when they were in Syria so we were too far apart.

- The wives of his comrades did not gather at your house?

- Men and women did not mix in our house.

- But in the first interview you said that women approached the Sheikh to inquire about matters of Sharia' and other consultations?

- Oh, yes, they came to inquire about some religious issues. Once I saw them in the guest room. My father sat down sideways to avoid looking at them. They said to him 'lift your head up so we can see your eyes'. He would then look at them and answer their questions. Once, after they had gone, he said that he did not like to see their hair uncovered and that they should pull something over their hair as if they did they might go to heaven.

- Do you remember the sort of issues they discussed with him?

- Most of the time it was marital problems. He also worked as a marriage official.

- Did he use this job to get to know more people?

- Exactly; he wanted to know as many people as possible. He gave advice, visited poor people and gave them whatever they were short of; rice, sugar, whatever they needed.

- He gave things to people?

- He visited widows (..)

- Do you not remember people coming to visit him to discuss ordinary matters and then the conversation turning into a political debate?

- No, (..) No. It did not happen, and he did not allude to politics either. I did not understand, he was very careful (..)

- Was he cautious?

- I don't know.

- Did you hear about a group of women calling themselves the 'Al-Qassam Comrades'.

- I heard about that from you.

- You did not hear about them?

- I did not.

- You didn't?

- I never heard about them. When he had a meeting he needed someone to serve food outside of the house. He employed a woman for that purpose, they were registered as wife and husband but he never actually married her.

- Who was she?

- A woman.

- Was he supposed to marry her?

- He did not marry her.

- Where did she actually serve him and his guests?

- I did not know much about her (..)

- Where? Where?

- She served them in the mountains. I did not know where they held their meetings; they were registered husband and wife, but in fact they were not married.

Just for 'halal' and 'haram' reasons (to legitimize her being with him from a religious point of view).

- What was her name?

- I don't know; we were told about this matter after he died.

- Were there other women helping them?

- No, only her (..)

- Who would take the food to them?

- After his death we heard people saying 'Who will bring things to us?', 'Who will help us?'

- You never heard of a group called 'The comrades of Al-Qassam'?

- Never heard of them (..)

- I did not know (..) There only seemed (..)

- Did you hear of a woman named Ruqayya Al-Houri? (..)

- No, (..)

- You haven't heard of her? Do you remember whether the name is right? She was in Haifa!

- What did she do?

- She was, supposedly, one of Al-Qassam's female comrades.

- I really did not know of that.

- You did not hear about it? They were his work companions. What did you say was the name of the association that he founded?

- The Muslim Youth Association in Haifa.
- When did he found it?
- I think between 1935 and 1928

(Maymanah meant to say between 1928 and 1935 because he died in 1935.)

- What were the main activities of that Association?
- What was it? I really don't know.
- Was it involved in social activities or in charity work?
- Yes.
- Was its work public or secret?
- Yes, (..) its activities were secret. I don't know.
- You did not know anything about it?
- Each person knew about their own tasks.
- Did you feel like the Sheikh and his friends were involved in some sort of struggle? Did you sense there was a secret between them?
- We never felt anything as such, and he did not let on to us about anything.
- Of all the people who visited him, whom would you say were his closest friends?
- His sister, I don't know (showing signs of anger).
- Forgive me, but I mean close friends come and go more often than ordinary visitors.
- I don't know.
- Some people came to him to discuss marital matters, but I am not asking about those people. I am asking about the names of the people who visited him frequently?
- Our house was very spacious and there was no mixing between men and women or between those inside the house and those outside. Besides, the guest room was an external annex to the house.
- Once a man came to our house and left his daughter with us after he

Part 2: Women's Narrations

had quarreled with his wife. Those of us in the house never got involved in such affairs, never. We never mixed with people who we knew were his associates.

- What were they?
- His associates in the armed struggle.
- What about them? Were there any women?
- You should (..) No, no.
- Did you hear any names? Have any stayed in your mind?
- No.
- You did not hear any names?
- I did not know; I only knew about my own work.
- Shall I remind you of some of the names?
- Okay, please do.
- Do you remember, for instance, Ahmad Al-Ghalayeeni?
- I heard of the Ghalayeeni family (..) I don't know.
- You mean you remember that one of his friends was from the Ghalayeeni family?
- I don't know. He had so many friends (..)
- Did you ever hear of Abu Ibrahim Alkabeer?
- Yes, I heard of him, but I did not know him (..)
- What did you hear?
- I heard about him on the television, they showed some series, but I did not really watch it. I don't get involved. You see, bygones are bygones and now we are in the present.
- No, we are trying to establish who his friends were, for example (..)
- I am sorry but you can refer to the books; there are lots of books (..) about him and his friends. With regards to the women, and there were women, who took water and food to the insurgents (..) When you first asked me I told you I did not know, and I don't know.
- You don't know?

- At that time, I was very young, and he said to me 'I want to send you to the villages'. I replied 'No, I don't want them to call me the Sheikha'.

- Do you still remember the day when the Sheikh was martyred?

- Yes, in 1935.

- You remember that day?

- How could I ever forget?

- Tell us how you got the news? What really happened? (..) Tell us your memory of those times.

- There was a bang on the door. The person knocking on the door said 'Al-Qassam would like to see you; come on, the car is waiting outside'. There were actually a number of cars outside and we got into the cars with my mother. They started roaming around the roads of Haifa. He had already died and my clever mother knew that.

- The cars took you, your mother and your sisters?

- All of us including my aunt.

- Who came to get you in the car?

- I did not know them, but they were friends. As the car drove round and round the area my mother knew: some cried, others screamed, and somebody else fell to the ground. My mother finally said 'Oh, Allah, may Allah bless his soul; take us back to the house!'

- Did you see him then?

- Martyrs are not dead people (..) he remained until the morning. People smashed the window panes trying to enter the house (..)

- Who were those people?

- The people smashed the glass of the veranda as they jammed into the house (..)

- You mean they wanted to see him?

- They wanted to enter the house by any means possible, then it was the funeral (..)

- Tell us about the funeral…

(The second field researcher intervened asking 'Who else was killed

Part 2: Women's Narrations

alongside him?')

- I forgot.

- No, you told us earlier (..)

- Al Masri, Azzebawi and another person from one of the villages whose name I don't know; perhaps there were more than two.

- Can you tell us about the funeral?

- The funeral proceeded from the house, I don't remember how I found myself at the funeral nor do I know how it reached the graveyard; the time seemed to pass so swiftly.

- You mean you were at the funeral?

- Yes, I was.

- Were there other women?

- The whole town was at the funeral; at the new graveyard near the village of Yajour.

- How far was the village from Haifa?

- From Haifa to the village it took almost two and a half hours on foot (..) they carried the body and walked the whole time.

- The Sheikh and the other two or three martyrs alongside him?

- One of them – I forgot his name – was taken to be buried in the cemetery of his home village. However, Al Masri and Azzebawi were buried along with the Sheikh.

- Do you remember whether there were women at the funeral?

- Not only women, but men and women from many towns.

- Was there chanting at the funeral?

- There must have been some, but I am not sure (..)

- Can you remember what they chanted?

- No, I can't, but it was something good.

- I was not walking with them; I was in the car along with my mother, grandmother and aunt.

- But can't you remember anything chanted at the funeral?

- I am sure they said good things.

- After the death of the Sheikh, his fellow fighters were still fighting in the mountains for six months after the event. Did they return to their villages? Who supplied them with food and water?

- I wouldn't know, but I am sure there were still people helping them.

- You did not know, but didn't you hear about what was happening?

- Perhaps I wondered how they were surviving, but I had no idea.

- Didn't your mother talk about it?

- No, never; we were not involved and no-one could enter our house.

- His friends were still there, though (..)

- Not even the closest of friends entered the house (..)

- They must have dropped by to see how you were doing?

- Men coming into the house? No, no-one. A man came once and said he wanted to split his salary between us and himself but my mother refused (..)

- How was the activity in the house after he died?

- What activity?

- I mean what was happening in the house after his death?

- My mother, her three girls, a boy and my aunt lived in the house. I was teaching and we lived a decent life.

- Does that mean you were supporting the family with your salary?

- I really do not know who was supporting the house, but I know my salary was too small to do it. Who provided for us? I have no idea. My mother was well off and she always had money; there was always money on the table in the house and we never counted how much there was! Where did that money come from? I had no knowledge whatsoever. They say 'God forgets none'.

- It is true.

- When you were a teacher you took part in demonstrations and you told us that you did this once during the strike? That was during the strike after the Sheikh died?

- Yes, the six-month strike.

- Could you tell us about the strike and the role you played in it?

- Yes, they say I was involved and that I gave a speech; I really can't remember.

I swear on my honor that they told me you preached in a mosque (..) in Haifa, what was its name? Al-Jazzar?

- Yes, I remember something like that.

- Don't you remember that you spoke, or what you said?

- I don't know anything. I know I was patriotic but I cannot remember what I said! They say that I stood there at the (..)

- Apart from speaking, do you remember anything else? Did you participate in calling for the strike and urging shops close? Tell us anything about these kind of things, please talk (..)

- Yes, we did. I told you (in the preliminary interview).

- Tell us what you did?

- There is nothing to say; those who opened their shops were told to close down the shops.

- You mean you had some sort of a role in the strike?

- I was not alone.

- But you did?

- I might have done.

- Those people who were with you, were they men or women? Were there more men or more women with you?

- Women.

- Do you remember any of them? Surely you do.

- Once they wanted to know where I was and they could not find me. They looked for me and even asked the authorities about me, but were told that I had not been arrested and was not in their custody.

- Oh, you mean they thought you had been arrested?

- Yes, they were told to look for me at home and when they came to the house I was there people said 'Maymanah, Maymanah'.

- What were they saying? What did you do, for them to say 'Maymanah, Maymanah'?

- People were looking for me and when they could not find me they thought I was under arrest; there were, in fact, women who were under arrest. People then shouted for my release, but the authorities told them to go and look for me at home.

- What were the chants you shouted at marches and demonstrations in those days?

- I really don't know, there were pressures (..) I don't remember but I probably spoke the least of all.

- What did other people say? What did those people who were with you say?

- I can't remember. We spoke off the top of our heads.

- But did you participate in demonstrations? Do you remember?

- I did, yes I did.

- You remember that? Were there many women with you?

- Yes, (..) many (..) many.

- Did you ever confront the British soldiers or even Jewish settlers? Did anyone ever assault you?

- No, no-one ever assaulted me.

- No-one? Do you remember any confrontations occurring during a demonstration?

- If such a thing happened, I was not there; I was always very careful.

- Do you remember the names of women who were martyred during that period?

- No, I don't. After the death of my father I stayed in the house.

- But the strike and the revolt happened after the death of your father?

- I did not do much. Had I been active they (the authorities) would not have stood by idly; they would not have let me get away with it.

(Maymanah's daughter interrupted saying 'Why mother? What had you done?')

- They said I was under arrest, but I turned out to be at home.

- O.K. you mentioned a very important issue to do with the conference; so you received an invitation and then you travelled to Cairo, do you remember any details about what went on with regards to the conference?

- I attended the conference as I was chosen as the representative of Haifa.

- Firstly, where did you get the invitation from?

- The women's societies that decided to attend the conference insisted that I should attend. They found somebody to accompany me and they discussed the issue with my mother. My mother said she would refuse to send me so then they informed her that somebody would accompany me, i.e., somebody would travel with me (..)

- Who was the person who travelled with you? Was it Sathej Nassar.

- Yes that's correct she was the one, god bless you how did you know? She was from Haifa, of Iranian origin (..)

- So you got one invitation for the conference in Cairo, or did you receive more than one?

- When I arrived in Cairo?

- No, to attend the conference.

- Invitations did not come from Cairo; the conference was in Palestine.

- Do you mean the first conference which was held in Jerusalem. Which conference are you actually talking about?

- The conference in Cairo (..)

- Did you receive the invitation from Cairo (..)?

- The associations attended the conference and I was amongst them.

- You mean you were nominated?

- Upon arrival in Cairo I was well received and got invitations from three different parties.

- Okay, who were they?

- I made a choice; forget about it![1]

- We want to know who thought so highly of you? Who invited you?

- I was visited by a delegation from King Farouk and a delegation from Huda Sha'rawi.

- You mean an invitation? You were invited by them?

- They wanted me to be their guest; the Palestinian deportees also invited me, I received three invitations. I was young then and I was confused. So I said to myself if I accept the King's invitation, or the deportees, people would suspect my motives. So I decided to accept Huda's invitation.

- Huda, so you accepted Huda Sha'rawi's invitation?

- Yes, I was her guest (...)

- You went and attended the conference? Were you representing Haifa or an association?

- No, I represented the City of Haifa.

- So you represented Haifa, who else was present in the Palestinian delegation?

- Who?

- Who was there with you in the delegation, do you remember?

- They were many from Jerusalem.

- Do you remember any names?

---

1. The interviewer notes that in a preliminary interview Maymanah mentioned that she received three invitations from Egypt: the first from King Farouq, the second from Huda Sha'rawi and a third from the exiled Palestinian community. Maymanah wondered which one to accept and finally decided to accept Huda Sha'rawi's

Part 2: Women's Narrations

- I remember that 'Abdul-Qader Al-Huseini's wife (Wajeeha) was one of the delegates, in addition to the directors of the women's societies, you know them (..)

- No, remind me of them.

- I don't remember their names.

(Her daughter intervenes to say 'That one, Um Iyad, whose husband died whilst you were still in Cairo')

- Al-Dajani (..) Al-Dajani

- So how many Palestinian delegates were at the conference, do you know? (..)

- There were many of us, nearly forty women. Jordanian women were part of the delegation too.

(The researcher Dr. Faiha[1] intervened saying 'Do you remember a woman called Tarab Abdulhadi?')

- Of course I do (....)

Faiha: Bless her soul, Tarab died.

- The wife of the solicitor?

- Yes, Awni; he was my uncle.

- Are you from Abdulhadi Family?

- Awni is my uncle and Tarab was his wife. They told me about you.

- Bless her soul, bless her soul. I have never forgotten her (speaking with emotion). So you know some of the names?

- She (Tarab) told us the wives of the presidents of Syria and Lebanon were with you?

- Oh, I cannot remember their names, but yes the wives of the Presidents of Lebanon and Syria. I don't remember their names exactly and so I don't want to sound as if I am lying and give you the wrong names.

---

1. It was noted that Dr. Faiha Abdulhadi had to be there because Maymanah refused the interview after the preliminary interview. Therefore, the two interviewers called upon Dr. Faiha to persuade Maymanah to cooperate with them

- So who delivered the speech on behalf of the Palestinian women? I mean who delivered the speech from the Palestinian delegation?

- Which speech?

- In the conference wasn't there a woman who was asked to deliver the speech on behalf of Palestinian women? Was it you who gave the speech for instance?

- Well I wasn't alone, I wasn't the only one; there were forty women there, some from the most prominent Palestinian families.

- Okay. So all of them would have been very knowledgeable and well-known? Who were their fathers, their grandfathers and their mothers, etc.?

- People did not appreciate and respect each other, some were jealous, so they spread some rumors about other women. May God have mercy on his soul, the man who died, what was his name

- You mean Akram Zuaiter?

- Yes, Akram Zuaiter said to me whilst we were at the zoo 'There has been some talk about some of the women who came to Egypt to attend the conference. What's the solution, what should we do?' I told him 'Whatever you suggest!' So he said we should write a speech that I could deliver, and we would show the whole world what Palestinian women can do and how respectful and intelligent they are.

- Yes, of course

- Akram was a well-known writer of course and he was far more knowledgeable than me. He wrote the speech but I did contribute a bit and I was the one who delivered it. It was published in books (..)

- Do you remember anything from the speech?

- I remember the first few sentences of it.

- Go on then, try to remember and say it (....)

- *Ladies and Gentlemen (..) Do you know who I am?*

It was very difficult for me to talk, I was mad, I was angry; I wanted to give them an idea about myself and people like me. I said 'Do you know who I am?' and they all nodded.

I am the daughter of the one who knocked on the door of freedom with his bare bloodstained hands, and there, in the land of Palestine, is my resting place. (She spoke in a careful, punctuated tone).

(..) This is what I recall (..)

- What was the reaction of people towards your speech?

- They stopped talking about the women in the delegation and after a few days the newspapers stopped writing and slandering.

- What was the slander?

- You know, Akram, God bless his soul, told me that they might talk.

- About the women who participated in the conference?

- They talked about some members (..) not everybody. They talked about some; actually about most of us. My speech had some value because after it people were deterred and they came to their senses. My father was a great character and he spent his lifetime solving people's problems (..) it has been sixty years now since that conference happened; we wish everyone well and don't feel bitterness towards anybody.

- Did you hear about another conference that took place in Cairo?

- No

- What were the main recommendations which that conference - the one you attended - came up with? What plan of action did the conference put forward once it had finished?

- Perhaps they spoke of their cause, Palestine and the state of affairs of the Palestinian people but I did not hear (..)

- You mean there were recommendations with respect to Palestine?

- I mean a person will always have someone opposing them regardless of what they say.

- No, for the interest of Palestine?

- For the interest of Palestine? That conference was for the benefit of the Palestinians, the needy, and money was collected for that purpose (..) The most important point is that the money was never received; it was all diverted.

- Meaning what?

- Meaning that all the money collected went to Palestinian officials (..)

- What was the money collected for?
- It was collected for Palestine because conditions were difficult then.
- The money was collected for the cause of Palestine (..)
- All the money collected was diverted to officials.
- Did you hear about the second conference which took place in Cairo?
- I neither heard of it nor participated in it.
- You did not hear about it?
- No, I did not.
- Do you think those conferences were of any tangible value or use?
- They must have been of some value.
- Do you think that the participation of a large delegation of Palestinian women in this conference had any value?
- Yes, a considerable value. Nobody criticized the Palestinian women's delegation to the conference; well, maybe a few people did, but it was valuable because they were all (..)
- Do you believe that women's participation in that sort of conferences was a kind of struggle?
- Every charitable work is a struggle; every charitable work is a struggle.
- What happened when Palestine was partitioned?
- We did not hear anything, I did not hear anything (..)
- Didn't any demonstrations happen?
- I was not involved.
- You stayed in Haifa?
- Pardon?
- Did you stay in Haifa?
- What is she saying?
- You remained in Haifa?
- Yes, we stayed in Haifa.

Part 2: Women's Narrations

- Until what year? Until when?
- Until the year we came over to Jordan.
- What year was that? 1947 or 1948?
- In 1948.
- You did not go to Tulkarm first?
- No, we did not move to Tulkarm.
- You didn't go to Tulkarm?
- We left Haifa. We had been in Tulkarm previously.
- Prior to going to Haifa?
- No, we lived in Haifa first, but when my father died we left for Tulkarm.
- How long were you in Tulkarm for?
- We stayed for a while then we returned to Haifa.
- Did you work as a teacher whilst in Tulkarm?
- No, I didn't.
- You did not work? Were you part of any associations in Tulkarm?
- No, I don't recall that I was.
- It is mentioned in the books that you participated in the activities of certain associations. It is okay, Aunt Maymanah, don't worry, there is nothing to it.
- Maybe I did but I can't remember.
- Associations are okay, many people take part in their activities, and it is mentioned that you were in an association with Wadee'a Qaddourah Khartabil in Tulkarm?
- It is possible they included my name.
- Please try to remember; one sometimes forgets (..)
- By the almighty Allah, I don't wish to say anything. I am trying to remember something but I don't really remember it all that well. The people of Tulkarm were good people and they suggested that I work in the association.

- During your experience as a teacher, did you ever encourage your pupils to go out and take part in demonstrations?

- Never.

- You did not march with them, spontaneously, on any occasion?

- I never did and they all knew that I wouldn't.

- Never at all?

- They did but I did not.

- For you teaching was just teaching and not a matter of raising awareness?

- Nothing else (emphasizing), only giving lessons. Thanks to Allah, my fifth grade girls were accepted into the American University (in Beirut). I once bumped into one of them in a bank and she greeted me. When I asked her who she was, she told me I had taught her in fifth grade and she said 'What you taught me in school was then taught to us in university'. One does like to teach people something useful.

- Of course.

- I was thinking to myself, such and such, but nobody was listening. I could not teach at home and make money, because then people would say 'look, this and that person went into the house'. I didn't want the money and one could not get herself involved in everything.

- When you were still a teacher, did you ever start a political discussion with the girls?

- No, never. I taught composition; I would tell a story, write it on the board, let the girls read it, and then ask the girls to write it down. Once a complaint was submitted to the ministry and the official asked 'against whom is the complaint?' The girl replied 'Maymanah' and he took the complaint, tore it into little pieces and threw it into the rubbish bin.

- Really?!

- Yes, really.

- Nobody could say a thing against you?

- Not a thing. At one point the authorities sacked all the married teachers except me; that actually happened.

Part 2: Women's Narrations

- When did you actually get married?

- In 1948 or 1946, actually I think it was in 1944. What do you want to know?

- Tell us what happened?

- They sacked of all the married women except me. Every day the teachers would buy the newspaper to see if my name was in it but they never found anything. A teacher went to the Ministry and when she returned she told me, in front of everyone, 'I saw your name on the list', but I knew she had made it up. I heard that and I was depressed, but I did not show it. The teachers objected but they were told 'Al-Qassam's daughter will be promoted every year and that is none of your business'.

When His Majesty issues a decree to the effect that Maymanah will receive promotions on annual basis what can you do about that? I pretended that I knew nothing about it (..) Must we lie? Lying is not my manner. I don't remember ever lying in my life. A teacher once lost her salary and I found it – I thanked God that it was me who found it – and handed it to the head mistress. The following day that teacher came to school looking sad. I asked her what was wrong and she said 'Why do you ask?' I told her not to worry because her salary was with the headteacher. I never lie or steal, and I have never offended or talked ill about anyone. I don't gossip but I might give advice when I see wrongdoing. There was a woman who left her children and husband and I advised her to go back to them and she did. The woman was upset with her husband and became ill. She needed hospital treatment but she wouldn't go. Her father talked to me and I asked him to leave the matter to me. I took her to the clinic and she recovered and went back to her husband. I saw her a few days ago and I asked her how things were? She assured me that all is well and her children are now big boys and girls, thanks to Allah for his mercy.

- Were you ever a member of some kind of organization?

(Maymanah shook her head to express denial).

- Never, (..)?

- You are a child of the Sheikh, you must have been (..)

- It is even more natural that you were active in one of the military organizations. The Sheikh was the first one who really believed in the armed struggle. He was the first to call for the military struggle (..) isn't that correct? (..)

- Correct (..) several women enlisted for the armed struggle; I am prepared to join King Hussein's Army today, are you happy now? By Allah, I mean it.

- Were you ever a member of the Futuwwa or Najjadah organizations?

- Who? (..)

- I mean groups that were involved in military activities?[1] (..)

- I have heard of them but I never got involved (..)

- You heard about them but never got involved?

- I heard about the Futuwwa.

- What did you hear?

- I don't know, they said Futuwwa (..) if I knew I would have told you.

- What kind of activities were they involved in? Do you know?

- No it is enough that I taught in Haifa (..) I taught (..)

- Education is a form of struggle too and you like to talk about education most of all (..)

- I like talking about religion but nobody likes to listen, (..)

Faiha: Your father was a preacher and he used his religious preaching to raise people's political awareness (..) isn't that true?

- Yes, that is true (..). Once, whilst he was teaching, a man walked in and asked him 'What do you teach them (..) how to pray? The Sheikh relied 'I don't teach people how to pray, people already know that'.

- And you used a similar method? (..) Aunt Maymanah, have you heard of a group, or a women's organization, called Zahrat Al Oqhuan?

---

1. The Futuwwa and Najjadah were scout organizations that gave military training to participants

Part 2: Women's Narrations

- I've heard of it, but I don't know (..)
- What did you hear?
- I don't know, I just heard things, at that time I was very young (..)
- Try to remember (..)
- You knew from the name that it was a worthy organization (..) it was named Zahrat Al Oqhuan (..)
- But you heard about their activities (..)? Who were they? (..)
- Of course, that group did great work; we cannot measure the work they did! The name had great connotations (..)
- What about other women organizations (..) did you hear of any (..)?
- There were so many associations in Haifa (..)
- What were they called?
- I don't know?
- What about in Tulkarm?
- They asked me to join them but I did not go (..)
- Do you think they put your name down in your absence?
- I don't know, do you mean that you have seen my name (..)?

(I felt that she didn't want to talk more about this subject)

- Tell us about the day of your engagement (..)
- Why? We should not be talking about that (..)

(Her daughter intervened saying 'tell us about when they gave you the poetry test')

- Our school was called *Madares Aljame'yah Al Islamiyah* (The Islamic Association Schools). It had a reputation for having low standards. The people in charge of the school called eighteen of the education inspectors to see the school for themselves. Some of the inspectors were ministers from Saudi Arabia and my father was with them. They started with a girl called Munirah in fourth grade, in my class, and asked her to recite some verses. She had a beautiful voice and read so well. My father then wrote some poems on the board and asked the girls to explain the meanings and the grammar of the verses.

- Who was the poet?

- He did not say the name of the poet (..), the girls did (..), do you want me to tell you?

- It is okay, we are sure you can.

- There was one word which none of the girls knew what it meant; each girl said something different. I put my hand up and told them the meaning. They asked me what my name was and I answered 'Maymanah Ezzedin Al-Qassam' and they all shouted 'the daughter of Al-Qassam!' At home my father asked me how I had known the word and I told him 'I knew it because the prerequisites for attaining knowledge are intellect, interest, stamina, money, a diligent teacher, and time, and I deduced from the context that the meaning of the word was money. I told him it occurred to me because every morning you tell us to take money from the purse; we were very content in that respect. Once my mother complained to my father that I had taken money from the safe. He asked 'from the neighbor's safe, or our safe?' She answered 'our safe' and he told her 'Maymanah was not at fault by doing so; she took from her own money'. My mother was not being a miser; rather she wanted us to ask before taking.

- Do you remember the names of any women who were active in politics or in the struggle during your lifetime? Are there some names that have been mentioned to you repeatedly?

- There must have been, but they were older than me; I don't know the names of women of my own age (..)

- Names which were mentioned again and again must have stayed in your mind? There were women who were active and had played an important role? (..)

- Yes, many but I can't remember names.

- I mean women like Wadee'a Qaddourah Khartabil, do you remember her?

- I have only heard of her.

- How did you leave home in 1948? (..)

- The situation was getting a bit dangerous (..) and we were worried about what could happen to the young ones (..) so we left, people received us, and we found a house (..) After that the camps were founded

Part 2: Women's Narrations

and we built a house in the camp.
- Which camp (..)?
- Al-Zarqa' camp (..)
- How were you treated in Jordan?
- (..) The Prophet - peace be upon him - said: "Ask not, but if given return not, for giving is a gift and gifts are not to be returned" (..) The King summoned me and I complied (..) The question put to me as soon as I entered was 'By order of his Majesty King Hussein, what are your demands?' I said 'I am grateful for your concern, but I have no demands'. I left empty-handed. The ladies in the locality said I was mad. My cousin in Syria read about my visit to the palace and said 'you were an honor to us'. My cousin was a graduate of the Azhar.
- When did that happen?
- Around 1958, something like that (..) I can't remember whether I was retired or still teaching.
- We like poetry (..) can you recite some more?
- You want poetry? I will give you some.

Oh, you the best of kings and most generous of those who paid (recited with the utmost eloquence and meticulousness).
- Was that by Sheikh Al-Qassam (..)?
- No, (..)
- Did the Sheikh write poems?
- God knows, I knew he was interested in religion and Arabic language.
- What about you? Did you write poetry?
- No, I am not a poet, but I know some of it:

Say what you may of lies and counterfeits

By wisdom I shall not hear but my ear's not deaf.

I shall not be concerned were I to be superseded,

For Neptune is farther than the sun from earth.

(She recited the poem then explained: one must be content when somebody else goes higher than them because the sun, though lower than Neptune, it is more useful for the earth than Neptune).

- You told us some poetry, do you have any songs?
- They sang *Mawtini, Mawtini* (..) I forget (..) I can't remember.
- They say if you know poetry you can learn songs easily (..)
- Thank you so much for your time.

End of Interview

Name of Narrator	Wadee'a Qaddourah Khartabil[1]

Date of Birth 1915
Recording location .... Narrator's House
Date of Recording 11/09/1998
Address of Narrator .... Beirut – Lebanon

Tape No. **2**

Tape Duration .... **90 Minutes**

Field Researcher: ...... **Suhair Al-Uzom**

Researcher: Having taken the necessary information for the questionnaire, we would like to ask you firstly about the family circumstances into which you were born, the things mentioned in your book, and how you were heavily influenced by your aunt, perhaps (…)

Narrator: I was born to a family who was greatly interested in knowledge and culture. This is the family of Qaddourah, the majority of them were doctors and pharmacists. Both, the men and women were educated; we were the first women to graduate from college. We studied and we pursued life based on our nationalistic upbringing.

- Lady Wadee'a, it is interesting that you were brought up in an Islamic environment.
- An Arab Islamic environment.
- Exactly.
- Arab [environment].
- There was another big family, but rules were more strictly applied in your family that that other one.

---

1. Wadee'a Khartabil passed away in Beirut on: 14 April 2007

- Yes, very much so.

- You mentioned in your book that many people objected to your enrollment in foreign schools.

- Many people objected and spoke to my father about it, yes, they did, but he did not care about what they said.

- What did you study?

- I had studied elementary medicine and was about to enroll for my first year in medical college. However, that year I got engaged and married.

- You mean you did not complete your studies.

- Yes, I left for Palestine.

- In those days how did you feel about entering college in a conservative environment? Some of your family members had gone to university before; did that make things easier for you?

- Yes, my aunt, and there was also my elder sister who finished college. I mean I was not the first.

- Did you have any special feelings about going to a foreign school?

- Yes, of course, we were enormously pleased. That was quite an accomplishment – you know what I mean. We were learning from foreigners in order to enrich our national identity as Arabs.

- You did not feel there was a contradiction?

- On the contrary, no.

- While you were in University, were there activities of a nationalistic nature that you participated in?

- Yes, we took part in nationalist action.

- Within the University?

- Yes, exactly, we took part in such activities, but the question of Palestine was not yet an issue as such

- But there were activities in Lebanon at the wider national level?

- Yes.

- When you left for Palestine you lived firstly in Tiberius?

- Yes.

- How did you feel about living in Tiberius? You said in your book that it was prettier, cleaner and livelier than Beirut.

- Yes, quite.

- What differences did you see between Tiberius and Lebanon?

- It was not prettier than Beirut, but it was a lot more interesting and cleaner. I mean there were so many foreigners in Tiberius, Jews – you know what I mean – and the British who tend to modernize wherever they go.

- Okay, so you stayed there for about a year then you moved on?

- We moved to Jerusalem where my husband worked as a doctor. We stayed there for a few months, whilst he was training for the job, because he was not employed at that point, then we went to Nablus.

- To Nablus or Tulkarm first?

- First to Nablus, yes, we stayed in Nablus – it is in the book – for a while, and then we moved to Gaza where we stayed for almost a year. In Gaza I lost a daughter, so we left and stayed in Tulkarm.

- During this period of time, was there participation in nationalist activities?

- Not much; the revolt hadn't started yet. But, there was some national social work, you know what I mean.

- What was your role in that work?

- I did as much as I could, which was not a lot in the beginning. I started work when I returned to Nablus, and then when I went to Tulkarm (..)

- When you took charge of the association?

- I established a branch of an association called the Union of Arab Palestinian Women. Its main headquarters was in Jerusalem and it had branches throughout Palestine. I established the branch in Tulkarm and it was where I worked all my life.

- But prior to that, when you lived in Tulkarm, you were invited to take charge of the Women's Charity Association?

- Yes, that was the one. The Union of Arab Palestinian Women.

- The Women's Charity Association?

- Yes. When I first lived in Tulkarm they asked me to work at that Association. I worked there and I renamed it the Union of Arab Palestinian Women.

- Ah, so it is the same one?

- Yes, it is the same one, yes.

- Where did the name come from? At that time the General Union of Arab Women had not been founded yet.

- No, it did exist at that time, and my Aunt Ebtihaj was its Director in Beirut. The Union had many branches in a number of Arab countries.

- Did it not come into existence in (..)

- (Interrupting) The General Union of Arab Women was already in existence – you know what I mean – and I grew up knowing about it. Yes, and I founded a branch of the Union of Arab Palestinian Women whose headquarters was in Jerusalem.

- Zulaikha Al-Shihabi?[1]

- Zulaikha Al-Shihabi is mentioned in here (pointing to her book).

- You were in Tulkarm at the beginning of the revolt in 1936?

- During the revolt in 1936 we gave assistance to the young men. Men involved in the revolt came to us for assistance and so we helped them, both symbolically and materially, and we also helped their families.

- How did you help them?

- We gave them money.

---

1. The Narrator thought it was necessary to bring up this name in the middle of the conversation to end the apparent overlapping in the Narrator's memory. The first Union of Palestinian Women was established by Zulaikha Al-Shihabi in 1921. However, the Union of Arab Women was established in 1944 by Huda Sha'rawi in Egypt following the General Conference which she called for. Ebtihaj Qaddourah, Aunt of the Narrator, did not take over the leadership of the Union until after Huda Sha'rawi died in 1947. The interviewer's question was about the precise date on which the Union of the Arab Palestinian Women was established

- I mean, as an association, where did you get the money from?
- We collected donations from people.
- From people in Tulkarm? What about from the members?
- The members would collect money from the families who wished to donate, and they were happy to give money because they knew what the money was going towards; the national struggle.
- People had faith in you?
- They trusted us immensely and we could not have succeeded had we not had the faith of the people. We had enormous success and we worked throughout the revolt in Palestine. We helped them with food, clothing and nursing, and supported their families and the widows; yes, we helped them all.
- When you arrived in Tulkarm, I believe from reading your book that the Charity Association already existed?
- There was a charity association.
- Did they ask you to join them?
- Yes, they asked me to join. I worked with them and changed it from the Charity Association to the Union of Arab Palestinian Women.
- When did you make it the Union? When did you change the name?
- Perhaps a few months after I joined the association.
- Very quickly after you joined the Association?
- Yes, almost straight after I joined them.
- Did they know at that point that you were Lebanese?
- Yes.
- Did you feel that they treated you differently because of that?
- No.
- On what basis did they invite you to join them?
- It just happened.
- But in the beginning you were not well known for your nationalist work? You were new to them?

Part 2: Women's Narrations

- What do you mean in the beginning?
- I mean when you had just come to Palestine.
- They knew about my nationalist work and that I was coming from university, the University of Lebanon, and that is why they wanted me to join them. A group of them came over to me and made me the offer and I accepted. They decided to elect me as head of the association right there and then.
- Do you remember who those women were? I am asking because this is not mentioned in the book.
- I really cannot remember all of the members.
- Could you try to give us a few clues as to who were they?
- The members from Tulkarm?
- Can you remember some of their names?
- One was from the Samara family, Almeqdadi, Hannoum or Hannoun, and from the family of (..) I mean they were from all the families there.
- The big names (families) generally.
- The big families, yes.
- How frequent were your meetings?
- Our meetings were very good. We met often and made work plans, assisted people, helped the children by creating a kindergarten. That was our work. The revolt had started and we were ready to assist women as well as the insurgents.
- Did you have a special place designated for the meetings, or did you meet in your own homes?
- We had a special place for the school children, but we met in our houses and most of the time we met at my home, yes.
- Did you have a house? Did you have children then?
- Yes, I had two boys.
- During the 1936 revolt you formed village awareness committees?
- Yes.

- Could we talk more about this particular point?
- We formed committees which visited the villages, especially the women there. We tried to raise awareness of the cause and we would find out how we could assist them and try to maintain relations with the entire district of Tulkarm and with the insurgents.
- Which villages did you actually visit?
- Thinnaba, Taibeh, Bala'a; several of them.
- Was the Galilee region within the area that you covered?
- How do you mean?
- Did you have any activities in the Galilee region?
- No, we just operated in Tulkarm.
- You mean Tulkarm, the city and the surrounding villages?
- Yes, because there were similar associations operating in other towns such as Nablus and Jerusalem.
- You mean you each operated in certain areas?
- Yes, in those regions where there were associations our workload was reduced.
- You mentioned that you formed the Union of Arab Women? That implies that your area of operations got broader and broader?
- It became broader.
- Your operations were not limited to Tulkarm?
- There were meetings in Jerusalem and we also met in different towns throughout Palestine.
- In town and villages?
- In those meetings we took decisions. We decided to change the name of the organization to the Union of Arab Palestinian Women, headed by Zulaikha Al-Shihabi, with branches all over Palestine.
- In what year was that?
- When? I think in 1935.
- That means it was before the revolt. How were the relationships

Part 2: Women's Narrations

between the women inside the movement?

- We had great relationships. We all met in Jerusalem and we would take decisions and do all the planning together, including all the branches and unions; we all worked together.

- You mean you felt that you had a common cause?

- We had one concern and one cause; we were defending the cause, the land and the country.

- What about your differences? I mean, as you know, Palestinians have strong family ties and they have a history riddled with conflicts between different families?

- Families?!

- Most of the associations you founded (interruption)

- I can proudly claim that the Union of Palestinian Women included many different families, like the Husseinis and Nashashibis in Jerusalem, despite their differences. We had members from all over; we the women were united and partners in our work, yes we were.

- How are we to understand this? The men from the different families were at odds but the women were in agreement?

- Yes, women's work was charitable, social and in support of other women. That is why they did not get involved in the various families' conflicting (political) interests. Besides, when the war began in Palestine nearly all Palestinians set aside their differences.

- Certainly, they set their differences aside.

- Yes, the tension between the families almost disappeared completely.

- That was around 1944, when Huda Sha'rawi, in Egypt, called for a conference for the General Union of Arab Women?

- Yes.

- First of all, how do you evaluate that conference, especially given the fact that a number of other conferences had taken place prior to 1944?

- It is true that many other conferences happened before 1944, some were held in Beirut, others (..)

- I meant for the General Union of Arab Women?

- Yes, many took place.
- Before 1944?
- In 1944, that was the one which was held in Cairo and we all attended.
- Were you there representing Palestine?
- I went as a representative of Palestine along with Zulaikha Al-Shihabi. There were also others from different Arab countries.
- Did you view the conference as a turning point for women's work in Palestine? Did it provide significant support for Palestinian women?
- Yes, it gave us a deep sense of togetherness and the feeling that we should be working in harmony and stand united against our common enemy, the Zionists.
- When the conference ended was there a sense of triumph?
- Yes.
- After the revolt in Palestine ended, and the British White Paper was issued, were Palestinians happy?
- Yes.
- But it was afterwards that illegal Jewish immigration to Palestine started?
- Jewish immigration, yes, yes.
- There were a number of declarations, like the one by Nahom Goldman which called for the establishment of a Jewish State?
- Yes, exactly.
- These declarations coincided with the conference in Cairo?
- The conference for the General Union of Arab Women, yes.
- Can you give us a description of the general public mood, in the midst of that environment; the mood surrounding the struggle and the attitude towards the Jews?
- Huda Sha'rawi and all the other Arab women were interested in the Palestinian cause, which was the central issue at the conference table. We worked on the basis that women share with men a duty towards

Part 2: Women's Narrations

their country. This was the main issue that made the conference so significant.

- In what sense was the conference distinct? What new proposals were made at the conference?

- How do you mean?

- What new topics were raised at the conference? What did you discuss with regards to the challenges you faced at that point in history?

- We discussed all sorts of general topics concerning the Arabs; we spoke about Zionism and Israel. My presentation, for example, I am not sure if it is there, in the book?

- "Searching for Homeland"?

- Yes, "Searching for Homeland", I urged greater awareness and for people to rise up and work for Palestine.

- As women, did you really feel that there was something you could do?

- Yes, we did as much as we could. I mean men fought the battle whilst we fought to take care of our society through charity work. For this reason we could cooperate with men and we stood together as one.

- Did you take part in the Dublin Conference? It came to my attention that the issue of equality between men and women was raised at this conference, but you mentioned that you did not attend it?

- No, I didn't.

- The Dublin conference happened during the 1960s?

- Yes.

- If we were to make a comparison, we could suggest that in the 1940s, women participated in conferences, were enthusiastic and felt quite capable of doing things, but when it came to the issue of women's equality with men nobody seemed to want to get involved.

- Yes, not so much.

- How do you feel those ideas changed? Did Arab women feel that whilst women might share the work with men they are not necessarily equal partners?

- Not really, women felt the need to share the work with men and the need for equality as well. The members of our organization were invited and some made contributions, but not all Arab countries received invitations. Yes we were part of international conferences and all for the service of the cause; the Palestinian cause. We promoted the cause.

- Does that mean those who did not attend were not invited rather than them choosing not to attend?

- Yes, that's what it was.

- Because they were not part of your clique?

- Yes, they did not go because they were not invited.

- What was women's attitude towards men in those days? You said there was a division of responsibilities; the men went to battle and you worked in the hospitals treating the wounded?

- This is true.

- Why? Why didn't you think about fighting yourselves?

- Fighting? Because we did not see any real need for us to fight while there were still enough men who could do the task. Women those days were as advanced and developed as they are now. Do you see what I am saying? I mean our work was extraordinary; we took a great leap forward and carved out the freedom for ourselves to choose such work. The concept of women fighters was still unheard of.

- You mean that it was the maximum women could do?

- Yes.

- Under the circumstances of the time?

- Yes, in those days men needed women to play that role. Men absent in battle needed someone to pay their household expenditures and care for their widows and orphans.

- I want to ask you a question which isn't strictly about your own experience; we conducted interviews with people living in villages in Galilee, and they had a different view to you. The villagers in Galilee said that because they were peasants nobody really cared about what they actually needed and that all the associations worked in the towns. How do you feel about this view that the women's movement had a leadership that did not concern itself with the villages even when they were most in need of assistance?

- Believe me we did not withhold aid from where it was needed or where we could reach. Peasant women took part in the revolt by helping men with water and food, and carrying messages. They played a big role; most of them did.

- That was their role in the battle because their sons were fighting in the mountains?

- Yes, their sons and brothers.

- Was it spontaneous participation?

- Yes, they were concerned and they took part.

- Such a role was very important, but perhaps if there had been better organization they wouldn't have participated in the way they did?

- Yes, they were not well organized at that time, they were not educated. These women could not participate. In some villages women had a positive attitude towards the movement's work but not many.

- You mean in Tulkarm there were no village women in the association?

- No, none from the villages. Oh, actually there were a few from the villages; from Thinnaba, and from Taybeh.

- Do you remember their names, or how they were referred to?

- Yes, I remember one.

- Is it one of the names you mentioned?

- It is written here.

- No, it is not mentioned here.

- It is not written there? I can't remember her name. That woman was very active, but that was sixty or seventy years ago.

- It is not really important; we just want to confirm the idea that women's participation in social activities was exclusive to the big families.

- Hajjeh (..) Hajjeh, she was a great woman (still trying to remember).

- What else do you remember?

- She passed through my mind today but I could not remember her name.

- Was her brother a leader?

- I was thinking of her today. I could not remember her name.

- But what can you remember?

- Haven't I written it in the book?

- No.

- I wrote down some names. I mean some of the names in my memoirs are written in the book.

- Yes, certainly, there are many (names).

- Hajjeh Halimeh (..) Oh God, oh God, Hajjeh Halimeh (very happily).

- What can we say about Hajjeh Halimeh?

- She was great. She was taller than me by this much(..)

- About twenty centimeters taller than you were?

- She had the height and the looks; she was a leader – you know what I mean. She was very energetic and strong; she was such a personality. She was from Thinnaba.

- She was from Thinnaba?

- Yes.

- What did she do? I mean what was she in charge of?

- She used to come along with us to the villages, and we would travel around the rural regions and visit the fighters. We would visit those most in need. When the Israelis raided the West Bank and there was colossal destruction we took food, water and clothes to the affected people. I mean that was our job; we tried to help the villages, to keep them alive, and to let them know that there were people thinking about them.

- And Hajjeh Halimeh, how did you get to know her? Did she approach you at the association?

- Yes, exactly. We worked together; all of us worked together. When I arrived in Tulkarm, a delegation from the Charity Association

Part 2: Women's Narrations

approached me and asked me to join them and so I did. They wanted me to take charge of the association and I accepted.

- Did women from Tulkarm and its outskirts approach you, or did you take the initiative to visit them?

- Both, they would come to us and we would go to them.

- Did they come just to visit or when they wanted to ask for something?

- No, they came when they had requests to make; when they needed assistance for the villages, or they wanted help for their families and children.

- What were the sources of your funding? Did you say you collected money from wealthy people?

- From people who were able to contribute; they donated happily and willingly. We were never short of money.

- How many of you were there in the association?

- I can't really say how many.

- Approximately, how many?[1]

- People donated money generously.

- I don't mean how much money was collected, rather how many members were there?

- Oh, in the association? There were 15 women.

- 15 women?

- Yes.

- At that time, since we were talking about Halimeh and women like her, there was a women's organization called the Al-Qassam Comrades (…)

- Who?

- Al-Qassam, Ezzedin Al-Qassam?

- Ezzedin Al-Qassam, yes, of course. We cooperated with him too. We cooperated with all the leaders of the revolt. We had relations with

---

1. The Narrator thought the question was about the sums of money collected, whereas the question was about how many members were in the association

everybody and we helped everybody, yes, we did.

- Do you remember how you met Ezzedin Al-Qassam? How did you cooperate with him?

- We cooperated with them by helping their families. We helped their children with food and clothing; we even gave them money to buy weapons.

- How did you know that they were Al-Qassam people?

- They came to visit us; we had delegates from them approach us.

- Men?

- Men, I will tell you something interesting, but I am not sure if you want to record it?

- Please do!

- It was difficult to meet with men in those days. We met and spoke with men from behind closed doors. They always approached me. They used to come when my husband left for work; they would come asking for some sort of help.

- They came to your house?

- Yes, they would come to the house. I gave them all that I could; as much as I possibly could. Once my husband was leaving for work, but one of his shirt's buttons fell off and he decided to come back and have it fixed. It was late when he left again and as he left he met four tall and well built young men coming to the house. He asked them what they wanted – the British used to spy on us to see who was cooperating with the insurgents - and they told him 'we need medical assistance from the lady of the house'. My husband said 'If you wanted medicine come ask for it from the hospital, I would be happy to oblige', then he carried on to his work. After he had gone they came and told me what happened and I was really angered by what I heard. When he returned, I told him 'Look, these men would not dare go and ask a government employee for help. They come to us because they feel safe asking us'. My husband replied 'What do you expect me to do when I see three gangly looking men? I thought they might want to rob the house or be spying on you; they could cause you so much trouble'. That's how he found out I was helping men.

Part 2: Women's Narrations

- They came to your house, to you personally? Did you help them with your own money?

- No.

- Or through the association?

- They came through the Union with their requests.

- And they expected you to offer (..)

- They approached me with their requests for some sort of help. They also approached others in the association, such as women from the Miqdady and Hajj Ibrahim families. Those women had people approaching them for help too, but being the head of the association naturally more people would approach me.

- Those people who were approaching you, were they from the Al-Qassam group or the insurgents in general?

- The insurgents in general.

- Did you say that your uncle, or your father-in-law, tried to impose the *hijab* (head cover) on you, or did he simply ask you?

- No he did not try to impose it, but he thought it would be a good idea for me to cover my head. I told him that I wouldn't do so, ever.

- Okay, that was in Tiberius, but what about when you went to Tulkarm?

- In Tulkarm I never covered my head.

- Did your colleagues in the association cover their heads?

- No they did not. Most of them let their hair be seen.

- It struck me when I was reading your book that it was women from the big families who were the ones who covered their heads more (..)

- Yes they wore head covers.

- The peasant women only wore small headscarves when they went outside?

- Yes, they were *safirat* (they did not wear a head cover). In the city there were only a few women who went around without their heads covered but after a few years they increased in number.

-188-

- Didn't that affect your relationship with the insurgents, or other men for that matter?

- No, it did not affect relations because we were respectable women and the way we conducted ourselves was very much respected.

- As we are talking about revolutionaries, during that period, were you approached by, or did you hear of a group of women called the Al-Qassam comrades? Perhaps these women were the wives of martyrs?

- Yes we were approached by the wives of martyrs.

- So were they an independent women's organization?

- No, but we used to help those women.

- But did you hear of an organization named the Al-Qassam Comrades?

- No, we never heard of them.

- As an independent organization?

- No.

- I am trying to collect material on these women but it seems no one knows anything about them (..)

- I did not hear of them in Tulkarm; no, never. I would have written about them in the book if I had.

- I looked for them in your book and found nothing about them.

- Yes, I would have written about them.

- Let's move on to 1946. Do you have anything to say about the period from 1936 to 1946? Do you remember something important which you witnessed. Was there a particular thing or incident that occurred while you were still in Palestine?

- As a woman I worked and did the most a woman could do in terms of offering help. I participated in the revolt fully. We stayed until the second armistice.

- The second armistice at the end of July?

- Yes, I mean I stopped operations only when the revolt stopped. At that moment in time I thought to myself 'my children and I no longer have a life here'. My children were in Ramallah and Haifa so I hired a car and took them back to Beirut to be with my family.

Part 2: Women's Narrations

- Was that in 1948?
- That was in 1949.
- In 1949?
- Yeah, towards the end of 1948; yes, the end of 1948.
- The war for Palestine had ended then?
- The war was over.
- You mean you stayed in Palestine until the end of the war?
- Until the end of the war; the end of the revolt.
- We say the 1936 revolt, and we say the Palestine war when we talk about 1948.
- In 1948.
- Which one are we talking about now?
- We are talking about the 1948 war, yes.
- You remained (in Palestine) until the end of 1948?
- Yes, indeed.
- Until November.
- I sent the children to Beirut and then I returned to our house in Tulkarm, which was a hospital for the treatment of the wounded.
- Between 1944-1945 when the Second World War was about to end and 1947, what was the nature of your work and activities inside Palestine?
- We did several things; not only the association but all the women in Palestine. Zulaikha Al-Shihabi, the chief in Jerusalem, was bursting with energy; she ran all the branches, yes, she was very energetic.
- Were things different from the way they were during the 1936 revolt?
- No, not really.
- Did you get aid from outside Palestine?
- Very little. My aunt Ebtihaj sent some medicines and clothes - things like that - from Beirut to the association in Tulkarm.

- To Tulkarm? You mean not to the Union?

- No, to Tulkarm, because she sent what she did because I requested it; yes, she sent what I requested.

- You requested things for the hospital you worked in?

- For the hospital and for the families of the martyrs; for the villages which were destroyed by the Zionists during the war.

- When was this approximately? Before the war?

- One or two years before the war. Those two years after 1944-45 were the hardest.

- You mean in 1946-47?

- Yes.

- In your book you mention that there was a demonstration in Tulkarm.

- Yes.

- And you gave a speech in front of the crowds?

- Yes.

- Can we talk about that demonstration and its aims? How did the crowd assemble and how did you decide to demonstrate?

- It was like all other demonstrations; we called for a demonstration to express our dismay and rejection of the idea of partitioning Palestine.

- You mean that demonstration was prior to the partition plan, when they were still preparing the resolution?

- Yes, when there was talk of partitioning Palestine; it was not a resolution yet.

- Okay, before the resolution.

- I wrote in the book that we called for a big demonstration. It was in fact a great one, especially when all the mosques joined in by raising the Athan and the churches rang their bells. The entire town walked in that demonstration. We stopped at the entrance of the Municipality and it was there that I gave my speech.

- Who asked you to speak to the demonstrators?

Part 2: Women's Narrations

- Who?

- Did someone ask if you could speak?

- No, nobody did. As the head of the Union it was part of my duty. I called for Jihad; I called upon women to help men in their battle and their sacrifice. Those words, at the time, echoed and had an impact. People were affected by such words. I stood at the top of the stairway of the municipality and I spoke. Oh, God those days have gone now, gone.

- Since it was the Union who called for the demonstration, were there many women in it?

- Pardon me?

- Because the Union called for the demonstration a lot of women must have participated?

- Yes, of course.

- No other institution called for the demonstration?

- No, it was the Union who called upon the prominent personalities in the town and the entire District to organize the demonstration. Many women took part; they dressed in black and covered their heads with black veils.

- You mean they were dressed as though they were in mourning?

- Mourning; yes, yes.

- But, perhaps not mourning; rather expressing anger?

- Boycott and anger, yes.

- But the Partition resolution had not been passed yet?

- Yes, true. But with Israel we had become accustomed to the fact that when it wanted something done, it happened; which meant it was really just a matter of time before the resolution became a reality.

- Were there many women in the demonstration?

- Yes, many women. Some who never usually took part in public events came out to participate in the demonstration.

- Was it a silent march or did you chant slogans?

- No, we marched through the main roads of the town and then returned to the Municipality headquarters, where I gave the speech.

- Where did the march take off from?

- Sorry what?

- Where did you gather before the march started?

- From the Tulkarm public square.

- Did the committees created by the Union inform the villages of the demonstration?

- Yes, we informed all of them.

- How did the idea of turning your house into a hospital occur to you?

- My house consisted of two floors. The lower floor was made up of five rooms and that served as my husband's clinic. We lived on the upper floor. After I sent my boys to Beirut I was alone with just the cook and some servants. My husband donated his clinic to the project and he treated the wounded. We bought beds for the rest of the rooms and turned it all into a hospital. It was full of patients, and all the doctors in the district volunteered to work at the hospital; they all came and helped.

- The idea (of having a hospital in the house) gives me goose pimples.

- Yes, every night I think of those days, even now. I just can't believe how it happened. We operated until the revolt ended; until the war ended. Then I looked around and saw that everything had gone except my husband. I finished my work there and I decided to return to Beirut to look after my children and their schooling. I came to Beirut in 1949. This very house was still being built. I rented it then went back to Tulkarm to bring my furniture. Oh, I forgot to tell you, the guest room on the upper floor was also part of the hospital. The lower floor was not enough.

- The lower floor wasn't enough?

- No it was not. I sent my furniture to Amman, where my married daughter lived. The furniture remained there until the war ended. Then we collected it all and furnished this house in Beirut.

- Is this the furniture you brought with you from Palestine?

Part 2: Women's Narrations

- No, this is new. I used that furniture for ten or fifteen years then I sent it to the Jabal (the Mountain) years ago (laughing).

- For how long did your house operate as a hospital? For how many months?

- It was for a year or so, perhaps two years.

- Shall we say from 1948 to (..)

- We cooked for the patients and fed them. We made it like a hospital. Can you imagine how much work that took? How many nurses we needed? How much the cost of running a hospital was in those days?

- I'd really like to ask you some more questions. Who helped you?

- The members of the association worked as nurses, and the people of the town came and made generous donations. Women in the town came and helped with the cooking and cleaning, and sent meals to the patients as well. We worked together, hand-in-hand.

- What about the costs of that undertaking?

- The Union paid off the costs.

- The Union paid for all of it?

- The Union was prepared to cover the entire cost.

- Who were the doctors working at the hospital? Were there women doctors at the hospital?

- No, there weren't any women doctors. There were women nurses though (the members of the association).

- Were you one of the nurses?

- Yes, we women were the nurses.

- Perhaps because you were preparing to become a doctor?

- Yes, I knew a few things about nursing and I did well, I think.

- Did some of the wounded die?

- Yes, some died.

- Were there women among the wounded?

- No, there were none.

- Most of them were men?
- They were all men; there was no section for women in the hospital.
- Let us suppose that a woman was wounded in battle (..)
- My husband would treat her in the clinic and then she would be sent back to her home.
- You mean no wounded women stayed overnight at the hospital?
- Yes, no female patients stayed overnight.
- During this period of time, since we are talking about hospitals and medication (..)
- Yes
- In Yaffa, a women's organization by the name of Zahrat Al Oqhuwan was founded in 1947.
- Okay.
- It is thought that the people who founded this organization were women who helped out in the hospitals. Did you hear of them?
- Okay, okay.
- Did you know of their existence? What did they do exactly?
- No, but I heard about them.
- Oh, you have heard of them?
- Yeah.
- Where did they work?
- In Yaffa and its outskirts.
- In the entire Yaffa region?
- Yes.
- What did you hear about them? Were they distinguished? Did they participate in political activities?
- I do not know much about them. Perhaps I knew more back then but I have forgotten.
- How did you know about them? Who told you about them?

Part 2: Women's Narrations

- From the news in Palestine, and through the Union; we used to get all sorts of news and information.

- You mean through your branch of the Union?

- In Yaffa there was a big branch, and there were other big branches in Haifa and in Nazareth. Yes, we used to cooperate with one another.

- During that period of time, in 1951-52, there was another institution founded in Syria – I am sure you know about it because you wrote about it in your book – it was called Returnees and was founded by Sa'adeh Al-Kilani.

- Returnees? What was that?

- Returnees was an organization founded by a woman called Sa'adeh Al-Kilani. She was well known and participated (..)

- Sa'adeh Al-Kilani? Yes, of course. Yes, I know; I know.

- Was that organization only in Syria? Do you know more about it?

- No, it was just in Syria, but there were relations between us and them.

- What was the nature of your relationship with Returnees?

- We met sometimes at conferences; we had a moral relationship.

- You mean there was cooperation between you?

- No, there was no cooperation because Syria was separate.

- Were you so disciplined that no one encroached upon each other's work?

- Yes, each organization knew its bounds.

- Do you mean you heard about each other's news?

- Exactly, we called and visited each other.

- Why do you think that an organization run by a lady like Sa'adeh Al-Kilani, who was a very big name in the women's movement, could not last?

- Yes, it did not last.

- You and others in the movement managed to last (..)

-196-

- How did I last? I came and moved the Union here (to Beirut) before it died. I felt it was going to die in Jerusalem; it was on the verge of collapsing.

- That was after it came under Jordanian control?

- Yes, before King Hussein and King Abdullah tightened their grip on the union, it is written here in the book. King Abdullah even sent my husband into exile.

- You mentioned that the King made his life difficult?

- He exiled him, he exiled him. The king tightened his grip on him because he did not subscribe to his policies. My husband stuck to Palestinian policies (..) What were we saying?

- You were talking about your fears about the demise of the Women's Union, and that you thought it was dying in Jerusalem.

- Oh (..) Yeah, I came here (to Beirut) and I revived the Women's Union. I mean, when I returned to Beirut, I was in a seriously distressed state, because of what happened with the hospital, the patients, and the wounded. All this caused my stress and ill health and my husband said that I should not return until my condition improved.

- You mean because of your stress?

- Yes, my anxiety and anger (..) I was immensely angry because we had lost Palestine. We were broken, we had lost and the cause was lost. This was the end result of so much death and sacrifice?! Those Arab states, from whom we had expected assistance, did not give as much help as they should have done; they did not do what they should have done in terms of providing assistance. Yes, that is why I became so ill; I was ill for sometime after I came back to Beirut. That is why I had to bring my children here. I stayed in this house with my children, but my husband stayed behind in Tulkarm. He said 'I will not leave because they need me here; I will be the last to leave'.

- Did you give birth to any of your children here or were they all born in Palestine?

- My children?

- Were your children all born in Palestine or were some born here?

- No, they were all born in Palestine; some in Nablus, some in Tulkarm

Part 2: Women's Narrations

and the others were born in Yaffa.

- How blessed you are; how many children do you have?

- I had two boys and two girls. One of the boys died when he was only twenty-two.

- Was that Marwan?

- Marwan. You read my book?

- I was really moved by the incident.

- Yes it was Marwan; Marwan was larger than life. What can I tell you about him? He was a student in America, and a leader of the students. Nobody could do what he did. He returned to work at the Emile Bustani Company. Frankly speaking, Marwan wanted to take advantage of working for Bustani to be able to carry out patriotic activities. Some men were waiting for him in Jordan; they were planning to carry out military operations inside Palestine. But the airplane crashed as it was landing and he died at the age of twenty-two.

- I wanted to ask you about this particular incident. Did you know that he was going to carry out an operation in Palestine?

- No, he never mentioned anything whatsoever about it. He was very discreet with what he did or wanted to do. However, I knew he was a very proactive student and tried to promote the cause in America; he made a lot of speeches there and talked to others about the Palestinian cause. But, he never spoke about conducting operations in Palestine. Just before he was leaving, his father spoke to him saying 'I don't like you travelling with Emile Bustani'. Marwan asked him why and his father replied 'those planes are very small and dangerous'. Marwan asked his father 'am I worth more than Emile Bustani?' His father answered 'No, but I can only talk to you as my son; not to him'. He spent about half an hour arguing with his father, who then told him 'Okay if they are waiting for you I guess you have to go'.

- Did he want to go to Jordan and then from there to Palestine?

- He wanted to enter into Palestine with the youth, but then he was taken in that disaster.

- What about your other son and your two daughters?

- Farouq worked here, and my daughter was married to Dr. Adib Al-

Dawoudy. I think I wrote about him. He was a political advisor for President Assad in Syria for a few years. Then he asked to be posted abroad. He took his family to live in Switzerland where he was posted as Syria's ambassador in Geneva. They used to come here to visit but because it is hot in the summer they prefer not to come then. When they next visit I will call you so you can meet them.

- Yes, sure, I would like to meet them.

- Yes, you'll like my daughter. She received her BA from the American University; she is everything you could ask for in a woman.

- What about your second daughter?

- I don't have a second daughter.

- You have one girl and three boys?

- Yes. My second son is Hisham, his wife and children live here but he works in Jeddah. He takes care of me and looks after all my responsibilities. His wife works here with me in the Union.

- How about the third son? We spoke about Marwan, God bless him, and Hisham and (..)

- Farouq, he is in America.

- I see, Farouq is the one in America. Now, let's move to the last question (..) I must be making you so tired?

- No, no, it's okay; you must be tired of me.

- No, of course not. On the contrary I am so pleased that we finally got to meet.

- It has been a wonderful hour.

- Thank you. In this last part of the interview can we go back and talk about when you came back to Beirut in 1952 and revived the Union's branch here? You mentioned that you contacted Palestinian women (..)

- Yes I sent out an invitation to as many women as possible and we met in my house. I told them about the idea, and it seemed agreeable to everyone. Then we elected sixteen women to represent the Union of Palestinian Women and we formed a committee and got to work. At first we held our meetings in our houses because otherwise it would have been very costly. We met and worked in the refugee camps where we gave assistance to the children of Palestinians and martyrs. Later we rented a place in Suq Al-Gharb, which we subsequently managed to purchase and renovate. It was a house and a school which we named the Esa'ad Attufulah House. It consisted of 500-600 children, most of whom were the children of martyrs and the dispossessed. The school had two sections: one for Palestinian children and another for Lebanese children. Since we were in Lebanon we thought it was only fair not to discriminate between people. Isn't that true?

- Indeed, because they all lived through a common tragedy. When did this happen?

- That was in 1954-55.

- Was it the one which later became the school of Suq Al Gharb?

- Yes, it was the School of Suq Al Gharb itself.

- Do you wish to add anything to this discussion, say, anything to your home in Tiberius?

- Oh, my home in Tiberius! I wish that before I die, that I spend an hour there. We lost Tiberius, we lost Palestine; but, Palestine has courageous and strong willing men, do you know?

- Yes, I heard

- Yes, you are one of them, (The Researcher laughed), their men and their women, I mean.

- Thank you so much for your time

- It is my pleasure, you are doing a great job, God bless you

End of Interview

| Name of Narrator | Issam Hamdi Al-Huseini[1] |

Date of Birth 1919
Recording location .... Narrator's House
Date of Recording 31/08/ 1998
Address of Narrator .... Gaza – Al-remal

Record No. .... **One**

Tape Duration .... **50 Minutes**

Field Researcher: .... **Iman Amer Radwan**

Researcher: I would like to ask you firstly about your childhood and the things you remember about women's involvement in politics?

Narrator: I was born after the First World War, at the beginning of this century; a little after the Balfour Declaration. I was brought up in a house where you heard talk of nothing but Palestine, the Balfour Declaration, the British, the liberation of Palestine and Zionism. All through my early life, I knew about nothing other than my country and the tragic circumstances surrounding it. I heard nothing from my father except talk about our home country and I heard nothing from my mother except talk about the defence of our home country. It was not a stable upbringing because my father moved from one town to another and from one area to another, sometimes under the pretext of looking for work, and sometimes for other reasons that I didn't understand, for he was involved in politics since childhood.

My life started with me looking at the world more than looking at myself, I thought about my country more than I thought about my family, so I was born believing in community work. When I was a

---
1. Issam Al-Husseini Passed away in Gaza City on 06/01/2005

child I received tuition and instruction from my father through reading and he chose for me the most beneficial and useful books that would consolidate my knowledge and support my activities until the time was right for me to join the teachers' (training) institute.

Prior to that, I moved from one town to another: from Gaza to Yaffa, then to Haifa, to Nazareth and to Ramallah. It was exile; being in those places was like being in exile. During my studies I put all my time and effort into studying, but I was a rebellious sort of person especially with the outbreak of the 1936 revolt. We had English teachers living in the flat beneath us, which was a wood store, and I tried to make a practical contribution to the revolt by burning it, thinking that my action would be a form of participation in the revolt against the British and the Jews. After that I graduated from the institute and worked as a teacher in Gaza's elementary school for girls; the sole elementary school in the southern part of the Gaza Strip.

I started trying to carry out the revolutionary message that I had learned, but English laws forbids teachers from engaging in public work, cultural or social activities, or anything beyond teaching. I took advantage, however, of school parties and school meetings where I could pass on whatever ideas I wanted to the girls.

After four years of teaching, I was promoted to the position of school headmistress and here I seized the opportunity to do more. I began to write for the newspapers and work at the Palestinian broadcaster, Jerusalem Radio, where I presented a program entitled "from girl to girl" twice a week. The programs were advisory, educational and cultural; targeted towards the new generation of young people. I tried to do these programs for a long period of time. I also wrote in the newspapers on public issues: social, moral and cultural, for example the veil, which were all of importance to society, the country and the people. I wrote out of a sense of duty towards my country and people. This situation continued until 1948. During those years we tried to establish a secondary school but only a few of the pupils made it to 12th grade. However during that time we were able to offer first aid and nursing courses; the trainees would work as volunteers at Al-Maidan Hospital which was taken over by our Egyptian brothers. We worked in the Hospital for a long time, and I established a new association – in addition to two others that already existed – called "Women Progress", which offered assistance to refugees arriving in Gaza. They needed help and so we collected money and donations and distributed them to needy refugees. There was no other source of help except from the Quakers, who gave some assistance; so we formed a committee made up of the three societies and we worked in cooperation with the Quakers. The situation remained like this until the United Nations UNRWA Agency took over and then we abandoned this type of work. We embarked upon other public work, political and social, and we produced our first theatrical work in 1948 which was performed onstage in 1950. I wrote the play and it was entitled "Jihad Filestine" (the struggle of Palestine). It was the only play I ever wrote in my life. The play spoke about Al-Nakba (the 1948 Palestine tragedy) describing what happened right from the beginning until the time when people fled their homes; a time we lived through day-by-day and hour-by-hour.

The play was performed at Al-Samer Cinema in Gaza, and was attended by the Governor General who was really impressed by it because he felt it reflected the everyday reality on the ground. Afterwards, the Association turned to other sorts of activities – cultural and social activities, holding public meetings and ceremonies, and sometimes lectures – any means through which they could keep me in contact with the people. In addition to that, whilst Gaza was under Egyptian control our activities went beyond the Strip. I arranged a trip to schools and other institutions in Egypt in order to learn more about education in Egypt because our knowledge was limited and our schools were (..). I stayed in Egypt for a two week educational course, accompanying the educational course inspector, Dorreyah Shafiq, sister of Mrs. Aminah Saeed, and then I returned to Gaza. Then we began to develop a school education system in Gaza. Fifteen girls joined the secondary school level in 1950, and all graduated successfully. That was the starting point for secondary education in Gaza. After that we continued our public activities. I worked in Khan Yunis as head of a secondary school and during the three years I spent there I introduced some social activities, gave public lectures, took part in demonstrations (outside the city) and gave a speech, despite the fact that Khan Yunis was less open to accepting such behaviour than Gaza. But things carried on in a satisfactory way, praise the lord. I remained in Khan Yunis until the early 1960s, and then returned to Gaza, for I had pledged not to stay there for more than three years. Upon returning to Gaza I worked as an inspector for Arabic language and religion, and spent two to three years as Director of the Department of Education. Then I took charge of the administration of a teachers' training institute which had been founded and begun work. I spent two years at the institute and saw the first group graduate. Then the (1967) tragedy happened and that was when I decided to terminated my activities in the educational field because I could not work with Jews. I could not work with my enemy. When they asked me to continue working I refused. The Israeli in charge said to me 'Don't you want to work with us?' and I said '*no, no I won't*' (strong emphasis). He replied 'look, all of these people will cooperate' and I said to him '*no*, they have no choice, it is not because they are keen to cooperate with you! It is because they have families! I however will resign to my house and live with my father under his auspices'. Whilst at home my activities shrunk, except for a few lectures at the start, on occasions like International Child Day and Women's Day. I participated in some occasions but my public activities were drastically reduced. Prior to that, we had taken part in demonstrations. Under the Egyptians we commemorated the expulsion of the Jews in 1957. Each year we held ceremonials at the site of the unknown soldiers' where people would gather and give speeches, including myself. We participated in many activities in many different fields. During the Egyptian era I had the chance to attend a conference in Beirut in 1963. Because transportation between the two countries was difficult, the Governor General ordered a plane belonging to UNRWA to take me to Beirut for the conference; I attended the event and gave a speech there. We then agreed that the next conference should be held in Gaza. That was in 1963, and we were all aware of the political changes happening and looming in the region. While I was there I got to know and meet a number of Palestinian women who had come from all over, representatives from Egypt, Jordan and Iraq; many exiles were able to meet together. It was a nice opportunity for us to meet. There was also Hajj Amin Al-Huseini, who we of course knew; he and his wife and daughter attended the conference. Later he invited us all to dinner; all the guests at the conference. We did all we could do. I gave a speech and wrote pieces for the papers, some of which I still have and others I do not. I heeded my father's saying that "he who says does not and he who does says not". Therefore, we used to do rather than just say, and Allah knows it is true. Following that, during the same year, a conference for working women was held in Egypt, and I was invited to attend by the Egyptian Minister (for Social Affairs), Hikmat Abu Zeid. I went and attended on behalf of the Gaza Strip and presented a paper. At that time, in November, a meeting was held in commemoration of the Palestine Partition Plan and the Partition of Palestine in 1947. The meeting was attended by many Palestinians and Arabs, and I was among them. I had not prepared anything to say before the meeting, but I spoke offhand. President Nasser, may Allah bless him, heard my speech on the radio and he seemed impressed by what I said. He asked the Minister for Social Affairs to arrange for me to meet with him. The following day she invited me along with representatives of Kuwait and the representative of Algeria and we went to visit the President. The president commented lengthily on my speech and talked a great deal with me, expressing his approval of us. I then invited him to visit the Gaza Strip but he apologized and said he wouldn't be able to make such a trip. So I invited the Minister and he gave permission for her to visit Gaza. The Minister came with me to Gaza and stayed for a few days travelling around the Strip to see its conditions.

In Egypt, I was also engaged in social activities as I had several friends in the upper echelons of society, such as Dr. Hikmat, as I mentioned, and Ayesha Abdulrahman, Bent Eshshati', Saniyyah Qarra'a. I remember this name well as the name Saniyyah is also my mother's name. I have always been fond of this name and I recall when I was young that Saniyyah Qarra'a wrote a book entitled *Famous Women in the Islamic World*. I read it perhaps three or four times a day. We finally met at the age of sixty and became close friends. Jathebeyah Sudqi, who was also one of Egypt's literary figures, is someone else I got to know and I accompanied her during a tour to Gaza. I mean I had lots of contacts. I also knew several men whom I need not mention. The few years when Egyptians lived with us was the time when we really felt like we were Arabs. They were in charge of us and met all our needs. Those times were the happiest for us despite all the harshness and bitterness that we endured. We awaited a real revolt and the end of the bitter era, but the bitter era has been repeated and repeated and repeated.

- Have you ever heard of a women's organisation called Al-Qassam Comrades?

- No, I have not heard of that organization, I used to follow the news about Al-Qassam, but this group did not exist.

- You told us about the wife of Najeeb Nassar before we started recording.

- Najeeb Nassar was a journalist and I think he had a newspaper called 'Mirror of the East'. With regards to his wife I think I heard that she was involved in some women's activities, but where and how I don't know; I was so young that I didn't really understand such things.

Part 2: Women's Narrations

- Do you recall the names of any woman who worked with the Al-Qassam group?

- Regrettably I do not remember any names. That does not mean none participated, but my knowledge of those times is limited.

- What are your memories of the 1936-1939 revolt in Palestine?

- The revolution broke out in 1936 with the general strike, and it escalated from there. They would stop the British trains, damage things and kill several of the British. I remember times when we were travelling to Yaffa and my father would say 'here we killed six British, here we killed four'. Indeed there were many British victims (..) no not victims; we should not say they were victims. The revolt swept throughout most of Palestine. The revolutionary movement grew up from the early 1920s, they used to say 1921 or 1922, but I'm not sure of the precise year because I was not involved; I was just a child and didn't know any details. However, there was a movement and I know it began during the 1920s.

- Do you remember the role played by women during the revolt?

- The 1936 revolt was more than demonstrations and movements; what could a woman do? The women involved in these activities were limited and there were not many educated women because not all those who reached school age were actually sent to school; it was not deemed necessary because they would marry. Therefore, I do not think there were really any women who participated in the true meaning of the word.

- What are your memories of the six-month strike which was declared on the 19th of April 1936?

- I was a school girl and I used to hear the news about strikes and the revolution from my family. My sister Rabab even took part in a demonstration, perhaps the only demonstration. My mother sewed an Arab flag for her to carry and she gave a fiery speech at the Great Mosque in Gaza to encourage the crowd. Then she threw the flag down to the people demonstrating and urged them to go and fight. The young men picked it up and went on the march. One of the demonstrators lost his life at the hands of the British that day and then Rabab gave a speech at the church, causing the British to call on our father, intent on arresting him because his daughter had led the demonstration. However he convinced them that he had nothing to do with the matter.

I myself was at the teacher's institute where the spirit of the revolution was raging pretty strongly. School ended when someone attempted to burn the English teachers. We had a staff of English teachers living in a flat above a store for fire wood. This gave the arsonist a chance to burn the wood and the teachers with it, but in the end the wood burned without damaging the school or injuring the staff. The arsonist was arrested and imprisoned for a few days until some good people testified that the prisoner had no connection with the incident. It was me who was the arsonist.

- How did women deal with the 1936 general strike and what were the different roles they played during the strike?

- Women responded fully to the circumstances and weighed in to support the strike from within their houses by being good housewives; but they were not directly involved in activities in the field, and in Gaza the field was limited anyway.

- Do you remember anything about the Arab conferences which were held in support of the Palestinian issue, like the one held in Beirut in April 1930?

- I do not remember such conferences, although there were several of them. Even in Palestine, six or seven such conferences were held, and all of them were, of course, concerned with the issue of Palestine. Nonetheless, we were still young and distanced from politics and public affairs. References to those events are available in the history books. However, I imagine there is nothing in them indicating that there was a tangible role for women in those times.

- Did you believe in the usefulness of those conferences? (..) like those held in Baghdad and Damascus in October 1932?

- Events of that sort are forums where discussions, arguments and dialogues are laid down, provoking ideas and counter ideas, and this must at least have some use, however slight that might be.

- Do you think the downturn in the 1939 revolt affected women's activities in Palestine?

- In any event that was in Palestine, whether in Jerusalem or in the north. There were women's groupings but of course we were far away from them. There was, for instance, the Union of Women's Association that once held a conference; I cannot remember when precisely. I attended it in Jerusalem by sheer accident and there were ladies like Zulaikha Al-Shihabi and Andaleeb Al-Amad there. They carried out some activities

Part 2: Women's Narrations

during the 1920s but their impact, I would guess, was very limited because at that point in history the role of women was limited.

- What was the role of women during the period between 1939 when the revolution ended and 1947, just before the partition resolution was passed? You mentioned to us that during that period you, in Gaza, were transporting weapons and hiding them in a mosque. Could you tell us more about that?

- Ah, well the Palestinians predicted the intentions of the Jews and that the Mandate would be terminated, so they prepared for a revolution, for battle and confrontation with the Jews. Therefore there were several groups who prepared themselves and got weapons ready – I should not mention their names – and some of them sold their land to buy weaponry. Some of them were very closely related to us.

- Mentioning the names is very important.

- My father happily sold his land and he sold some of my mother's land to buy arms which he hid in the mosque near us, as I mentioned, but that did not only happen in the 1940s; it happened right from the beginning of the revolution.

- But what was your role? Where did you bury the arms?

- Right next to our house, it was easier than it seems, the place was safe and secure because the mosque was adjacent to the back of our house. Besides, all the people living around there were our families and countrymen; our beloved who would never betray us. I would ask somebody to come along to dig for me; people had faith in one another and none dared to betray that trust. During the 1936 revolt many men lost their lives because of their betrayal; I mean when a person was suspected of being an informer that person would be killed. We all know that many faced death because they were alleged informers or land sales agents. Palestine was on guard and, despite their simplicity and limited resources, people were very aware.

- Did you take part in the endeavour to boycott Israeli goods?

- Ever since I was born, throughout our whole lives, we were against purchasing foreign goods, let alone Israeli goods. Each one of us would buy things and bring them for the house but no one ever bought Israeli products. We were the sort of people who liked to buy and wear expensive things, but never Israeli products. I boycotted Israeli goods to the extent that I once made a dress for myself from a peasant woman's head cover. I actually have a photo of me wearing it. I also made school curtains from striped cloth made in Gaza and I still have some of the cloth in Gaza. When my mother, bless her, wanted to buy us things she went to Jerusalem to buy from one-hundred percent Arab shops. Even when we bought the clothes for my sisters' wedding we got them from Jerusalem and Yaffa but not from Tel Aviv. I remember after 1967, my father, bless him, asked me to buy him a pair of slippers when I went to the market. I looked around and they were all Israeli made. When I returned I told him there are slippers but they were Israeli made and he replied 'no, no, I don't want them; I would rather walk bare footed'. I wrote to my sisters abroad who then sent him four pairs of slippers. On one occasion, while in Egypt, I wanted to buy wool fabric to have it made into a dress. The shopkeeper noticed I was looking for something good quality and he pointed out to me that he had some English wool. I told him I wanted Egyptian wool. He replied 'but Madam, it is better'. I said 'I know it is, but I want the worse one, our product'. He was astonished by my attitude to the extent that he asked me 'where are you from Madam?' I told him 'I am an Arab woman who wants Arab made wool'. I got what I wanted and tailored the best dress ever. Similarly, once in Amman in the early 1970s, I went to buy some socks and the shopkeeper showed me different designs for different prices. I asked him 'why is this cheaper than that?', 'It is Israeli' he said. Imagine, Arab states importing Israeli goods in the early seventies. I told the shopkeeper 'I am from Gaza and I buy from Amman to avoid Israeli goods and yet their goods are in your shops'. The shopkeeper was embarrassed and then he inquired who I was. He became more embarrassed when he realised who I was because he knew my father, and then he told me who he was.

- Did you take part in the semi-military activities during that period, such as the Futuwwah and Najjadah?

- Naturally Futuwwah was in the schools, and it was students in the Futuwwah groups. I was the scout's leader. I was responsible for the scouts but I did not participate in the Najjadah.

- Did you participate in the League of National Liberation? The new Arab Marxist organization which was formed as a result of the split of the Arab group from the Palestinian Communist Party in 1943? Did you hear about it?

- Honestly, I have no idea what or where that was!

- It was here in Palestine.

- In Palestine? I do not remember much of 1943, we were still blockaded then; you can ask me about anything after 1948, that is when I sprung into action and started working, prior to that it was forbidden and no-one could move.

- Did you hear about the Second Arab Women's conference, held in support of Palestine, which was led by Huda Sha'rawi in 1944?

- I don't know of that one either.

- What was the impact of Ernest Bevin's declaration in November 1945 (allowing Jewish immigration) on Palestinian women's activities?

- Whenever there is a decision contravening our interests, we erupt and revolt and raise hell, but very soon after that we cool off again. The Jews understood that we are reactionary people. Unlike us, they are able to react to decisions which are against their interests calmly and operate smoothly, just like the way things are done today. For example we erupted over the tunnel issue and they left it to work on Mount Abu Ghneim. We in turn erupted over Abu Ghneim and they went back to work on the tunnel. Of course, no one is happy about what happens, but then again what matters is not one's feelings as much as one's deeds! Can you or can you not act? Regrettably we talk but we don't act.

- What was the impact on Palestinian women of the UN Partition Resolution of Palestine on 29th November 1947?

- We revolted and raised hell on earth, and we still remember the event year after year, but what have we been able to do?!

- But you have particular memories of that resolution?

- You did not live in my days; back then we believed that all of Palestine was ours which meant we rejected partition. According to some reports, when we went to war people chanted "wish they had partitioned, wish they had partitioned" because it seemed as though they got more under the partition plan than they got after the war. But that was a pack of lies. They just wanted to take Palestine and the partition could not have been accepted. Palestine was rightfully ours and we refused to share it with strangers. Unfortunately what was really implemented in the end was far worse than partitioning Palestine.

- But during the partition did you do something particular?

- No, I did not do anything specific. I swear to Allah, at that time I was only talking about the situation; I told you we talk a lot.

- Do you remember a public demonstration in which women strongly participated?

- There were women at the celebrations held on the 13th of March, when the Jews left here. Each year there used to be some sort of demonstration when school girls and boys would gather in front of the Unknown Soldier. I mean there were demonstrations against something, I don't remember what exactly. When Jamal Abdul Nasser died people demonstrated too. Sometimes there were small demonstrations in support of the detainees; but none of them were demonstrations in the real sense of the word. You, the new generation, think well of us then!

- Did you hear of a secret Women's Association formed on the 20th February 1947 in Yaffa, with the name Zahrat Al Oqhwan?

- No, I did not.

- But you mentioned to me that you heard of women like Mohiba Khourshid, Arabiyya Khourshid (Nariman) and Adla Fatayer?

- I have heard of Mohiba Khourshid, and I heard she participated in the revolution. But that is all I knew of her, and that is why I respected her. However, I do not remember meeting her.

- Do you remember what types of women's activities there were in Palestine during the 1950s?

- I really do not recall anything particularly memorable. Women's associations did the things they were supposed to do, like charitable and social work etc., but nothing surprising. During the fifties I was in the field and at the forefront of activities. However, the fact that I do not remember does not necessarily mean there wasn't anything happening.

- Okay, what about the sixties? Do you remember some forms of women's activities then?

Part 2: Women's Narrations

- I am not sure what you mean by women's activities? They used to do their duties.

- Could you give names or details about the various women's societies and associations?

- We already spoke about them! You know people's opinions are not always correct or perfect. Sometimes knowledge is limited and others opinions differ. The truth is women are fully culpable and they need to start all over again. Women ought to transform themselves completely, starting from the beginning. I want women to be mothers who bring up boys and girls to do what they can for their countries.

- Do you remember any names of women who were particularly active in unions, organisations, political parties, movements or other political activities during the fifties and sixties?

- If their activities were political, they would have been clandestine; so for that reason I would not have known about them!

- Would you tell us if you did know about them?

- I don't think so.

- Try to stimulate your memory, please?

- Once a journalist came and asked my father about how they conducted the revolution and how they went about fighting the Jews and the British. He looked at her and although he replied clearly and openly he managed to speak without giving an answer. When the Journalist left, I asked him 'why did you not give any answers?' He replied 'We might need to apply the same methods again in the future'. Look though, whenever an individual entered the field of politics and made an impact we all knew and heard about them.

- Do you remember the names of any female political prisoners?

- I have no memory of their names, but they were all well-known. Most of them were mentioned by name and they were honoured, not long ago now there was a ceremony; they were wonderful!

- What were the names of the female martyrs?

- Look, I'm not mentioning their names not because I don't want to, but because I really cannot remember them. I mean although the tongue may not remember them the mind and heart do.

- What was the main factor that pushed you into public work?

- The main factor? As I mentioned earlier, my father awakened me to it. The deep sense of duty I felt towards my country since I was a child was also a powerful factor. I pledged my entire life to this cause and that was the main reason I did not marry.

- What was the nature of your work for the nation?

- It was educational and advisory. In whatever I did and whenever I met with women – formally or otherwise – I would take an issue of public concern and deal with it. I always thought that the people in charge ought to devise practical and useful ways of raising women's awareness; something that would be of use to women and help make them worthy humans.

- Did you receive encouragement from your family members?

- I got a lot of encouragement, especially from my parents; they would have been dismayed if I hadn't been doing something. Women in those days did not like what their husbands were doing though, so imagine how they felt about their sons and daughters?! But my mother, honestly, respected their work. We were once playing and making noises next to the room where my father was sitting. My mother asked us to play further away saying 'let your father do his thinking'. That was the extent to which she respected his work. Then, as I was sitting on the doorstep of the house a man came and asked me 'Is your dad home?' I said yes and when he asked what he was doing I replied 'he is thinking' and the man looked at me and said 'Yes, he is'.

- Do you have any specific memories of them encouraging you? How did they encourage you with regards to your education for example?

- Of course, education is essential, but my father also encouraged me to rely on myself when doing my work. I remember I started school in Yaffa at the age of five or six. When my father and I reached the school entrance, he told me to go on my own and knock on Headmistress's door and tell her that I wanted to register myself. When I knocked the woman at the door asked me what I wanted and I said I wanted to see the head teacher. She asked me what I wanted her for and I told her it was an urgent matter. I knew I could not retreat because, if I did, I would have been punished by my father. I entered the room and said 'I have come to register myself at the school'. She asked me where my father was and

Part 2: Women's Narrations

I told her that he had told me to come alone. When I told her who my father was they all knew him. My father used to go from Yaffa to Gaza and he would take me with him, although he never usually travelled with children. He actually wanted me to be a messenger, taking messages and letters to different people. I was once under surveillance from the secret police because they suspected my father was using me for his work. I remember an incident, after I moved from the nuns' school in Yaffa to the nuns' school in Nazareth, when a vicar approached me and gave me a letter for my father. The letter contained a request to meet with my father. It was revealed later that the vicar had been sent by Stalin to meet with people in Palestine to discuss some form of cooperation in the war efforts against the British. When the supposed vicar met my father he told him about the true purpose of their meeting and my father was so angry at him and told him there was no difference between British or Italian colonialism. Such matters used to charge up the patriotism in us.

- Which of your family members supported you the most?

- My family members (..) may Allah bless all of them, my father and mother supported me enormously from the very start (*she spoke in a sad voice and shed a tear*). When I moved from Yaffa to Nazareth I failed my maths examination. It was such a shock to me because I thought I was very intelligent and to me failing in maths meant I was not. It also meant that I would have to retake the exam. I asked my father, when we were at the beach in Yaffa, is it not true that an intelligent person must be good at maths? He said 'No, not necessarily, sometimes pupils go through difficult circumstances and they might fail something'. I went silent and he asked me 'have you failed in maths?' I said yes and he replied 'So what? You moved from Gaza to Yaffa, to Nazareth; you simply have to retake the exam'. I did indeed retake it and I scored 95%. That continued to be my average until I entered the teachers' institute. The head teacher used to take my composition book and show it to people, saying: look what a third year elementary schoolgirl wrote! But at the nuns' school we did not learn much grammar like they did in state schools. My father asked me about my grammar studies once and I told him 'I am wondering why sometimes they say this word is a verb and other times they say it is adverb; how am I to know if it is this or that?' My father said it was easy and that he would show me. He gave me an Arabic book and he would say a sentence to me and then ask me about its grammar and I learnt how to do it. I mean they used to encourage me at every stage. To tell the truth my father even taught me about those things which people would not ordinarily speak about to a girl; he wouldn't speak to me directly but he gave me books to read about sexual matters, for example. Those books were for adults not children. He helped me a lot; yes, in many respects it was him who made me the way I am.

- Was there anyone who used to dampen your aspirations?

- Dishearten me? No, no-one could do that. As long as my parents were my guide, no-one had the tiniest bit of authority over me.

- How did society view your work?

- They approved of me; which was strange. In 1950, I considered removing my head veil but I was reluctant. I had written in the newspaper about this matter. My father did not mind and he said to me 'the day when you might have to take your veil off is coming'. I volunteered for work in Al-Maidan Hospital and visited several camps but with the veil on. My father was working in Egypt then, at the League of Arab States, so I did not take the veil off then because people might have thought I was doing so against my father's will, taking advantage of his absence. However, when he returned we spoke together about the veil and I got his permission to take it off. He allowed me to do it. I asked him to permit me to leave and I left the house unveiled and walked back and forth along Omar Al Mukhtar Street. I did not notice any negative attitude towards me. On the contrary, many women did the same; they took their veils off too. In Khan Yunis, however, people were a lot more conservative. They once rebuked Soad Al-A'athamy simply because she held a party. I don't know why, perhaps accusing her of being irresponsible or insensitive to society's sentiments. I went there and forbid them from wearing the masks they wore, giving them an alternative head cover instead. Every year I held parties and exhibitions and gave speeches. Girls who wanted to participate in these activities were allowed provided they brought a letter of approval signed by their spouses. People in general encouraged me and gave me their support. In Egyptian newspapers and magazines they wrote about me and interviewed me; they all knew me. I was bursting with energy back then. That energy oozed away and dampened when times were bleakest and when I should (..) but that was the will of my country.

- Thank you so much for your time.

Part 2: Women's Narrations

- You are welcome. I only told some of what I know (laughter). You know, I hope that you do whatever that you can to prepare the new generation, and I would be ready to help and volunteer.

- Thank you very much

- By God, by God, all that I care for is the service of our country. I am not impressed by the state of our country nowadays because there is so much apathy and irresponsibility. Mediocrity; that is all there is. You arrange to do something about that and count me in.

- Thanks a lot, really (laughter).

The Second Section of the Interview

Researcher: Earlier you mentioned to us a number of associations; could you please name them and tell us about them?

Narrator: Until the 1940s, Gaza did not have any associations. However, in the early 1940s, women working in education in Gaza began to form a women's movement. Prior to that date they were forbidden from doing so by the Mandate authorities. The first society was founded by Um Issam Al-Shawwa and was named the 'Renaissance Women's Society'; the secretary was Ameenah Tarazy. A short while later another society was formed, this time a branch of the Women's Union which was well known throughout Palestine. It was established by Um Al-Taher Al-Sebasi and Saniyyah Al-Sebasi and the secretary was Mary Al-Taweel, wife of Shafiq Tarazy. Almost three years later, in 1948, when the mandate ended, we started work. After a while we established the Women's Progress society. What we meant by Progress was that the women's movement was marching on more than front. The three societies worked with us on charitable matters as there were refugees flooding into the Strip. A joint committee consisting of members from the different societies was assigned to look after refugees, giving them the necessary assistance, visiting their camps and providing the services that the refugees needed most, especially before UNRWA began operating in the camps. Alongside us were the Quakers and the

Egyptian Red Crescent who also provided assistance for Palestinian refugees. A branch of the Red Crescent was allowed to establish itself in Gaza, headed by the wife of the Egyptian Governor General.

The Women's Progress Society also did other things on top of its charity work such as holding exhibitions, meetings, speeches, lectures, parties and plays. The lifting of the veil began there in 1950 and I was the first to do it in Gaza. I was veiled because the nature of the work I did demanded that I wear veil. For example in 1945 I had to give a lecture before an audience of men; it was the first lecture by a woman in Gaza. That was nature of the work of the Women's Progress Society. It was only our Society that used to receive invitations from abroad like the one we received from the Working Women's Conference in Cairo, and I alone was invited by name. Our activities were purposeful and went beyond charitable work: they were educational, cultural, and historical. After that the Women's Union Society continued to develop, even after 1967.

(Intervention by the researcher to ensure that the society being talked about was actually the Union of Women's Society. The Narrator consented).

- The branch of the Union of Women's Society is still there, but the Renaissance finished a long time ago. It is the only women's association in Gaza. Progress ended due to the political circumstances. The Renaissance Women's Society ended after Um Issam, bless her. The Union is still working, by God it is working, but it is restricted and governed by current circumstances.

- Who led the Women's Progress Association?

- I did; I was elected for the position. When the idea occurred to me I called upon some female friends, some of those I thought might be in favour of what I wanted to do. One of them was my friend Hind Farah. She is the mother of May Sayegh; you might know May Sayegh? She was my friend, an enlightened friend.

- Can you tell us some of the names of the Association's members?

- Most of the names escape me now. Some of the ladies were from the Shoheibar family, Al-Shawwa, but I cannot remember their names.

- You mentioned elections in the Association, how were they conducted?

- I remember the last election; we got together and asked who would like to nominate herself, and then we voted.

- You mentioned stage performances as an example of your activities? What other forms did the Association's political activities take?

- We did some acting, recited poetry, foreign dances, etc.

- Do you remember any of those poems?

- I do not but most of them were patriotic songs.

- None what so ever?

- All my life I have always been known as someone who doesn't participate in singing or chanting.

- Is it possible to tell us what the songs were in the form of a poem?

- I can't remember; they are all well-known today, patriotic rhymes etc.

- Last question, you spoke about the Futuwweh and Najjadeh (scouts) in schools and you spoke about supervisors. What was the nature of the Futuwweh and Najjadeh in those days? What was the nature of your work as a supervisor?

- The Futuwweh and Najjadeh were teams of female pupils who received physical training. We were hoping that it would be developed to become a military regiment one day, but that never happened. With regards to the supervisors, they were part of the youth supervisory movement - scouts for men and supervisors for women - which was charged with the administrative side of those matters. I was not jumping up and down with them.

- Lady Issam, thank you ever so much. We shall stay in contact, always. Do you have a last word you want to say?

- I really wish you all well, and hope that we will all continue our work for our country. I do aspire to see more cultural direction in our association, I care so much about our social infrastructure, and I can see our generation is in a state of loss. Educating women using different means is important. I am with you all the way and ready to help with what knowledge I have; I believe I know something.

End of Interview

Name of Narrator	Samiha Khaleel[1] (Samiha Yusef Mustafa Al Qubbaj)

Date of Birth..................... 1923
Recording location .... The Narrator's House
Date of Recording............. 15/12/1998
Address of Narrator.......... Al-Bireh/Ramallah

Tape No..................... 2

Tape Duration........... 80 Minutes

Field Researcher........ Hala Abu Hashhash

Narrator: I completed second preparatory grade, and then my family had me married when I was seventeen. I had five children and as they got older I began to think about going back to study. I sat for the Tawjihi (12th grade) with my son. I did special studies and passed alongside my son Saji. His average was better than mine; I was too busy and I could not remember everything. At the start of the academic year I was busy laying the foundations for the Family Care Association. I was also a trustee of the General Union for Palestinian Women in the PLO.

Researcher: Did you ever think of going into higher education after the Tawjihi?

- Yes, I registered at University to study Arabic literature, but following June 1967, Israel occupied the West Bank and did not allow me to leave the country to sit my third year exams.

- Which University?

- The Arab University of Beirut.

- Were you studying as a non-attending student?

---

1. Samiha Khaleel passsed away in Ramallah on: 27/2/1999

Part 2: Women's Narrations

- That is right.
- Did you ever hear of group called Al-Qassam Comrades?
- (She continued her talk without paying attention to the question) We were at that time. I remember it was the first time I took part in a demonstration, a march. The young men gathered at the mosque; they were not so obvious there. I met them at the mosque and I gave a small speech. I remember it was really noisy and I had to shout so loudly that my neck swelled; I swear no one heard a thing I said. However, I was so happy that I served my country by speaking against the Balfour Declaration and against the sale of land [to the Jewish-Zionists] in 1936.
- You mean the 1936 revolt was ongoing?
- Oh, yes, it was. One day my father was downstairs with us in the lower floor of the house where people would bring donations in the form of sacks of rice, wheat and sugar. My father was the head of the distribution committee; he distributed donations to individuals enlisting for the revolution. Suddenly we heard a big bang on the door and several British soldiers entered and ransacked the store. They dumped the sacks into the water well and my father was shouting at them loudly. One of them pushed my father and he fell in the well. Then, in 1936, they closed all the schools so my parents sent me to a boarding school, Friends School, to complete my schooling. At the school I caused them so much trouble: whenever foreign guests came to the school I would mobilize the girls and we would shout at them thinking they were the Americans or the British who pushed my father into the well. Subsequently, the ladies in charge of the school would send me to work in the library or keep me busy with something whenever they were expecting foreign guests.
- How old were you in 1936?
- What do you mean how old I was in 1936?
- I mean when the incident happened, when they ransacked the store and pushed your father into the well?
- I was perhaps sixteen or seventeen.
- Do you remember the names of the girls who took part in these events; is there anyone who comes to mind?
- They had a society, a women's society headed by Wadee'a Khartabil,

a Lebanese woman, and my mother; everyone was part of the assistance efforts.

- What was the nature of the society's work exactly?
- It was of a political nature, revolving around issues such as land sale and people collaborating with the Jews. Things like that.
- Were you not yet a member of that society?
- No, they were all ladies, older than me.
- Were they distributing leaflets and declarations, or doing other public things?
- Very little, I mean when they knew someone was collaborating or was a traitor they would give us - the younger ones - leaflets to distribute on the streets and to shops.
- How many members did the society have?
- The whole town; all the women.
- You mean it was organized randomly?
- Yes, it was not organized. The women in charge would gather people in a house and I would tell them my political views on the situation and people would say "down with Balfour declaration". We used to say "Mr. Del (Bel), fix it for us, you might have the solution". The High Commissioner, you see, wanted to resolve the issue and we lacked his expertise. But now we would not accept such a thing.
- Do you still remember the six-month strike?
- During the strike no shops were open; all of them went on strike. The insurgents were in the mountains. We used to go to Anabta (in the District of Tulkarm) and find the whole town busy; one day this family would prepare food for the insurgents, the next day that family would do it and so on and so forth. People would take food to the mountains and when the British entered the town someone would signal with a white flag to the insurgents and they would escape to another town, etc.
- What was the role played by women in the revolt?
- Women cooked the food and carried it on their heads; the villagers fetched food for the insurgents and carried out all their instructions.
- Besides cooking, what else did women do?

Part 2: Women's Narrations

- Child rearing, housework and they worked on the farms because the men were absent; families split the responsibilities, some worked for the insurgents and others cared for the land and animals.

- But they were not involved in military activities?

- They cleaned weaponry, loaded it and sent it to the insurgents.

- Aunt Samiha, do you remember the Arab conferences which were held in support of Palestine, such as those held in Beirut, Damascus and Baghdad, and the big women's conference in the 1930s?

- No, the first conference I attended was in 1968 in Egypt. It was organized by the PLO for the Union of Palestinian Students. The PLO had three Unions: The Students' Union, The Workers' Union and The Women's Union.

- That was a conference you personally attended. What about before that? Did you hear about any conferences even if you did not attend them yourself?

- Not really. The media was not as widespread in those days. I used to hear about Huda Sha'rawi and Zulaikha Al-Shihabi. I heard of them but I don't know what they were famous for.

- What was the impact of the failure of the revolt on Palestinian women's activities?

- Which revolt? In the 1936 revolt everyone - men, women and children - were with the Fidaeyyeen (insurgents), the Mujahideen; everyone provided them with all they could.

- When the revolution declined, how did that impact on women?

- No one admitted that the revolution was waning. All people knew was that the British were against us; they helped the Jews, killed our men and confiscated our land.

- You mean the Palestinians themselves didn't admit that their revolution had collapsed, and the result was (..)

- We did not hear about things and we did not know the revolt had collapsed; we did not know a thing. There was no media. I remember my father saying to me 'Those British are our worst enemies, they made the Balfour Declaration'. He told me once 'Your cousins and their friends went to picnic on a hill and spend the night in a cave.

As they were going into the cave they bumped into something. So they didn't enter the cave until the morning when they found around seventy or eighty packets filled with ID cards signed by the High Commissioner due to be given to Jewish immigrants entering into Palestine secretly by sea.'

- Were they fake IDs?

- No they weren't fake IDs, they were printed by the British for immigrant Jews. They hid them in the countryside so Palestinians wouldn't know about them. He told me how the British helped the Jews to come and settle in Palestine and supported them against us just like the Americans are doing nowadays.

- What role did women have after 1936, prior to the Partition in 1947?

- Among the main roles played by women were things like raising funding and providing food, then after 1948 women started the real work; they fought with men in the war.

- Did you contribute to the boycott efforts?

- Yes I did, and I used to give lectures telling people why they should not buy Jewish goods. We still boycott their goods and if any of these girls (pointing to the girls in the room with her who were working at In'ash Al-Usra Society) bought Israeli Coca Cola we would rebuke and penalize them.

- Did you ever take part in any semi-military activities? Were you a member of the *Futuwweh and Najjadeh* or did you participate in military courses?

- Politics and incitement run in my blood but I did not do physical training, Karate, or anything like that. Now we send our girls to learn Karate and everything else at the Family Care Association.

- Why do you have them learn this?

- To start their military training.

- Did you hear about the conference in support of Palestine which was held in Cairo and headed by Huda Sha'rawi in 1944 and 1951?

- No.

- Did you participate in or subscribe to the League of National Liberation?

Part 2: Women's Narrations

- I was never a member of any party, and that remains true today. Whenever they tried to get me to join a party I would say that I wanted to stay outside of the party-framework. I would say that those who are good shall have my support and that when I am not in a party I can see its mistakes; from the inside I may not be able to do that.

- Did you hear about Earnest Bevin's declaration of 1945, which opened the doors for Jewish immigration to Palestine? What impact did it have on women's activities?

- Oh, yes, we resisted; we talked and condemned and did what we could.

- What about when the Head of the Zionist International Congress, Nahom Goldman, declared readiness to allow Britain and the United States to have military bases if they agreed to give the Jews a state on 65% of Palestine?

- The impact was not on women and men separately; it wasn't like that in the past, we were all the same. Unlike today when you carry women on your shoulders and run around with them.

- You mean this is a new phenomenon?

- It has evolved in the last ten or fifteen years; before that people never said 'the women', never. Men and women were both thought of as citizens.

- Do you really feel women were more sincere in their struggle in those days than they are now? Are you saying that there are associations nowadays that are promoting women's causes?

- Today all the talk is about women but it is not women's struggle; it is about the women themselves. In my time women really did struggle; in 1948 we attended conferences abroad and worked here and there. Our associations were political; I was the only female member in the National Front against the Jews, and we were sent to prison. Then, because we suffered a lot in prison, it was decided that the work of the National Front should be done in secrecy. Also I was the only woman working with men on the National Guidance Committee (1976). However I managed all the women who worked with me. We met, for example, to decide what to do about the question of freedom-fighters (*fidaeyyeen*). I mean I used to represent women in those committees.

-224-

- But were you the only woman in that Committee?

- Oh, yeah, I was the only women's representative, but women participated in all activities and they could not get things going without us. They all worked but I represented them in men's associations.

- What do you think was the impact of the UN Partition Resolution on women and how did they confront it?

- I am telling you sister, I am against those who say 'women'. Why women particularly? Women are like men in their thoughts and activities, in fact, in everything, there are only some things women did not do because they could not.

- True, they are the same, but history wrote about men and forgot and ignored women!

- Many books have been written about women. Once I had an elderly aunt whose son was killed in Dir Ghassaneh. She went and brought his body from Dir Ghassaneh to Anabta where she buried him; she walked at night and slept during the day.

- What year did that happen?

- That was in 1938.

- Has anybody written about that event? Was it ever reported in the newspapers?

- Nobody wrote about it anywhere; but they neither wrote about men nor about women. It was forbidden. But, then again, not much has been written about our entire revolution.

- Did you take part in the mob attacks and clashes which occurred between the Arabs and the Jewish settlers?

- We walked in marches and wrote leaflets, we stood at the gates of embassies; we took part in everything.

- Can you remember a demonstration where there was a large amount of female participation?

- Most of them were large.

- Did you take part in a demonstration which involved a large number of women?

- Yes, there was a demonstration in Jerusalem; we marched through all the streets of Jerusalem.

Part 2: Women's Narrations

- When? What was the occasion?

- I think that was in 1953, and then the biggest of all was the demonstration against the Baghdad Pact in 1956: women from everywhere in Palestine participated. On the first day we marched in the Ramallah area and from Ramallah to Jerusalem, demonstrating against the Baghdad Pact, and we killed it. You see, America made this pact consisting of Iraq, Iran, and I think Pakistan, too. This was a military pact against the Arabs. We marched as Jamal Abdul Nasser was giving his speech about the pact. About 15 women were from Al-Bireh and they were wearing the traditional dress. By the time we reached Al Manarah Square there was over five hundred of us. I sent some women to call upon the girls at the teachers' institute to join us. It was such a huge gathering at Al Manarah Square. There were many vehicles waiting to carry us to Jerusalem. When we arrived, we went to the office of the Governor of Jerusalem who said to me 'Lady Samiha, you are the wife of an educated man and you are roaming the streets with these girls; get them off the streets and take them back to their schools. Otherwise you are jeopardizing their future'. The following day we organized another demonstration in which people from 27 villages took part. We continued in this way until we killed off the Baghdad Pact. They used to write about me, not in newspapers, I mean the Jordanian Government used to write against me. When Israel occupied the territories, they did not burn the documents. On the day when the Jews destroyed Al-Samu' village about one thousand women went to Al-Samu' to show support.[1] We went there and found people's houses and furniture torn to pieces, and women sitting outside with no shelter.

- What year was this?

- That was Al-Samu', I think in 1969 or 1970 (1966), something like that. Five days after the 1967 war a group of Israelis barged into the association. One of them asked 'where is Samiha Khaleel?' and someone pointed me out. He said 'you're the boss here'. Everything I had done in the past was documented with them. I did not want them to come to the association. Saleh Abduljawwad told me that the governor or the lieutenant wanted to visit the association and I told him I could not accept that. The governor kept going back and forth for two weeks wanting to

---

1. She is referring to events on November 13, 1966 when there was an Israeli military attack on the Jordanian-Controlled West Bank village of Al-Samu'

visit the association. Eventually he said he would close it down if his order was not met. People came to me and tried to reassure me that as long as they were willing to license the association it would not be closed down. The occupation did not seem to be leaving any time soon, and so finally I allowed him to visit. He, the Israeli, came and sat down and I sat staring intently at his face. He asked to see the nursery and I told him that the infants in the nursery were the children of villagers who were forced to flee from war (from Amwas, Beit Nuba, and Yalou). I said 'we opened it for them; do you want to see the happy children?!' The governor said to Abduljawwad 'if she keeps on talking we will close it down'. I gave him a hard time and from then onwards I was never far from their minds. All the marches in Ramallah were organized and led by me. During the occupation, the Israelis imprisoned me six times.

- When was the first time you were sent to prison?

- After 1967 they arrested girls, locked them up and abused them. I organized a big march in support of the girls in prison. I sent Saleh Abduljawwad to them with a fifty-seven page letter and they told him 'take this back, this paper is indecent'. After that they denied me the right to leave the territories to see my children and denied my children the right to enter to see me. Each time someone would speak to them (the Israelis), they would tell them 'all her sons have escaped abroad, she can go with them instead of them coming over'.

- Did you ever hear about a women's society called the Zahret Aluqhuwan (Daisy Flower)?

- I heard about it but I don't know much about it.

- But, you have heard of it?

- Oh, yes, I heard of the Comrades of Al-Qassam'[1], the media spoke a lot about it, but not here as much as in the Galilee area.

- Did you hear about it from the written media or from people?

- No, from people, the media did not speak about it (here in Ramallah), and it was not widespread.

- Did you know the precise role of that association, or did you just know of its existence?

---

1. There seems to be confusion between the names: Al-Qassam Comrades and the «Daisy Flower» Society in the mind of the narrator

Part 2: Women's Narrations

- No, all the associations founded were against Balfour, against the sale of land, against Jews murdering people and confiscating land, and against the British.

- Do you know the names of the prominent women members of a group called 'The Comrades of Al-Qassam'?

- No, not many; I heard of Zulaikha Al-Shihabi.

- Were you a member of the (Daisy Flower) Society?

- She was here in Jerusalem; what's her name (..) Al-Amad, Shash Al-Amad[1] was in Nablus. All of them are old ladies. We are the next generation. These women played a big role during those times.

- Do you remember the days of the Arab exodus in 1948?

- Yes, of course, I remember those days the most.

- Can you recall for us your memories of those days?

- Of course, my husband was head of a secondary school in Al-Majdal and when 1948 happened, we were told that Gaza was not receiving much shelling, so we went to Gaza where my husband's cousin worked for the municipality. We went to him and he offered us one of the two rooms in his house. As we sat in the house we heard the sounds of a bombardment of gunfire. Those were days of hardship. I sold my jewelry to buy food for the children. Before the armistice I told my husband to go to our house in Al-Majdal and bring us some clothes. We hired a car and drove home but as he was about to turn the key to open the door, a group of Jews approached him and asked him 'what's happening?' He said he wanted to fetch some clothes for his children and they told him 'go back it is not your home'. We could not retrieve a thing; our food stuff, clothing and furniture, the family diaries and mementos of the children's birthdays. I mean the chairs and tables can be replaced but those diaries and mementos are irreplaceable. Even now I am still sad that they stole our belongings and history.

- Do you remember a particular massacre committed in 1948?

---

1. The researcher noted that Samiha meant Andaleeb Al-Amad who was the president of the Women Union in Nablus city

- A massacre?! Massacres! There was the Emwas massacre in 1948[1]; in Yaffa and in Haifa they killed and maimed. They littered the roads with bombs, we planted bombs too, but in Lod the Jews brought a bed sheet in a car and filled it with jewelry stolen from women; they really were criminals. That is why people ran away, leaving their homes and belongings. Some walked until they reached Ramallah.

- Did you witness a massacre with your own eyes?

- Yes, in Yaffa, they said they planted a bomb which killed many people.

- But did you see it with your own eyes?

- No.

- What were the types of activities were carried out by women in the 1950s?

- In the 1950s, we founded the Family Care Association for the Union of Women (Association), which people in Ramallah subscribed to.

- What about around the West Bank?

- Yes, associations were being founded in every town, I established the Union of Barreyyah Association in 1952, and the Care for Family Association in 1965.

- What kind of activities did women participate in during the 1960s?

- From 1952, up until this day, women's activities have remained the same; in 1965 we formed the first executive committee for the Union of Women. I was a member and we attended lots of conferences in which we spoke about the question of Palestine.

- Who were the most well-known women in those days?

- I remember Ameenah Al-Huseini (she passed away), Zulaikha Al-Shihabi, and Lidia Al-A'araj (in Bethlehem), Yusra Shawar (in Hebron), Sarah Hannoun (died in Tulkarm), and many more.

- In your mind, what do you associate these names with?

---

1. Emwas is now Canada Park (2001). In 1967 Israel destroyed the Palestinian village of Emwas and two other neighboring Palestinian villages, Yalo and Beit Nuba, forcing their residents to flee

Part 2: Women's Narrations

- They are connected with resistance to the Israeli occupation.
- What was the political role of these women?
- We were political in every aspect of our lives. We worked to combat illiteracy in rural areas and through this we promoted political awareness.
- Do you know the names of women who were imprisoned for political reasons?
- There were many: Aa'yesha Oudeh, Rasmeyyieh Oudeh, Latifah Alhajj Ibrahim, Ameenah Al-Huseini and her daughter, and myself.
- How about names of women who were killed?
- Several were killed, but I can't remember their names just now.

(Whilst talking Samiha pointed towards the television screen saying that her uncle Abu Ammar (Yasser Arafat) is in France)

- What was the main factor that prompted you to become involved in national work?
- Our homes, land and personal belongings were stolen by Jews right in front of our eyes; when we were in Gaza people slept in scrap cars, mosques, and churches, without food or water. Living conditions were absolutely tragic.
- Did you receive encouragement for what you did from your family?
- I was never discouraged and I never gave up. I believe that people must, one day, regain their rights regardless of the immensity of the repression they are subjected to. All my life I have been optimistic that we shall overcome injustice and I say this to your generation too.
- Did your family encourage you, or did they object your activities?
- No, they never objected to or obstructed what I was doing, but they always feared that something bad might happen to me; I was imprisoned not once but six times.
- Which member of your family gave you the most support?
- All of them supported me, perhaps in their minds they wondered about what I was doing, but neither they nor my husband ever objected.
- How did society view the work you did?
- People were behind me; my husband (Abdallah) was with the Nationalist Arabs, and Ba'athism started here. Al Rimawi used to send

me leaflets to distribute and I would say to him 'People are against the Jews and I am with those who are against our enemies but I cannot subscribe to one (ideology) or another'. I used to work with more than just their members; I worked with anybody I thought was doing the right thing. I was never a member in any particular organization and I have remained like that until this day.

- Is there anything that you feel you did not do and you would still like to do?

- There was nothing which was offered to me and needed to be done that I did not do. I was very daring in everything I did.

- Generally speaking, do you feel women reached important positions and played significant roles in political parties and other movements?

- Yes, of course, just like men, and that was apparent during the Intifada, when women shared all roles and activities with men.

- What was the percentage of women participation?

- Not very high; but during the Intifada for instance, most people, both men and women were out on the streets.

- Did women reach high positions in the political parties?

- We can't deny that political parties did a lot of work, but internal competition prevented their ability to progress.

- Prevented whose ability to progress? Women or the parties?

- No, the parties themselves; competition in a party did not always help further the cause of the party. I mean if all the parties had united we would have been able to progress much further.

- I am asking about the women who belonged to political parties or associations, could they reach high positions?

- Yes, they did, but they did not accomplish what men did.

- So what do you think the problem is?

- There is not a problem. Girls nowadays think there is a problem, but everyone does what he or she can in accordance with his or her ability. Men are stronger but women have more endurance. There was nothing that women were able to do and refrained from or were prevented from doing. I read that several of our women's associations did things that

Part 2: Women's Narrations

American and English women did not do in those times. I mean 40-42% of women have sons and daughters in university, yet they don't have a laundry machine. One of those would become a doctor, another an engineer and the third a pharmacist and so on, but most are men. I mean the status of our woman is improving, but just like in foreign countries the majority of the high positions are still occupied by men. Thatcher was a woman among twenty or thirty men. Women are by no means inferior to men; we are just like them. Here in Palestine we have a lot of women who are completing their Doctorate. My daughter has a BA Degree and is married. She recently completed her MA and is now working on her Doctorate.

- Does your daughter have an interest in politics?

- I have one daughter and four sons and they all have an interest in politics. Samir was imprisoned in Jordan, Saeda lived in the diaspora and she was active in the students' union in Egypt. When she returned, the Israeli authorities gave her 24 hours to leave the West Bank. Her brother was studying medicine in Romania and we sent her to complete her education there. Her brother lived in mixed student accommodation, but he left it to live independently with his sister. We tried to arrange for a "family-reunion" in order for her to come and live with us but when she arrived at Allenby Bridge the Israelis did not allow her to enter Palestine.

- Did that happen because they were your children?

- No, not really. Each of them has their own political views and ideology. What I did was to feed them love of this country alongside their milk when they were little. Even now I regret that they did not enjoy their childhood more. I mean women played a role and men played another: men were out fighting in the mountains whilst women looked after the cattle and farms, reared the children and cooked. They made money and bought weapons for the insurgents. Life was so difficult without the breadwinner.

(The Narrator then said she would like to recite some of the poems she wrote)

In Yaffa, we have memories

Of Haifa, we were told stories and tales.

Books wrote so much about us

About people peaceful and tranquil at home
Rules and laws so oppressive, and taxes of all kinds,
Repatriation, Bridge, Permit and IDs.
Oh home, if for so long I do not see you
If I do not play in your alleys and lanes
They forbade me from tasting your oranges
I only hear of you and wish to see you
I want to touch your soil
In darkness now we live
Both peace and settlement building they call for
But we the children won't accept that
Won't you people agree with me?
Of course, you're all with me
Every graduate learned that
Do you people know that our money is in enemy safes?
Their cars run on our petrol
And, the petrol keeps them warm
Our armies can be seen on television
Dancing, alyadi... alyadi...
The Palestinian wondering, at war with the self
And, everyone against him, planning to kill him, why?
Why people? We are all Arabs
Why not work together and plan together
Think together... Our pain is one and our aspiration is one
I tell you how we suffer when crossing the bridge
Hours upon hours of repression and indignation
Suffering from head to bottom
Because of that we resist and sit steadfast
We burn tires, we throw stones

Part 2: Women's Narrations

> **Land swallows, high prices kill and people abandon... what more**
>
> **Extended our hand for peace**
>
> **They refused, we gave in and in, and that made them more stubborn**
>
> **Briefly,**
>
> **Respond or don't**
>
> **There is nothing left but war ... nothing but resolve**
>
> **To end the epidemic ... and kill the locusts**
>
> **To protect our honor, wipe off disgrace and regain our land**
>
> **To live free**

- I used to get up at night and write about many issues; I wrote about the blind in Beit Sahour and Sabra and Shatilla refugee camps.
- About Beit Sahour, when was that?
- That was when we declared civil disobedience and people refused to pay taxes and so the Israelis took materials belonging to associations and medicines from pharmacies. The tax authorities went to an elderly woman and asked her to pay at least one Shekel but she refused, saying that it is a question of principle. Not many people followed in her footsteps. The following poem sounds like a meejanah (Palestinian folklore song).

> Ya Meejanah, ya mejanah, like lions none can beat us
>
> Oh mother, we hear the news, talking about children
>
> About children everywhere ... in the papers, in the news and all are jubilant
>
> Now the New Year and new dress all are happy
>
> Oh mother! Our children are not ... oh mother they are not like children
>
> Oh mother, oh brother, let us be happy with them, let us play with them
>
> Mother, why dad left us and did not wait for us to say good bye
>
> We need him ... we want him for the Eid
>
> Wait my child, my darling heart, I will tell you what happened
>
> In the night and in the dark, in the middle of the night

He and friends went to battle ... into the unknown he went

He said as he left hurriedly... take care of the children

And the garden and the house... his voyage and absence have been long

I will come back and erase the shame... his voice is still

Echoing in my ear...we men have the duty to avenge

Another child: Mother and we sleep! Who stands by us and who brings us happiness?

We have ourselves, we have the land, and we have the birds of the sky standing by us

Soon you will be older and bigger and avenge for father, brother and uncle

You will then return to the house, to the garden and to the family, proud

Like your dad who died, oh mother we want to return to the garden

Sell the harvest and buy toys like children

Oh mother, look our land marked and barb wired...and the good men in prison

They left it among the stones loaded.

Another girl: why are you wondering? Haven't you heard the news... oh mother, people endure and endure, but there are limits to how much one can endure, then people will start to document... and learn what he an the others wrote. There will come the day when the people through the width and breadth of the country and question the criminals, and the nimrod will yell and roar the earth beneath the feet of his oppressor. People, isn't it injustice that people eat from the bowl of flames and other eat caviar? Oppressor, your day has come... he's before you folded his teeth and took flight (the shah of Iran). His masters abandoned him and dumped him and told their other agent (Sadat) celebrate his arrival.

Hell awaits the enemy of his people, hell awaits he who oppresses his people; his days would be darker than paraffin. Oh my children, the garden and the land will return and the house and the flag of Palestine will fly high on the rooftop of each house and all the

> revolutionaries and free men will jubilate.
>
> We declare our rejection to all conferences; we declared refusal of negotiations and we refused the elections. So long as we are united we are are not afraid… so long as we are determined and believe nothing is impossible, Palestine must return to her rightful owners.

- We put on a play in Al-Bireh Garden and after the show ended people were charged up and marched in a demonstration. They shot live ammunition at the demonstrators. Five of them were injured, and subsequently we were not allowed to perform any more plays.

(Samiha goes on to read on a new poem she wrote)

> In Iran, (President) Carter roared and condemned Islam, but in Afghenistan he became a Moslem before all, and the crocodile tears fell and slapped his own face and committed suicide. What foxes are those people, what wolves, what barbarians for the sake of self interest and position; they change colors like a chameleon. There he is canvassing and assembling his friends and aides… Britain, Belgium, and Holland… and what a shame, France, is with them too. Carter told them to forget the intricacy of Vietnam and hide that of Iran.
>
> Let us make a military pact and sign it… quickly today not tomorrow.
>
> We plan and design the world… to conquer all the nations of the world.
>
> Carter flew his plane at night thinking he would bring out the hostages.
>
> Victorious by the support of the Zionists and Sadat and his spies but he failed and retreated, and it was jubilation for the people, and the oppressor's day shall soon be coming; he dug his own grave.
>
> Where are my Arab Brothers? Seems like they faded, failed, got mad, jumping around in confusion with no consciousness and no dignity… they buried their own faces in the mud from this day until the end of time. Oh brothers, you who are living on your land (I say) he whose hand is in the fire is not like that blowing air onto it. Oh our people… Oh, Palestinians… Oh, our family… Oh, you Canaanites, have you seen any more repressive than the Zionists?

Have you seen terrorism like the Israeli terrorism? Wholesale land confiscation, they ousted people from their houses and in Hebron they poisoned crops, and in Qarawa they chopped the trees down, and thieved the olive harvest in Qatannah and told the people of Qatannah… do you know what they said? Sign that the land is not yours, neither today nor tomorrow nor ever. But the brave people of Qatannah (town) refused to betray their land. And they told them take it you damned. Our land at your time went astray. God shall have you punished for the injustice you have committed, depriving and denying children their source of livelihood. Was it not enough that you cut our leaders' legs, exiled them and imprisoned the others, Bassam Al-Shak'a and others. In the midst of the dark you attacked them; you terrorists and against your nose they returned. We shall remain with them and amongst them standing and steadfastly until we accomplish our rights. Our rights are: an independent state, return of the refugees, return of the deportees. Our brave men are our leaders; like it or loath it. They say we are terrorists. Oh people, Oh world, do we know who the terrorists are? They who implant bombs in the cars of Bassam, Ibrahim and Kareem are the terrorists. We all heard of the exiled Qawasmi, Melhem and Tamimi; they all enjoyed tranquility on their land, we all saw with our very own eyes bullets killing men and women. They are not to blame but our Arabs are, whose armies we saw every night on television dancing as though they liberated the country and bearing flag of victory in his right hand and the remainder of the army murdering his brethrens instead of turning to his unjust enemy; you care for America and Europe and you have betrayed long time back. When you come to us you claim patriotism; in the night and in the day you declare you are sincere… had you the honor and the dignity you would have broken that tap and turned you backs to America to deserve being called the children of Canaan and Qahtan. But, we are worlds apart: you build Palaces of gold and we mourn our martyrs. Oh Arabs, have you heard of the Begin vow that he will inherit us whilst we are a live. He wants the West Bank and Gaza; he wants Jerusalem and the Golan. President Assad said: Begin, shut up the defense force decided to succumb to oppression. Worse than that, the Americans are maneuvering force Assad to withdraw missiles from Lebanon to allow their fighter jets to roam the skies and return to safety, having destroyed homed at the heads of the young and elderly.

Part 2: Women's Narrations

- Is this poetry book in libraries?
- No, we did not dare to publish it.
- You mean it has remained with you unpublished?
- Only close friends and relatives could read it (..) this is a nice poem, 'When the Gliding plane left Lebanon':

> Oh flying bird, where are you going to and where are you coming from; you know these territories or are you a stranger or a foreigner. You seem one of us and your eye lights up with anger, you got my heart trembling. We see you fly with determination; Oh Son, so long it has been since you've been home, I thought you forgot this land, forgot the fragrance of your land and forgot the Qatayef (home-made dessert). The gliding plane turned around looking at me and said: perhaps we left the land and the soil, but my blood is blended with the soil of my folks and beloved ones. Oh Aunt, by God I forgot I am Palestinian; the Palestinian never forgets no matter the length of absence and wherever he goes he stays resolute. Oh Aunt, were I have time to tell my story; a story that turns our youth turn grey people. To tell you the story of how we were exiled into the diasporas, from town to town; how we starved and endured all sorts of despair; then the world became too tight and life got too bleak; no light at the horizon. I see my grandpas wandering and my little brother crying from hunger, seeking out a piece of bread in garbage bag. I miss the stench of the taboon (a place for baking bread used in the past), and embrace the children and family in the garden with the breeze gently passing through, and sleep under trees. One of those nights I dreamed I had returned and there was dancing chanting and I saw tears of happy people falling; I opened my eyes and said to myself: one lives once, one dies once; come on boy, and I rode my sail and flew so high shouting so loud: home, here I am come and will avenge for brother Sakhar, and Oh Haniyyah, I will avenge for you all and let happen what may. I found a pile of those ghosts of death and began to spray them with bullets; I looked around to see none left but one hiding against a wall. I said to him: you desecrated the land and he who starts is the unjust one; as he quivered in fear he said: we had orders, and we are tired of raiding houses at night and arresting

youth, but those disobeying orders gets killed and most of us want peace and safety. When I finished the job – I was not unfair – for, an eye for an eye and a tooth for a tooth is what our Quran says is justice. After I saw he died and his face glowed with light like the moon I kissed his face and said: son, you sacrificed your life, youth and soul for your country. Now you are alive in every mind, in every house, in every tent; you made people know there is nothing a Palestinian can not do. Each one of our people began to wonder why are we suffering all these tragedies? He did a miracle and so can we; with bravery he defeated the enemy and left them wandering about, blaming one another, reshuffling military posts, and instilled fear in their public, their remainders went to hospitals and hid in their fortresses. They collapsed, and the traitors, Army of Lebanon, and the electrified wires, and all their top personnel confessed: Palestinians can do all, they neither fear death nor surrender their land no matter the hardship they may suffer. Our people rose up and threw their fists in the air, declaring they no longer can bear; each has a sad tale to tell, that lost his land; that lost his trees and crops; that lost his house and that lost his children. The accumulation of calamities and suffering caused the Intifada: each suffered at the hands of the enemy his agents; our courageous people will take them out even if they were in the enemy's armored cars, but you Arabs, only if you could see our children as they fight the enemy bare-chested and how they fail despite their weapons and armors; our people struggle, one erects a road block, another throes stones and the other burns tires; our brave laborers don't go to work and honorable shopkeepers are on strike and their children are hungry. We suffered but laugh not at us because we are determined to sacrifice our souls until we liberate our country and shall awaken the dead consciousness of all. We want you, Arabs to defend with us because you know our enemy is wanton and your turn shall be the next and you, however you let us down we would never do the same; we promise to defend with you with our stones and the tears of widows.

- Each time there was a tragedy somewhere I would write. When the massacres happened in the Sabra and Shatilla refugee camps I would get up at two o'clock in the morning and write.

Part 2: Women's Narrations

- Have you written anything recently?

- Yes, I wrote something about the Wyes Plantation (Wye River Agreement Negotiations: 1998) but I am still finishing it. I write about anything I feel strongly about. It is these poems which got to the Israelis and they sentenced me because of them.

- What happened?

- They called upon me and asked me 'Are you preparing for War?' That was a reference to a statement I made saying that Jihad (struggle) in the name of Allah is a virtue. That was the statement they emphasized during my interrogation. Each time something was about to happen in the town, like the remembrance of the Balfour Declaration, they would ask me 'Miss Khaleel what have you prepared?' and I would say 'I haven't thought about it yet'. They would ask again 'What have you prepared? We know the country is at the tip of your finger. What have the municipalities prepared?' They would keep people waiting from eight in the morning until three in the afternoon then they would tell them that the governor is busy and to come back tomorrow. Sometimes they summoned me on three consecutive days to meet them at ten a.m. and I would go every day on time. After ten minutes of waiting I would say to the secretary 'Tell your boss Um Khaleel (Samiha Khaleel) waited for ten minutes and she has a lot to do'. The second time I was summoned he said apologetically 'Miss Khaleel I am one minute late'. I never showed weakness.

As I sat down he said "'think not of those killed in the cause of Allah as dead' you should write 'whoever does an atom's weight of good shall see it'", they know the Quran well, damn them. They used to tell Abduljawwad (Abduljawwad Saleh) 'Um Khaleel works against us more than the Palestinian Authority and the PLO; more than Arafat'. When they closed down the association they came in the middle of the night and took me. The man instructed me to get into the car and I said 'I do not get into your cars'. He said 'follow us in your own car, then' and I told him I didn't have a car. He said 'you sort that out yourself; the Governor and others are waiting at the association'. I told him I needed to tell my friend and he let me but she (Rima Tarazy) took a long time to answer. Then he told me that he would take me to her place. I said no and started walking very slowly, like a bride. When I got to her house I found Rima (Rima Tarazy) and her husband (Dr. Antwan Tarazy) waiting. We drove towards the association and when we reached it they started to take pictures. I said 'Who asked you to take pictures?', I was wearing my sleeping gown. We entered the association and they started taking documents and wrapping them in blankets. They took about six blankets filled with documents and records and put them in one of their vehicles. That day I screamed so much and so loudly 'You criminals, Allah is great', but they did not utter a single word. That was exactly like when they put me in prison; they did not speak to me at all.

- They imprisoned you when they raided the association?

- Yes, the following day, but they could not close down the association. The nursery remained open; that night we had moved all the equipment to the martyrs children's centre and we did not stop work. We also held a press conference with the National, an hour after they said at their press conference that they had found inflammatory material.

- Was that prior to the Intifada?

- Yes, that was shortly before the outbreak of the Intifada (8 Dec 1987). Journalists came and asked if I received money from the PLO and I told them that I didn't because if I did they would come and close the association, but the PLO is here in my heart I told them. Believe me Hala, I never bent down to anybody. When I was in prison the interrogator would say to me 'You are a women's union' and I said to him 'No, I am in family care'. He picked up the phone and spoke with the Ministry of Social Affairs, then he told me 'No, you are a women's union'. I screamed when they took me to prison. In the beginning they put me in a tiny room with an extremely high ceiling. There was a hole in the room, which served as a toilet. I felt like the world was closing in on me, so I started punching and kicking the door with my hands and feet. They came and found me and my blood pressure was very high. I must have fallen unconscious. They were terrified so they called some lady lieutenants to get me into a vehicle. I saw trees and slowly I began to regain consciousness. I was with the doctors in Hadassah Hospital for a couple of nights. I said 'Please tell them not to return me to the same room'. The person accompanying me said 'He is a doctor; he is not a policeman'. Then I was taken to Al-Maskubiyyah Prison to be with the lowly girls, the common criminals. I found all the girls in the nude. They held a broomstick and said to me 'Are you fatakh?' meaning Fattah (Palestinian National Liberation movement). I turned away and tried to avoid looking at them. The toilets had no doors and the girls used it standing up like men, it was repulsive, and they spoke foul language all the time. When the police officer brought me the blood pressure tablets I pushed at the door and told her I cannot go back with those girls. She replied that these are orders and I told her to go and tell the one who gives orders that Samiha refuses to obey. Another officer came and said these are orders coming from high above. I told him 'I don't care where they come from, but I will not stay with those vile girls'. Then they took me to be with our girls; our girls were angels, they could not believe I was among them. Damn them, how they got to you. Anyhow, our girls did not let me sweep the floor and when the guard told me to do something, they would all say in unison 'Aunt Um Khaleel (Samiha) does not sweep, tidy beds or anything else'. They really took good care of me; they brought me plenty of newspapers all of which were writing about me, and lots of letters, all of which we have kept.

- What about the leaflets, announcements and declarations issued by you?

- We still have them all, from the first one until the last one.

- Even those issued in the 1950s?

- No, only those issued by the unified leadership during the Intifada[1]; we have some of the old things but not much. From the time of the Intifada onwards everything is documented.

- But none of them date back to the 1950s?

- I think there are some documents but very few indeed. Most of our records are new. There are, for example, eleven files on the Hebron massacre; whatever we wrote to newspapers, on the streets, on walls, we have a great documentary library. Anything that happened to Palestinians in Lebanon and in Syria, or wherever is documented here with us.

- Thank you for your great effort and for your time.

End of Interview

---

1. The Unified National *Leadership* of the Uprising (UNLU) (al-Qiyada al Muwhhada) was a coalition of the Local Palestinian *leadership during* the First *Intifada* 1978

Name of Narrator	Najeyyah Barham [1]
	Date of Birth...................... 1924
Name of Narrator	Hasnah Salim Masoud
	Date of Birth...................... 1914
Name of Narrator	Zahidah Ahmad M. Mustafa
	Date of Birth...................... 1931
Name of Narrator	Sobhiyyah Ismael A. Barham
	Date of Birth...................... 1929
Name of Narrator	Sanajeq Mohammad A. Barham [2]
	Date of Birth...................... 1923

Recording Place:................ House of Rasheed Al-Ramini/ Ramin
Recording Date: 09/06/1999
Address of Narrators:.......... Ramin Village, District of Tulkarm

Tape No..................... 12

Tape Duration........... 90 Minutes

Field Researcher:....... Nida' Abu Taha

---

1. Najeyyah Barham passsed away in Ramin on 24/9/2004
2. Sanajeq Barham passsed away in Ramin on: 23/8/2012

Part 2: Women's Narrations

Najeyyah Barham

Resarcher: Could you please tell us about the days when you were a child?

NB: I will tell you about the time when we went to Thinnaba. We went back and forth, and as we arrived in Thinnaba and approached the house of Abu Kamal, a woman was stood there and she said 'Darlings, where do you come from?' We told her that we had come from Ramin and she said 'From Ramin?!' then she started welcoming us with a loud voice 'A village has come, a village has come; it has come!' Then she said 'Take the girls from Ramin and seat them together '. So we were all seated together. They had a big house and each room was full of people. I asked one of the girls, who was sat with me and who was my age, if she could follow me in reciting songs. The girl said that she could so I started by saying:

"From the heart of the house the white mare comes for Kamal."

Kamal's sister Sarah was sat right next to me as well, so I carried on saying:

"From the heart of the quarter the white mare comes for Sarah."

When the other women from Thinnaba started singing with loud voices, she (Sarah) said to them 'for God's sake, don't say it (say poetry and songs); let them (the women of Ramin) say it'. So we went on singing;

Abu Kamal crossed many seas and,

With his sword many towns he saved

Many seas, Abu Kamal crossed and,

With his sword many towns he conquered

Oh, mother Abu Al Rajeh toured the nations and,

He gave water and food (charitable)

(Poetry recitation and singing went on for a very long time)

We went on singing and reciting poetry from the moment we arrived in the afternoon until dawn. The women were saying 'we don't want the girls from Ramin to leave; let them stay'.

Researcher: Did you make up those songs for the insurgents?

NB: Yes for the insurgents; we went to and from Thinnaba walking on foot.

Researcher: From Thinnaba?

NB: Yes, from Thinnaba. They used to come there in a convoy of forty vehicles. They would laugh at us because as we walked we used to sing more songs, such as:

Syria sent its forces; long live Syria for its esteem

Oh, you Arabs, read its Journal

There can only be what will be

From the far distance came a car

Searching for the metal (guns)

A plane passed over Abu Kharroub

Seeking and searching all the paths of town

On board is an undercover agent who brought the news

Inevitably he will receive it between the eyes.

Researcher: Can we ask you about the nature of women's work in those days. What did they actually do?

NB: They looked after the insurgents. They gave them refuge in their homes. The town was totally united behind them; there were no traitors like those we see today. Some men once came and said Abu Kamal is besieged by the British in the town of Bala'a. The 10 guards immediately picked up their guns and went to his rescue. They kept firing and fighting until he could flee to safety. They rescued Abu Kamal. He was besieged once again in the village of Irtah, and killed the commander; I can't remember his whole name, but it was something 'Al- Ammoury' (Ibrahim Al-Ammoury).

They sang:

Oh, Arab daughter who carries the key do give a drink to the leader who was murdered in Irtah (Village)

Part 2: Women's Narrations

Hasna Salim Masoud

Researcher: Could you tell us about your past experiences and old memories?

HM: I will tell you first about my memories of the revolt in Palestine.

Researcher: Okay.

HM: When the revolt started they used to talk about Salim Abu Abdul Rahim, wasn't he the one they caught and threw in prison, the first time? They left Tulkarm at sunset and went to release him from prison using sticks; knocking at the prison door with these sticks. They were so naive; they could not get him out. The British soldiers shouted at them 'Go…Go'. At the start of the revolt it was not really a revolt as such yet. In the evening an old man came and asked us to give him money to buy a gun. Myself and Abu Rajeh from Beit Leed told him okay and he took the money and went to buy a gun. After that he and Abu Rajeh would go to a mountain top named Ras Alkalb which was the place they fired at the enemy from. First they would put up a road block and wait for the Jewish military to arrive and begin to remove it, and then they would shoot at them. When things improved financially they bought another gun, but the revolt had still not really started yet. The young men wanted to buy guns. Ten of them bought them but I really don't know who they were. They grew in numbers and strength, and that is when Abu Kamal appeared[1]. We did not know him prior to that and we had never heard of him either. Abu Kamal came and armed them.

Researcher: Was he your husband?

HM: No, Abu Kamal was the commander.

Researcher: Abdul Rahim?

HM: Yes, Abdul Rahim, Abu Kamal, he came and armed them. They started going to Al Ras to make road blocks and fire at the Jews and the military. They grew in number and went to the mountain together. They were not only from this village but also from Tulkarm, Anabta and Beit Leed; from all over the place.

---

1. The leader of 1936 revolt: Abdul Rahim Alhajj Muhammad

Researcher: Did you give money to your husband to buy weapons?

HM: Yes, I did.

Researcher: Why did you give him the money?

HM: Oh, God! (She laughed)

Researcher: Why? Tell me why you gave him the money?

HM: I gave him the money to buy a gun to defend the country and protect us.

Researcher: Did he train you on how to use weapons?

HM: No, he did not.

Researcher: What happened when they besieged Beit Leed?

HM: Abu Kamal's notebook had been dropped on the ground just before Beit Leed, and they found it.

Researcher: What notebook? What was in it?

HM: It contained their names.

Researcher: Whose names?

HM: The names of the ten.

Researcher: Were they his guards?

HM: Yes, the ten who guarded him.

Researcher: Who did they guard?

HM: They guarded Abdul Rahim. They were besieged for three days.

Researcher: Was the notebook then in the hands of the British?

HM: They came to the village from Azzoun on three consecutive days. On one of those days, when we were fast sleep just before dawn, we heard a knock on the door. It was Um Subhi.

Researcher: Who was Um Subhi?

HM: Um Subhi?

Researcher: What was her name?

HM: Um Subhi's name was Amina, Amina Al-Barham. One

day, she knocked on the door. I asked her what the matter was and she said the village had been besieged. She asked if Abu Muhammad was there and I confirmed that he was, and then she told me to 'get arranged'. I couldn't make up my mind what to do. The gun was over there and the pistol was over there, what should I do with them? Then, as soon as we stood up, the old woman, his mother, went to dig a hole in the taboon (a very small room of yellow mud where the traditional Palestinian fireplace was) to bury them. She buried them along with his uniform.

Researcher: That was Aamenah, Aminah?

HM: That was Aamenah, his mother. Once she had finished burying the weapons, she went to the houses of the ten men to warn them and to tell them to hide away their arms and uniforms. The military raided the village and ordered all the men to gather at the mosque.

Researcher: What did you do with your husband's weapon?

HM: I hid it in the taboon.

Researcher: How did you hide it? Please tell us.

HM: I dug a little into the ash and dust and placed the weapon down then covered it with more ash and dust (....).

Researcher: Did you light up the taboon afterwards?

HM: No, I did not light it up. I used animal remains to create a thick smoke and an awful smell to prevent them from searching in the taboon. They raided the houses of the ten men and caused damage to their houses. One of the sides of our house was demolished and the sight of it still bears witness to the event.

Researcher: What about the iron woman you mentioned? You told me she used weapons?

HM: Yes, she fired at them along with Sabha Al-yaqoub and Abu Yusef.

Researcher: Did they fire at the British?

HM: Yes, everyday they went to shoot at the British from Ras Abuhamad.

Researcher: They went to Ras Abuhamad?

HM: Yes, they went to fire at the Jews and block their roads. Abu Yusef would close the Sultanah road then start firing. Once one of my uncles from Qousin went to a woman from Beit Leed – I don't want to say from our town – with his military gear. As he entered her house, she was all over him taking off his clothes and weapons in order to hide them. The British were still in the town so she hid him in an empty well.

Researcher: Who was that woman?

HM: She was the wife of Asa'ad Al Khaleel, and her name was Hasnah; yes, Hasnah.

Researcher: Hasnah, what was her full name?

HM: Hasnah hid the man in the well and covered it with a metal sheet and on top of that she put a layer of cow dung. She kept giving him water and food for seven or eight days. After that she pulled him out and sent him off to his family who had thought he was dead.

Researcher: What was her full name?

HM: Hasnah is all I know. She and her husband are from our village, and they live in Beit Leed. Her name is Hasnah Asa'ad Khaleel.

Researcher: Oh, you mean Aamenah and Sabha?

HM: Yes, Aamenah and Sabha.

Researcher: Did they fire weapons?

HM: Yes, Heiger also took part in the shooting. When she went to send them food she participated in the shooting, but she was a lot younger than they were.

Researcher: Did they fire their weapons to give the impression that there were more insurgents?

HM: Yes, there were other people too.

Researcher: Not only the ten?

HM: Not just the ten. The insurgents escaped to Beit Amreen.

Researcher: What happened in Beit Amreen?

HM: The British military cordoned off Beit Amreen completely.

Suddenly a person started shouting that the insurgents were besieged in Beit Amreen and all the men and women said "let's go to their rescue!" The rescuers besieged the military and it became like a multilayered siege. They kept attacking them until they beat them. Two men and a woman from Burqah died in that battle.

Researcher: In those days you sang for the insurgents to raise their morale. What were some of those songs?

HM: Yes, I remember they went something like this:

Speak of the Beit Amreen battle! How many wounded, and how many fell?

Another day of battle when water containers were hit, and

Many men died whist others' who knows what fate they had?

Zahidah Mohammad A. Mustafa

Researcher: Could you please tell us about yourself and talk to us about the old days?

ZM: I was born in 1931. I was still very young when my uncle asked me to go with my cousin to the cave to fetch something. We asked him what the thing was and he told us it was a weapon. I went with him; he was the father of Shahirah (pointing to her). When we arrived he told us to go inside and take the things out. I started pulling out belts of ammunition and handing them over to him. One day he told me get them out and as I stretched my hand to pull the weapon out I touched something that sent shivers down my spine. I started screaming and he asked me what was wrong. I said 'there is something in there and I don't know what it is'. He said 'don't be afraid; that is the solid grease we use on the weapons to prevent them from rusting'. He asked me to hand it over to him then he cut off a piece of it and said 'let's go home'. The weapons my uncle hid in that cave were all used against the British soldiers. He would sit near that wild fig tree and shoot at them until he ran out of ammunition. The British would scream and shoot back. My uncle also came home to train the insurgents. My little brother and I, late one evening, heard loud bangs and we were so scared. We went back home and told my mother about the loud banging sounds and she said 'don't be afraid; that is your uncle training the insurgents'. He would then take them off out of town until they reached Bzzaria. On his way back my uncle met another group of insurgents coming from Kafr Allabad to Beit Leed so he took them to his house and gave them supper. As soon as they had finished their supper and changed their uniforms, they would leave. The two women, Om Yusef and Hafizah Alrajeh, would spend most of the night and the following day doing the washing.

Researcher: What did the two women do?

ZM: They washed the insurgents' uniforms.

Researcher: What were their names again?

ZM: Hafizah is Om Alrajeh, the wife of Alrajeh, and Om Yusef was the wife of Abu Yusef.

Researcher: What was the name of Om Yusef?

Part 2: Women's Narrations

ZM: Aayeshah, she was the daughter of Hassan Al-Othman from Anabta. My uncle had two herds of goats; he would ask someone to get a goat and have it cooked for the insurgents.

Researcher: You mean they cooked and washed for the insurgents?

ZM: They cooked the food, baked the bread and transported weapons from one place to another. They carried the weapons wrapped up in baby baskets.

Researcher: They carried weapons from one place to another for the insurgents?

ZM: Yes, Om Yusef and Om Abed (Hafizah) would walk with the weapons from one place to another for the insurgents. My father's house was made up of two compounds; in the first they had their horses and in the other they hid the weapons and ammunition. I was hungry one day and ran to the house to grab something to eat. As I walked into the house I saw a weapon and a military man there. Slowly I walked back and went to tell my father. My father told me it was Abu Kamal but I was too young to know who Abu Kamal was. The British surrounded the village and gathered the men and women in the mosque. They arrested the ten and ten more on top of that. My uncle was not home that night; he was in Beit Leed. As he was approaching the village he saw with his binoculars that the army had overwhelmed the place. He spent the night in the mountains. Among the men who were taken to prison was my father in-law.

Researcher: Did you transport weapons for the insurgents?

ZM: Yes, I did. I helped my cousins, but I did not have the strength to be involved in the fighting.

Researcher: Your cousin gave you a secret code for this work, what was it?

ZM: He would tell me to bring him this or that thing. He would tell me something and say 'this is a secret between you and me; never say anything to your brother or father'. He would say that we must go to the Ras to deliver or bring something and so on.

Researcher: How old were you then?

ZM: I was born in 1931 and when the insurgency ended I was probably seven or eight, maybe ten even. I can't tell you exactly.

Researcher: What were the names of the women who were trained to use arms?

ZM: I don't know, but they used to say – I very young then – Om Alrajeh, Heigar and this lady (pointing to her mother in law).

Researcher: And Aayeshah; who was she?

ZM: She was Om Yusef. She was the one who carried arms in baby baskets.

Researcher: How many were there?

ZM: Two.

Researcher: Can you repeat their names for me?

ZM: Hafizah Al-Sae'ed, the wife of Alrajeh and Aayeshah, daughter of Hassan Al-Othman, Om Yusef.

Researcher: What about Heigar?

ZM: She was his daughter.

Researcher: Was she trained to use arms?

ZM: Yes, she was trained and her step mother was as well.

Researcher: Tell us about the piece of paper which had the names of the ten on it?

ZM: Some said it was dropped at my cousin's house and others said it was lost on the way to Beit Leed. I can't tell you exactly what happened. The names were Abu Ahmad (Yusef Al-Dahdal), Abu Nasouh, Abu Ahmad Yusef (Fahmi); those three were from our clan. Then Salim Al-Sae'ed, the husband of this woman (pointing to the woman sitting next to her), Abu Mohammad and Maso'ud Abu Sami from the Salman clan. That makes six, I know them by their clans. Then there was Abu Ar-Ragheb, Ahmad Hajj Abed, and Al-Sae'ed Al-Rasheed, and finally Jeber Dar Ziedan. Those were the ten names in the paper.

Researcher: So the paper was with them?

ZM: I heard them say that the paper was with one of the insurgents' commanders. I really don't know exactly, but they say his name was Abu Nasouh.

Part 2: Women's Narrations

Researcher: You told me about a woman called Handoumeh Abdul Rahim, could you tell me more about her?

ZM: Her son was amongst the ten or more who were arrested and taken to jail. His name was Abbas Ezzat Mohammad Ezzat. During the siege, he told his mother to take care of the gun so she went and buried it in the taboon, as we were told to do by Om Mohammad. The ten were selected from amongst all the rest of the men and were taken to Akka. Her son was engaged but not married yet. She went to visit him in prison and he asked her 'Mother, my fiancé and her children are they still with you or did her family take her?'

Researcher: Was that a secret code?

ZM: The mother said 'she and her children are still with me'.

(Najeyyah Barham (NB) interrupted and started to discuss this topic)

NB: When she visited him, he asked her what had happened to his wife and her children? His mother told him that the wife had gone to her family's house but the children remained with her. He asked her 'did they take her?' and she said yes. She went to visit him once again after the first visit had ended; she was a clever old woman. The prison guard said to her 'you have just seen him' and she replied 'that was his mother who visited him, I am his step mother'.

Researcher: Why did she go back to visit him again?

NB: She wanted to see him; she wanted to sit with him.

Researcher: There wasn't something else?

NB: No, nothing else. The guns were collected by the insurgents who took them to use in the fighting.

Sanajeq Barham

Researcher: Can you tell us about the Palestinian insurgency and life during those days?

SB: When we came into the world the British were still here. Palestinians resisted the British for thirty years. After thirty years it was time for them to leave because they had created Israel. Some leaders of the Palestinian resistance movement initiated the revolt and opened the door for volunteers. Abu Kamal from the Dar Seif family was a leader; he was from Burqah but lived in Thinnaba. He came over to Ramin and asked Abu Rajeh if he would volunteer for the insurgency. Abu Rajeh told him 'why not, we are ready to call upon people and see who would like to join the insurgents'. So Abu Rajeh gathered the elders of the village and spoke to them, saying 'good people, whoever would like to volunteer to join the Palestinian revolt can find arms and ammunition available at my house; anyone who would like to enlist with the insurgents can find whatever they need at my house'.

Researcher: Were all of them men?

SB: Yes.

Researcher: Did women volunteer?

SB: Women?

Researcher: Yes.

SB: No, none of them were women. They stayed to help one another.

Researcher: Help with what?

SB: They helped their brothers, husbands and families; they cooked and took food to the insurgents and helped with the transportation of weapons and ammunition. Abu Kamal would bring equipment to Abu Rajeh and he would distribute it with the help of women. Ten of those who enlisted were from our village. Abu Rajeh hid the weapons in a place where the British could not reach them. The ten volunteers started fighting and dug themselves in at Ras Abu Hamad mount. A convoy of the British army would pass through the town at least once a day. The ten would spread themselves out on the mountain and wait for the convoy.

Part 2: Women's Narrations

Researcher: I thought Abdul Rahim Hajj Mohammad was from Thinnaba. Was he actually from here, Ramin?

SB: He used to come to Ramin.

Researcher: Did Abdul Rahim have a sister named Halima?

SB: Yes, Halima and Sarah.

Researcher: Did she work with the insurgents?

SB: Yes, she did.

Researcher: What did she do?

SB: They said that she was trained to use weapons and fix the guns.

Researcher: Who taught Halima?

SB: Her brother did; he was a leader in the insurgency.

Researcher: Did she shoot at the British?

SB: Yes, she shot at them alongside her brother when the insurgents were assigned to dig trenches in Ras Abu Hamad and Harikat Eid. They also set booby-traps for the British armored vehicles. When they pulled the wires you could see the vehicle lift up into the air and blow up.

Researcher: Where did Abdul Rahim Hajj Mohammad die?

SB: He died in Beit Amreen.

Researcher: In Beit Amreen or in Sanour?

SB: No, they said he was killed after (..) No, he was not killed in Beit Amreen. He stayed in Beit Amreen then withdrew to Sanour and that is where he was killed.

Researcher: So, he died in Sanour?

SB: Yes, they killed him there.

Researcher: Who transported his body from Sanour to Thinnaba to be buried?

SB: The people of Thinnaba and his sister.

Researcher: His sister Halima came to get the body?

SB: Halima came here to Abu Rajeh because he had a camel.

Researcher: Did Halima come along with people from Thinnaba?

SB: Yes, Halima came with a delegation that arrived from Thinnaba.

Researcher: Did they come in secret?

SB: Not really, but they did fear that the British might take the body.

Researcher: They brought a camel to carry the body?

SB: They feared the British might take the body so they came to Abu Rajeh who brought a camel from here in the village with him, as well as a group of people because at that time there was still less than ten of us.

Researcher: Was Halima with the delegation?

SB: Yes, she was with the delegation.

Researcher: What I am trying to understand is whether Halima was among the people who went to Sanour to bring back the body?

SB: Yes, she was and she went on foot.

Researcher: Walking?

SB: She walked but Abu Rajeh rode his horse.

Researcher: She walked?

SB: Yes, she went with the delegates who also walked on foot.

Researcher: They went to Sanour?

SB: They went to Sanour and found that his body had been hidden by the people there. They put the body on the back of the camel and returned to the village.

Researcher: Abu Rajeh and Halima?

SB: Abu Rajeh and a group of people, but not the ten insurgents who were still in prison. When they heard about his death they went on strike and mourned him in the prison.

Researcher: What happened when they brought back the body?

Part 2: Women's Narrations

SB: They brought him for a short while to the old house then they carried him discreetly to Thinnaba.

Researcher: They smuggled the body?

SB: Yes, they smuggled it.

Researcher: Abu Rajeh, the delegation and Halima?

SB: Yes, Abu Rajeh, the delegation and Halima passed through carrying him and said 'bury him before dawn; the British might raid the village and take him from us'. They dug a grave for him in the dark and buried him. Later everybody seemed to have heard the news and the whole town was in mourning.

Researcher: Was his sister's name, Halima Hajj Mohammad?

SB: Yes, and he also had a sister called Sarah.

Researcher: Sarah was his sister too?

SB: Sarah was his other sister and Kamal was his eldest son.

Researcher: Was Sarah trained to use weapons?

SB: No, she stayed at home.

Researcher: Only Halima was trained?

SB: Yes, only Halima went with the delegation; she had a manly attitude, she was manly.

Researcher: What was the full name of Ameenah?

SB: Her name was Ameenah Asa'ad Barham; she was my Aunt. One day, just before dawn, she went to fetch water from the spring and she saw that the British soldiers had cordoned off the cemetery area and some sort of a tape had been stretched around the graves. She was astonished to see the tape and said to the soldiers 'I want to pass through'. The soldiers told her 'you can't pass through here, go back home'. She said 'I want water, we need some water to drink' and they told her 'you can't get water; go back'.

Researcher: Where was she actually going to?

SB: She went to fetch water, but they made her turn back. On her way back she went to Om Abbas, her brother's wife, and told her that the village was full of British soldiers. Abu Abbas had returned from Ras Abu Hamad and his weapon was lying on the floor in the house. Ameenah asked where Abu Abbas was and Om Abbas said 'I think he is sleeping', so she took the weapon, wrapped it, and hid in the taboon.

Researcher: You mean she buried the weapon?

SB: Yes, my mother hid it. In the morning British soldiers came to the house and asked her to go to the gathering point at the mosque. She told the soldiers 'I am an old woman and I cannot go anywhere'. He told her 'I say you have to go to the mosque'. She was a brave woman and did not fear them. The whole village went to the mosque except my mother who stayed at home. The soldiers brought the Mukhtar (Abdul Aziz) to show them the house of Abbas. He pointed out which one it was and they entered the house which was filled with olive oil pots made of clay.

They pulled my brother Abbas by his hair and shouted at him 'boy, are you one of the ten insurgents?' He told them 'Palestine is our home and we want to liberate it from you; we will rid Palestine of you' and they started beating him so hard. My mother approached them to try to rescue him from the soldiers but the soldiers told her to go away. She said to them 'that is my son you are kicking' and they told her 'your son is a leader in the insurgency; he stole the weapons from Seilet Al-Thahr and gave them to the commander of the insurgents'.

Part 2: Women's Narrations

Sobhiyyah Ismael A. Barham & Zahida Mohammad A. Mustafa

Researcher: Sobhiyyah Barham from Ramin will now talk to us about her childhood memories.

Sobhiyyah: We had a piece of land opposite to a main road which was used by everyone; Arabs and the British. Once, as the women were sitting opposite the road they saw that the British soldiers were near Karm Aamer and were coming to the village. At that time we had a gun which belonged to my cousin Abu Nasouh. I ran to my mother to tell her and on my way my cousin Malik saw me and asked what was wrong? I told him 'the British are approaching the village and Abbas's gun is in our house; if they come in and find it they will demolish the house'. He told me to go get it for him. I said to him 'but what if they see me?' and he said 'don't worry, your mother will sort everything out'. I arrived at my house and told my mother that the British were coming and were already at Karm Aamer. My mother took out a belt filled with bullets and tied it around my waist, then she slung the gun across my shoulder, covered me with a sheet of cloth and told me to run. My cousin Asa'ad was watching and the moment I arrived at my uncle's house he came and asked me 'did you bring it?' I gave it all to him and told him to run. He asked me if I knew where the British were now and I told him they were very close to the quarter where we lived. 'Are you not afraid?' I said, 'if someone sees you he will come and take it'. He told me that he would not leave his house even if he had to stay until late in the night. He said that I should go then he cleared a space for the gun and placed some stones over it. He pretended to be working in the field digging stones out of the soil and throwing them onto the stone wall. When we heard that the British had gone I went to tell him and he retrieved the gun. He asked me 'Can you shoot?' and I told him it frightened me. He said 'don't be afraid, I will show you how to use it'. He loaded the gun and showed me how to turn the mechanism and pull the trigger. I shot it twice. He also had a 12mm pistol; the kind of gun I could handle more easily. He loaded it then handed it over to me and told me to shoot. I said to him 'people will think the British are raiding the village' and he said that I should know how to use it because when the men are away one never knows what could happen; that's why I should learn to use arms. Abbas, my second cousin, also taught me how to use guns for similar reasons. After that my Aunt rushed into the house and said 'anyone who has something should hide it!' We hid weapons in the taboon all the time; it was the Arab hiding place. When the insurgents used to come to the village they would ask for whatever they needed and people would happily oblige. People who were a little well off used to make them food and give them clothes. For example, there was a cave belonging to my Uncle Faris, where insurgents would hide, and my father and uncle sent them food more than a hundred times. That year several songs were sung in praise of my family, especially for Abu Rajeh. They went something like this:

Abu Rajeh may Allah give you power

All Arabs are behind you

The revolution men come to your house

You may stay defender of this country and fellow men.

You stay awake guarding, always and,

Abu rajah rode his horses

(After Sobhiyyah finished her singing I turned to speak to Hajjeh Zahidah and asked her about her childhood too).

Zahidah: My uncle used to hide the guns and ammunition in a cave. He would tell me to go with my cousin and fetch the guns. The entrance of the cave was very narrow and because I was small I could get inside and pull out the weapons and give them to my cousin, Abu Yusef; he was the father of Shahirah, and the son of Abu Rajeh. I kept pulling things out until I touched something soft and I screamed. 'What happened?' he asked and I said to him 'I think I felt a snake'. He assured me it was not a snake, it was the grease they used for lubricating guns to prevent them from rusting. When we returned home we found the house full of insurgents; the whole town was united to guard the house.

Researcher: Were there women training to use arms in those days?

Zahidah: I was too young to remember so I don't know, but I heard them say that Om Rajeh and Heigar were trained to use firearms.

Researcher: Om Rajeh's name was Sabha Al-yaqoub?

Zahidah: Yes, Sabha Al-yaqoub; she was my uncle's wife.

Researcher: Did you train to use firearms?

Part 2: Women's Narrations

Zahidah: No, I did not. The weapons were with the men and I was never trained to use them.

Researcher: Did you ever smuggle weapons?

Zahidah: Yes, I did.

Researcher: How and where did you smuggle weapons?

Zahidah: When someone told me to take a gun and meet them at a certain place or take it to the mountain (..) where all the insurgents used to hide, I would leave the weapon somewhere and then tell him to go and find it in that particular place.

Researcher: So you transported arms for the insurgents?

Zahidah: Abu Rajeh would send someone to the house to fetch something and I would give it to him.

Researcher: You mean you did not go with them?

Zahidah: No. I did not.

Researcher: Why not?

Zahidah: In those days Abu Kamal resided in Qatan Judeh, where my cousin Ayesha lived. One day he told her to go and say to Abu Yusef 'your father tells you to give me the thing which your father spoke to you about'. He said to Ayesha 'tell Abu Yusef the thing which your father spoke to you about will be brought by Abu Kamal who will be coming with some insurgents to the field where Abu Kamal resides'. It was raining so heavily and Abu Kamal could not stay because he feared surprise raids by the British. He asked him to wait a little to bring him something to put on to protect him from the rain. My father and uncle were like one. He said to him 'brother, he (Abu Kamal) wants the *a'bah*' (a garment men wore to protect them from the cold and rain). His brother told him 'here give him one of those two'. Abu Kamal wrapped himself with the a'bah and left. When they arrived at Sanour he was surprised by a regiment of British soldiers. The plain of Sanour was covered with piles of harvested wheat which he could hide behind. He pulled off the a'bah and lay it on a stone then started firing. They went to see the a'bah and found several bullet holes in it. He had escaped by zigzagging his way through the stacks of harvested wheat. One revolutionary who fought with Abu Kamal was killed in Sanour.

Researcher: Abdul Rahim died in Sanour but he was originally from Thinnaba and his sister Halima was with the insurgents is that correct?

Zahidah: I really don't know.

Researcher: Did you not hear about her?

Zahidah: They spoke of her but I did not know her.

Researcher: What did you hear about her?

Zahidah: I heard she mourned painfully when her brother was killed. When the revolt first broke out my husband and Abu Rajeh agreed to buy a gun together because they did not have enough money to buy one each. People were very poor then; they lived off whatever they could grow and harvest. He asked me to give him some money to buy a gun as he wanted to share the cost with Abu Rajeh. I gave him some money and they went and bought a gun from Beit Leed. Sometimes they went out together and other times each of them would go alone for a few days at a time.

Researcher: With the gun?

Zahidah: They bought that gun and later on the insurgents came and then Abu Kamal came along and brought them weapons and they all worked together. They were united, they all worked together as equals. Those who did not have a gun shared one with others; Abu Kamal brought them guns.

Researcher: Where did they hide their weapons?

Zahidah: They hid them wherever they could, in the taboon, for example, or anywhere they could bury them. Okay, what else do you want to know from me?

Researcher: Were there women training to use firearms?

Zahidah: No, there weren't; there were only two of them.

Researcher: Who were they?

Zahidah: Om Ahmad, and Sabha Al-yaqoub.

Researcher: What was the full name of Om Ahmad?

Zahidah: Her name was Amenah.

Researcher: Amenah what?

Part 2: Women's Narrations

Zahidah: Amenah Boolad.

Researcher: Did they shoot at the British?

Zahidah: Yes.

Researcher: Whom did they fire at?

Zahidah: They fired at the British.

Researcher: Did you sing for the insurgents in those days?

Zahidah: Yes, we did.

Researcher: Do you remember anything of the songs?

Zahidah: I do.

Researcher: Come on then, sing them for us?

Zahidah: (singing):

Revolutionaries of our country, Revolutionaries you are

Gather your strength, for the Zionists demand to take your country

So long as Abu Kamal defends you

Worry not for our Palestine

Never shall we succumb to Jewish rule

So long as our men hold the gun

Researcher: (Turning to Sanajeq Mohammad Barham) Hajjeh Sanajeq, tell us how the revolt broke out? How did the insurgents come to be in Ramin?

Sanajeq: Ramin was the place where the insurgents gathered because they felt a sense of security there. Abu Kamal used to say that Ramin was his home. Insurgents would come at night on horseback to see Abu Rajeh in Ramin. He would slaughter animals and cook for them, and the entire population of the village would come out to guard the insurgents against the British. They would bring their weapons and hide them in an old house used for storing hay. One night they gathered around Abu Rajeh, who said 'Men, whoever wants to enlist should give me his name'. The first to volunteer was Abu Nasouh, and then Ahmad Hajj Abed, Salim Ibn As-Sae'd, Jaber, and Abu Ragheb. In total there were ten volunteers alongside Abu Kamal. They were assigned to the outskirts Ramin to ambush the British regiments that passed by the village. When they returned we would give them a hero's welcome and ask what happened? They would say 'we are all safe'. One day Abu Kamal decided that they would ambush the British at midday. They hid between the olive groves and engaged with the British. Army planes came to the scene of the battle and the insurgents managed to shoot down one of the planes. The British brought a huge truck and carried the plane away from the area. We could see what was going on as we stood watching. People were shouting 'the insurgents of Ramin shot down a plane! Abu Kamal's men shot down a plane!'

Researcher: Where was Abu Kamal from?

Sanajeq: He was from Burqah, but he lived in Thinnaba and when the insurgency broke out he stayed in Thinnaba.

Researcher: Hajj Abdul Rahim had a sister, what was her name?

Sanajeq: He had a sister named Halima.

Researcher: What did Halima do?

Sanajeq: Halima was taught to use weapons alongside the insurgents, not her brother.

Researcher: Did they train her to use guns?

Sanajeq: Of course they did.

Researcher: Did she fire at the British?

Sanajeq: She did indeed.

Researcher: Where in Sanour did Abdul Rahim die? Who went to bring his body back from Sanour?

Sanajeq: Abu Rajeh took a camel from here and went along with a delegation.

Researcher: Was Halima with them?

Sanajeq: Yes, they sent for her and she came to help them protect the corpse from the British. They wanted to smuggle his body out of Sanour and bury him in Thinnaba. They rested for a while in Ramin then brought him to Thinnaba and buried him at night. In the morning everyone knew and they were very sad for the loss of such a man; the entire area was in mourning.

Part 2: Women's Narrations

Researcher: Which other women, apart from Halima, worked with the insurgents?

Sanajeq: From our village?

Researcher: Yes, who were they?

Sanajeq: Om Rajeh and some of her daughters-in-law.

Researcher: What were their names?

Sanajeq: Om Rajeh.

Researcher: What was the full name of Om Rajeh?

Sanajeq: Her name was Sabha Al-yaqoub. All the people in the house of Abu Rajeh took part in the insurgency. The mothers of the ten insurgents helped transport and hide the weapons. Even Abu Rajeh used to help; he could help more than Abu Kamal because he was from Ramin whilst Abu Kamal was from elsewhere. However, he used to say that he loved Ramin and that he considered it his home.

Researcher: (Turning to ask Najeyyah Barham) Tell us about the day when you went to mourn the death of Abdul Rahim Hajj Mohammad.

Najeyyah: We were singing the song they chanted at the house of Abdul Rahim:

The day Abu Kamal departed

The earth and the water shook with sadness

Abu Kamal is arriving,

So furnish the whole vicinity for him

From the Levant he brought ammunitions

He evenly distributed among fellow insurgents

(Najeyyah calls upon Om Mahmud to respond with a song)

Om Mahmud: (singing)

Break the damned radio up in the yard

It spoke about the Leader of Palestine

Break the damned radio up on the roof

It spoke about Abu Kamal

Abu Rajeh fed you mutton and fat

Oh, guests of midday come and rest in the shade.

Researcher: Thank you so much Hajjeh

Souriyyeh Issa Salman

Researcher: Your husband was the leader of the Ramin insurgents group, could you tell us about your memories of that great leader?

SS: I lived with him for fifteen years. He was old; my father had me married to him and in those days one could not choose or say 'I don't want this or that' (the women present laughed). Fathers in those days were all-powerful; one could not say a word in their presence, let alone oppose them. My brother Sari said to my Father 'that man is a chief (..) and a leader who is known in Burqah, Kafr Qaddoum, and throughout the whole district'. In the fifteen years I was with him we had five children; two died and three lived. When my husband died my eldest had not yet completed preparatory school. He used to tell me about Hajjeh Sabhah, Um Mustafa, who used to shoot guns.

During the war all the leaders met in Kafr Qaddoum, Burqah, Beit Amreen, Bala'a and Saffarin. When the army came to the town we would hide the insurgents' military equipment in the hay stacks. No one could ever find a thing hidden in the hay. The Abu Batha family lived near my brother's house. My husband used to say he wanted to die in the revolt for the sake of the cause. Of course one dies only when the time comes for that.

Researcher: Was he a great leader?

SS: Yes, he was.

Researcher: Did he train people to use arms?

SS: Yes, he trained them, taught them and gave them information. He trained the young and the old.

Researcher: Did he train you?

SS: I was too young when I married him. He was perhaps sixty when he married me, but my brother received training and had a gun called Sten. His name was Sari, Sari Issa Yusef.

Part 2: Women's Narrations

Shahirah Mahmud Muslihi[1]

SMM: I would like to say something about my grandfather Abu Rajeh. When we were really young we lived in this house and he lived in that one. He would gather us boys and girls together and play with us. My mother said her husband always treated her well, and her uncle (my grandfather) never called her by her name; instead he would speak to her using the expression 'Yaba' (father). When the insurgents came to the house and knocked on the door, my father and grandfather would receive and greet them. He would wake her up saying 'yaba, yaba may Allah bestow his grace upon you; please get up, the insurgents are here'. She would wake up and start cooking and preparing food for them. This is what Hajjeh Om Yusef and Ayesha Hassan Othman Qobbaj used to tell us. That night when the ten were imprisoned and they besieged the village, my mother told us that the ten were led to the mosque. She said that Ayesha Hassan had hidden the books in the drawer of the bureau. The British pulled out all of the drawers except the last one. It was thanks to God that they did not touch it. My mother was so nervous that she was beating my brother Yusef; she was so nervous that they might find the books. She feared for her father in law and for the house; if they found them they would imprison the men and demolish the house. She was praying and waiting but thankfully things turned out well, by the grace of God. My grandfather, Abu Rajeh, was good to everybody and we were too.

Researcher: How about your grandmother?

SMM: My grandmother Sabha? My mother said that she and my aunt Heigar used to clean the gun for her father (Abu Rajeh) and helped the insurgents and even fought with them.

Researcher: What was the name of your Aunt?

SMM: My aunt was Heigar Mustafa. She and aunt Hafizah and Ayesha cooked and washed for the insurgents and transported weapons to them in the baby baskets which they used to carry on their heads. They were all good and very active; each one was more active than the next.

End of Interview

---

1. from Azzahfer, Head of a Women's Society

Hasna Masoud   Sanajeq Barham

Najeyyah Barham

Dr. Faiha Abdulhadi   Zahida Mustafa

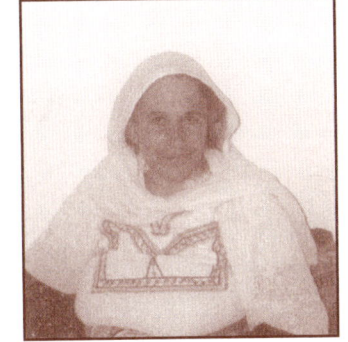

Sanajeq Barham

Narrators and Researchers/ Ramin Village

Annexes

- **List of Women Narrators**
- **Index**

List of Women Narrators

#	Name of Narrator	Date of Birth	Place of Birth	Place of Residence
(Palestine) (Above 75 Years Old)				
1	Adala Al-Aseer (Toukan)	1913	Turkey	Jinin
2	Afifeh Hijaz	1921	Anabta	Tulkarm
3	Awatef Abdulhadi	1925	Arraba	Jinin
4	Doumia al-Sakakini	1923	Jerusalem	Ramallah
5	Fatmeh Al-Khateeb	1912	Sha'ab-Acre	Ain Bit AL-Ma'-Nablus
6	Hamida Abu Rayyah	1922	Gaza	Al-Samu'-Hebron
7	Hasna Salim Masoud	1914	Ramin	Ramin-Tulkarm
8	Hilweh Jakaman	1913	Bethlehem	Bethlehem
9	Issam Hamdi Al-Huseini	1919	Gaza	Gaza
10	Jamila Muhamad Badran	1924	Dair Al-Ghsoun	Tulkarm
11	Jamila Ahmad Sabbah	1920	Qiffeen	Qiffeen-Tulkarm
12	Kamleh Abdul-Rahman Shneik	1912	Azzun	Azzun-Qalqilya
13	Karimah Ismail Barham		Ramin-Tulkarm	Ramin-Tulkarm
14	Khadra Mustafa Al-Sari	1917	Nazareth	Bir Al-Maksur-Haifa
15	Madeeha Al-Battah	1924	Al-Majdal	Gaza
16	Ma'zouzeh Qasem	1923	Beit Reema	Beit Reema-Ramallah
17	Najeyyah Barham	1924	Ramin	Ramin-Tulkarm
18	Sa'dah Dakar	1915	Deir el-Balah	Gaza
19	Salma Al-Huseini	1920	Jerusalem	Jerusalem
20	Samiha Al Qubbaj Khaleel	1923	Tulkarm	Al-Bireh

#	Name of Narrator	Date of Birth	Place of Birth	Place of Residence
21	Sanajeq Mohammad Barham	1929	Ramin	Ramin-Tulkarm
22	Shams Al-Titi	1920	Al-Falouja-Gaza	Al-Arroub Camp-Hebron
23	Sobhiyyah Ismael Barham	1920	Ramin	Ramin-Tulkarm
24	Su'ad Tawfeeq Abu So'ud	1925	Gaza	Gaza
25	Widad Al-Ayyoubi	1925	Jerusalem	Jerusalem
26	Yusra Al-Barbari	1923	Gaza	Gaza
27	Zeinab Aqel	1924	Jerusalem	Jerusalem
28	Zakiyeh Hulaileh	1916	Yazour-Jaffa	Jericho

(Palestine) (Above 55 Years Old)

#	Name of Narrator	Date of Birth	Place of Birth	Place of Residence
1	Afaf Al-Idreesi	1928	Nablus	Gaza
2	Farha-Al Barghouthi	1928	Kobar-Ramallah	Kobar-Ramallah
3	Latifa Mahmoud Darbas	1927	Tulkarm	Bal'a-Tulkarm
4	Mahira Al-Dajani	1930	Jerusalem	Jerusalem
5	Makram Al-Qasrawi	1939	Hebron	Hebron
6	Munawwar Dawood Husain Salah	1935	Jerusalem	Jericho
7	Nadeyyah Omar Hamed	1930	Tulkarm	Tulkarm
8	Rasmiyyeh Al-Barghouthi (Um Al-Abed)	1926	Safad	Al-Bireh
9	Samira Khoury	1929	Nazareth	Nazareth
10	Su'ad Qarman	1927	Haifa	Ibtin-Haifa
11	Ta'ah Awad	1930	Al-Falouja	Rafah-Gaza
12	Virginia Tarazy	1930	Gaza	Gaza
13	Wafiyyeh Al-Khayri	1929	Al-Ramlah	Ramallah
14	Zahidah Ahmad M.Mustafa	1931	Ramin	Ramin-Tulkarm

#	Name of Narrator	Date of Birth	Place of Birth	Place of Residence

(Lebanon)/ (Above 75 Years Old)

#	Name of Narrator	Date of Birth	Place of Birth	Place of Residence
1	Latifa Al-Taher	1914	Sha'ab-Acre	Beirut
2	Rafeeqa Hamada (Jafra)	1924	Kweikat-Acre	Lebanon
3	Wadee'a Qaddourah Khartabil	1915	Beirut	Beirut
4	Zakeyya Khaled (Shararah)	1939	Haifa	Beirut

(Lebanon)/ (Above 55 Years Old)

#	Name of Narrator	Date of Birth	Place of Birth	Place of Residence
1	Fatheyya Al-Bahsh	1926	Nablus	Beirut
2	Ulga Al-Aswad	1934	Haifa	Tyre

(Syria)/ (Above 75 Years Old)

#	Name of Narrator	Date of Birth	Place of Birth	Place of Residence
1	Amneh Al-Shinnawi	1924	Haifa	Damascus
2	Fattoum Al-Ghurairi	1920	Safad	Damascus
3	Huda Ibrahim Amer	1919	Jerusalem	Damascus
4	Khazneh Al-Khateeb	1917	Haifa	Al-Yarmouk Camp-Syria
5	Sa'adeh Al-Kilani	1920	Nablus	Syria-Jordan

(Egypt)/ (Above 75 Years Old)

#	Name of Narrator	Date of Birth	Place of Birth	Place of Residence
1	Amneh Al-Wenni	1924	Nablus	Cairo
2	Khadija Hedayah	1924	Jerusalem	Cairo

(Egypt) / (Above 55 Years Old)

#	Name of Narrator	Date of Birth	Place of Birth	Place of Residence
1	Arab Abdulhadi	1937	Jerusalem	Cairo
2	Fatima Al-Darhali	1928	Jaffa	Cairo
3	Izdihar Al-Shurafa	1930	Beersheba	Cairo
4	Samira Abu Ghazaleh	1928	Al-Ramlah	Cairo

#	Name of Narrator	Date of Birth	Place of Birth	Place of Residence
(Jordan)/ (Above 75 Years Old)				
1	Alice Elias Nawrasi	1923	Jaffa	Amman-Jordan
2	Fatima Musa Al-Budairi	1923	Jerusalem	Amman-Jordan
3	Haijar Mustafa Thafer	1914	Ramin-Tulkarm	Amman-Jordan
4	Maymanah Ezzedin Al-Qassam	1911	Syria	Amman-Jordan
(Jordan)/ (Above 55 Years Old)				
1	Isam Abdulhadi (Fatima)	1928	Nablus	Amman-Jordan
2	Widad Al-'Arouri	1941	Jerusalem	Amman-Jordan
(Men Narrators)				
1	Abdul-Qader Yaseen	1937	Jaffa	Cairo-Egypt
2	Ahmad Al-'Isawi	1909	Beit Hanina-Jerusalem	Isawiya-Jerusalem
3	Ahmad Mahmoud Al-Zaben	1913	Al-Teera-Haifa	Al-Yarmouk Camp-Syria
4	Ahmad Maw'ed	1923	Tsipori-Nazareth	Al-Yarmouk Camp-Syria
5	Ali Musa Abu Yousef	1932	Halhoul-Hebron	Halhoul-Hebron
6	Anis Al-Sayegh	1931	Tiberias	Beirut-Lebanon
7	Bahjat Abu Gharbiyah	1916	Hebron	Amman-Jordan
8	Daoud E'raikat	1934	Jericho	Jericho
9	Fouad Ibrahim Abbas	1924	Al-Majdal (Askalan)	Cairo-Egypt
10	Haroun Hashem Rasheed	1927	Gaza	Cairo-Egypt
11	Kamal Abdul Rahim	1925	Tulkarm	Tulkarm
12	Subhi Ghousheh	1927	Jerusalem	Amman-Jordan
13	Zuheir Al-Shawish	1925	Damascus	Lebanon

Index

A

'Aboud village	47
'Anata	48, 101
'Attil village	84
1948 areas (green line)	18, 19, 141
1948 war (Displacement)	190
Abbas, Fuad Ibrahim	69, 121, 134, 138, 274
Abdu, Mohammad	148
Abdul 'Al, Khadija	8, 131, 133
Abdul Aziz, Ahmad	259
Abdul Nasser, Jamal	211, 226
Abdul Rahim, Handoumeh	254
Abdul Rahim, Kamal	51, 129, 132, 137, 274
Abdul Rahim, Mahmoud	88
Abdul Rahim, Ruqayya Mahmoud	44, 88, 110, 111
Abdulhadi, Arab	53, 132, 273
Abdulhadi, Awatef	25, 106, 128, 271
Abdulhadi, Awni	105
Abdulhadi, Faiha	1, 127, 160, 269
Abdulhadi, Iffat	63
Abdulhadi, Isam	25, 28, 69, 92, 128, 129, 133, 136, 274
Abdulhadi, Taghreed	8, 128, 129, 132, 135, 136
Abdulhadi, Tarab	23, 25, 27, 53, 105, 160
Abdulhadi, Tawadud	106
Abduljawwad, Jamila (the mother of rebels)	48, 101
Abduljawwad, Saleh	226, 227

Abdulrahman, Ayesha (Bint Alshate')	205
Abed Rabbuh, Um Reem	99
Abu Al-Hamshari	114
Abu As'ad	38
Abu Gharbiyah, Bahjat	24, 34, 53, 61, 98, 128, 129, 132, 133, 136, 274
Abu Ghazaleh, Samira	25, 26, 28, 50, 51, 77, 128, 132, 134, 273
Abu Ghneim Mountain	210
Abu Hasaballah	84
Abu Hashhash, Hala	8, 130, 131, 135, 219
Abu Ibrahim Alkabeer	152
Abu Jeldah	84
Abu Rayyah, Ahmad	87
Abu Rayyah, Hamida	79, 86, 111, 122, 129, 132, 134, 135, 138, 271
Abu Reesheh, Suhaila (Al-Rimawi)	42, 106
Abu Sami, Maso'ud	253
Abu So'ud, Su'ad Tawfeeq	24, 128, 131, 132, 136, 272
Abu Taha, Nida'	8, 129, 130, 131, 132, 134, 135, 137, 243
Abu Yousef, Ali Musa	51, 66, 92, 98, 132, 133, 136, 274
Abu Zeid, Hikmat	204
Acre	25, 28, 37, 50, 105, 108, 120, 123
Adla Fatayer	211
Afghanistan	236
Ain Bit Al-Ma'-Nablus	271
Al-'Arouri, Widad	46, 61, 108, 116, 131, 133, 137, 274
Al-'Isawi, Ahmad	45, 46, 48, 100, 115, 131, 136, 137, 274

Al-A'araj, Lidia	229
Al-A'athamy, Soad	215
Al-Agha, Amaal	8, 130, 134
Al-Alami, Ruqayya	8, 143
Al-Ali, Sabha	84
Al-Amad, Andaleeb	207, 228
Al-Ammoury, Ibrahim	245
Al-Aref, Nader	106
Al-Arroub Camp	129, 272
Al-As'ad, Abdullah	84
Al-Aseer, Adala (Touqan)	26, 128, 271
Al-Aswad, Ulga	61, 106, 133, 273
Al-Athmeh, Bahira	69
Al-Ayyoubi, Widad	39, 64, 93, 130, 132, 136, 272
Al-Azhar	147, 148
Al-Bahsh, Fatheyya	117, 121, 137, 138, 273
Al-Barbari, Yusra	68, 69, 77, 78, 92, 133, 134, 272
Al-Barghouthi, Farha	45, 131, 272
Al-Barghouthi, Rasmiyyeh (Um Al-Abed)	32, 115, 137, 272
Al-Bassah school	120
Al-Bassah village	119, 120
Al-Battah, Madeeha	132, 271
Al-Bireh City	219, 236, 271, 272
Al-Budairi, Fatima	76, 134, 274
Al-Dahdal, Yusef	253
Al-Dajani, Ahmad Zaki	129
Al-Dajani, Mahira	61, 133, 272
Al-Dajani, Mu'taz	127
Al-Darhali, Fatima	47, 91, 131, 136, 273
Al-Dawoudy, Adib	198, 199

Al-Dazdar, Shahanda	107
Al-Fahoum, Saba	42. 105
Al-Falouja	25, 28, 108, 122, 272
Algeria	205
Al-Ghalayeeni, Ahmad	152
Al-Ghurairi, Fattoum	35, 88, 122, 130, 135, 138, 273
Alhajj Hasan, Khadra (Khadra Al-Sheikh Khaleel)	38
Alhajj Ibrahim, Latifah	230
Alhajj Muhammad, Abdul Rahim	246
Al-Hasna, Shamseh	102
Al-Houri, Ruqayya	25, 28, 150
Al-Houri, Um 'Isam	63
Al-Huseini, Abdul-Qader	56. 66. 108
Al-Huseini, Aisha	106
Al-Huseini, Ameen	93, 112
Al-Huseini, Ameenah	229, 230
Al-Huseini, Badreyya	107
Al-Huseini, Faisal	56, 66
Al-Huseini, Hussein Salim	56
Al-Huseini, Issam Hamdi	38, 40, 92. 106, 130. 201, 271
Al-Huseini, Khadija	106
Al-Huseini, Rabab (Al-Tamimi)	41, 42, 106
Al-Huseini, Salma Rajai	55, 66, 68, 69. 84, 93, 106, 107, 132. 133. 135, 136, 271
Al-Huseini, Wajeeha	66. 106
Al-Idreesi, Afaf	92, 136, 272
Al-Istiqlal Mosque	40
Al-Jazzar Mosque	156
Al-Jazzar, Hiba	106
Al-Khalidi, Samiha	69

Al-Khalidi, Wahida	69
Al-Khateeb, Fatmeh	34, 130, 137, 271
Al-Khateeb, Khazneh	26, 28, 52, 62, 88, 89, 129, 132, 133, 135, 136, 273
Al-Khayri, Wafiyyeh	63, 133, 272
Al-Khuffash, Sabah	8. 128, 131, 132
Al-Kilani, Sa'adeh	24, 25, 28, 55, 117, 128, 129, 132, 137, 196, 273
Al-Kurdi, Buthaina	8. 129, 130
Allouba, Nafeeseh Mohammad Ali	69
Al-Maidan Hospital	202, 215
Al-Majdal	228, 271, 274
Al-Makki, 'Aisha Alhajj Khaleel	65, 103
Al-Makki, Ruqayya Alhajj Khaleel	65, 103
Al-Maskubiyyah Prison	241
Al-Masri, Eiva Habib	70
Al-Mikhmasiyyeh, Fatima	101
Al-Na'nou', Aminah	146
Al-Nakba (the 1948 Palestine tragedy)	203
Al-Nashashibi, Fatima	64, 69
Al-Nashashibi, Zahiyyeh	64, 69
Al-Othman, Aayeshah Hassan	252, 253
Al-Qaddoumi, Ahmad	114
Al-Qasem, Rayya	70
Al-Qasrawi, Makram	117, 137, 272
Al-Qassam Comrades	17, 23, 24, 25, 27, 28, 125, 150, 205, 220, 227, 228
Al-Qassam revolt	26, 125
Al-Qassam, Ezzedin	25, 27, 28, 89
Al-Qassam, Maymanah Ezzedin	5, 40, 52, 66, 70, 71, 78, 134, 143, 157, 158, 159, 167, 169, 274

Al-Qassam, Zhafer Abdulmalek	148
Al-Qattouna, Hasna	101
Al-Ramini, Rasheed	243
Al-Ramlah	272, 273
Al-Rasheed, Al-Sae'ed	253
Al-Rimawi, Abdallah	42
Al-Sae'ed, Hafizah	253
Al-Sae'ed, Salim	253
Al-Safadi, Sumayya	8, 128, 129, 130, 131, 135
Al-Safouri, Salha	34
Al-Sakakini, Doumia	55, 132, 271
Al-Sakakini, Hala	51
Al-Salman, Latifa	101
Al-Samer Cinema	203
Al-Samu' village	129, 226, 271
Al-Sari, Khadra Mustafa	26, 30, 49, 78, 128, 130, 131, 132, 134, 271
Al-Sayegh, Anis	36, 105, 116, 119, 120, 130, 136, 137, 138, 274
Al-Sebasi, Saniyyah	216
Al-Sebasi, Um Al-Taher	216
Al-Shak'a, Bassam	237
Al-Shawish, Zuheir	69, 104, 119, 133, 136, 138, 274
Al-Shawwa, Um Issam	216, 217
Al-Sheikh Ahmad, Amina	87
Al-Sheikh Jarrah neighborhood (Jerusalem)	58
Al-Sheikhah, Gharibah	25, 28
Al-Shihabi, Zulaikha	25, 27, 64, 65, 69, 103, 105, 106, 107, 176, 179, 181 190, 207, 222, 228, 229
Al-Shinnawi, Amneh	49, 131, 273
Al-Shurafa, Izdihar	38, 115, 130, 137, 273

Al-Taher, Latifa	37, 109, 118, 130, 137, 138, 273
Al-Taji, Hamdi	63
Al-Tamimi, Maha	8, 128, 135
Al-Tamimi, Subhieh Raid	69
Al-Taweel, Mary	216
Al-Teera (Haifa)	25, 102, 116, 274
Al-Tel Prison	67
Al-Titi, Shams	30, 54, 79, 111, 129, 132, 134, 272
Al-Tur	101
Al-Uzom, Suhair	8, 130, 133, 137, 173
Al-Wenni, Amneh	42, 106, 130, 131, 134, 273
Al-yaqoub, Sabha (Om Rajeh)	248, 261, 263, 266
Al-Yarmouk Camp	24, 122, 128, 129, 130, 135, 138, 273, 274
Al-Zaben, Ahmad Mahmoud	25, 26, 28, 102, 116, 117, 128, 136, 137, 274
Al-Zahra School	41
Al-Zarqa' camp	170
Al-Zein, Nayefa	25
Amer, Huda	84, 115, 135, 137, 273
America (The United States of America)	67, 198, 199, 224, 226, 237
American University (in Beirut)	165, 199
Amman-Jordan	123, 127, 129, 133, 143, 144, 193, 209, 274
Ammouri, Maryam Husein	103
Anabta village	44, 87, 131, 135, 137, 221, 225, 252, 271
Anani, Aisha	99, 100
Aqel, Zeinab	117, 138, 272
Arab Ba'ath Party	21
Arab Nationalist Movement	21

Arab University of Beirut	219
Arab women Society in Jerusalem	57
Arab women's conferences	12
Arraba	271
Arafat, Yasser (Abu Ammar)	230
Association of Arab Palestinian Women in Jerusalem	23
Awad, Ta'ah	88, 129, 135, 272
Azzoun village	113, 129, 247, 271,

B

Bab Al-Amud (Jerusalem)	109
Bab Al-Sahira (Jerusalem)	103
Badran, Jamila	43, 44, 80, 131, 134, 271
Baghdad	56, 66, 68, 207, 222, 226
Baghdad Pact	226
Bal'a village	32, 33, 34, 39, 44, 54, 98, 129, 132, 272
Balfour Declaration	39, 78, 201, 220, 222, 240
Barham, Karimah Ismail	86, 89, 134, 135, 271
Barham, Najeyyah	5, 84, 88, 112, 135, 137, 243, 244, 254, 266, 272
Barham, Sanajeq Mohammad	243, 255, 256, 257, 258, 259, 264, 265, 266, 269, 272
Barham, Sobhiyyah Ismael	243, 260, 261, 272
Beersheba	273
Begin	237
Beirut	36, 55, 56, 63, 68, 127, 165, 173, 175, 176, 180, 189, 190, 193, 197, 199, 204, 207, 219, 222, 273, 274
Beit Amreen village	249, 250, 256, 267
Beit Attab village	109
Beit Hanina Neighporhood (East Jerusalem)	101, 274

Beit Leed village	246, 247, 249, 251, 252, 253, 263
Beit Nuba village	227, 229
Beit Rima village	46, 271
Beit Sahour Town	234
Belgium	236
Bethlehem	229, 271, 274
Bevin, Ernest	210
Bir Al-Maksur - Haifa	271
Birzeit Town	46
Birzeit University	20, 127
Bishara, Georgette	42
Boycott of Israeli goods	208, 223
Britain	67, 224, 236
British campaign	51
British colonialism	36, 38
British government	41, 52
British High Commissioner	147
British Mandate	37, 52, 78, 93, 99, 128, 166
Burqah village	250, 255, 265, 267
Bustani, Emile	198

C

Cairo	20, 22, 68, 69, 71, 129, 130, 134, 148, 158, 159, 160, 162, 163, 181, 217, 223, 273, 274
Cairo University	20
Carmel Mountain	25
Carter (Jimmy)	236
Communist Party	21
Coptic club of the Greek Orthodox Community	61

D

Dakar, Sa'dah	84, 135, 271
Damascus	24, 66, 68, 82, 104, 109, 112, 207, 222, 273, 274
Darbas, Latifa Mahmoud	33, 129, 132, 272
Darbas, Ragheb (Abu Durra)	34
Darwaza, Izzat	112
Darweesh, Nuzha	107
Deir Al-Balah	135, 271
Deir Lighsoon	131, 134, 271
Dublin Conference	182

E

Eastern Women for the Defense of Palestine Conference (1938)	67, 142
Egypt	8, 12, 18, 19, 20, 63, 73, 75, 128, 129, 130, 131, 132, 133, 134, 136, 137, 138, 141, 147, 159, 161, 176, 180, 203, 204, 205, 209, 215, 222, 232
Egyptian ministry of education	70
Egyptian Red Crescent	217
Eid, Harikat	256
Ein-Beitilma Camp	134, 137
Emwas massacre	229
Emwas village	229
Eraikat, Dawud	64, 103, 133, 136
Esa'ad Attufulah House	200
Europe	70, 237
Executive committee for the Union of Women (1965)	229
Ezzat, Abbas Ezzat Mohammad	254

F

Fadda, Um Ashraf	111
Family Care Association	219, 223, 229
Farah, Hind	217
Fattah (Palestinian National Liparation Movement)	241
Feminist perspective	11, 14, 15, 17, 22, 29
First Palestinian uprising (1987)	49
France	230, 236
Friends School	220
Futuwwa	167, 218, 223

G

Galilee	179, 183, 227
Gaza	8, 18, 19, 40, 41, 106, 128, 129, 130, 131, 132, 133, 134, 135, 136, 175, 201, 202, 203, 204, 205, 206, 207, 208, 209, 214, 216, 217, 228, 230, 237, 271, 272
Gaza strip	8, 19, 135, 202, 204, 205, 216
General Arab Women Union	93
General Union of Palestinian Women (Lebanon)	20
General Union of Palestinian Women in the PLO	219
Ghazal, Fatima	25, 28, 113, 114
Ghousheh, Subhi	69, 91, 97, 133, 136, 274

H

Hadassah Hospital	241

Haifa	25, 27, 28, 33, 40, 45, 55, 56, 64, 66, 70, 71, 72, 79, 88, 102, 105, 106, 110, 117, 128, 132, 148, 150, 151, 153, 154, 156, 158, 159, 163, 164, 167, 168, 189, 196, 202, 229, 232, 271, 272, 273, 274
Halhoul village	54, 132, 274
Hamada, Rafeeqa	49, 50, 131, 132, 273
Hamed, Nadeyyah Omar	85, 86, 135, 272
Hannoun, Sarah	229
Hashem, Maryam	69
Hebrew university	57
Hebron	51, 117, 129, 132, 133, 136, 137, 229, 237, 242, 271, 272, 274
Hebron massacre	242
Hedayah, Khadija	82, 134, 273
Hijab	109, 115, 122, 126, 188
Hijaz, Afifeh	44, 87, 110, 131, 135, 137, 271
Hulaileh, Zakiyeh	84, 135, 272

I

Ibrahim, Noah	121
Imran, Maryam Abdul-Fattah	99
Iran	70, 226, 235, 236
Iraq	70, 204, 226
Irribin Khirbat (Acre)	35
Irtah village	245
Isawiya-Jerusalem	274
Islamic (al-Fatat) Society	63, 64
Islamic Association Schools (Haifa)	168
Israel	182, 192, 219, 226, 229, 255
Israeli Goods	208, 209
Israeli occupation	230

J

Jabal Al-Khirba (Sofin-Qalqilia)	114
Jablah (Syria)	143, 144
Jaffa	43, 50, 53, 56, 62, 81, 105, 117, 129, 273, 274
Jakaman, Hilweh	7, 271
Jeddah	199
Jericho	103, 133, 134, 135, 136, 272, 274
Jerusalem	8, 18, 19, 23, 24, 39, 50, 55, 56, 57, 58, 60, 63, 64, 65, 66, 67, 72, 77, 84, 93, 97, 98, 99, 100, 103, 105, 107, 109, 118, 128, 130, 131, 132, 133, 135, 136, 137, 138, 141, 144, 158, 159, 175, 176, 179, 180, 190, 197, 202, 207, 209, 225, 226, 228, 237, 271, 272, 273, 274
Jerusalem Radio	202
Jewish immigration	181, 210, 224
Jewish neighborhoods	56
Jews	44, 52, 56, 57, 62, 70, 76, 95, 175, 181, 202, 204, 208, 210, 211, 212, 221, 222, 223, 224, 226, 228, 229, 230, 231, 246, 249
Jinin	271
Jordan	8, 18, 19, 20, 78, 122, 128, 129, 130, 131, 132, 133, 134, 135, 136, 137, 141, 143, 144, 164, 166, 170, 198, 204, 232, 273, 274
Jordan University	20

K

Kafr Qaddoum village	267
Khaled, Zakeyya (Shararah)	106, 107, 273
Khaleel, Samiha (Samiha Yusef Mustafa Al Qubbaj)	39, 65, 84, 130, 133, 135, 136, 219, 226, 228, 240, 242, 271

-287-

Khan Yunis	203, 215
Karm Aamer village	260
Khartabil, Farouq	199
Khartabil, Hisham	199
Khartabil, Marwan	198, 199
Khartabil, Wadee'a Qaddourah	36, 39, 65, 76, 106, 107, 130, 133, 134, 164, 169, 173, 220, 273
Khazneh, Ahmad	108
Kheil, Mary	69
Khourshid, Arabiyya (Nariman)	211
Khourshid, Mohiba	211
Khoury, Samira	42, 43, 130, 131, 272
King Farouk	70, 72, 159
King Hussein	167, 170, 197
Kobar village	45, 47, 272
Kufr 'Aboush Town	47
Kuwait	205
Kweikat village-Acre	50, 273

L	
League of National Liberation	209, 223
Lebanon	8, 18, 19, 20, 55, 56, 59, 66, 73, 78, 120, 121, 130, 131, 132, 133, 134, 136, 137, 138, 141, 160, 173, 174, 175, 178, 200, 237, 238, 239, 242, 273, 274
Lod	229
Lubia Village	127, 129

M	
Ma'touk, Jamila	107
Mackenzie (President of the Hebrew university)	57

Maghnam, Mateel	23, 105
Mahajneh, Muna	8, 128, 130, 131, 132, 133, 138
Mansour, Hala	8, 130, 131, 133, 136
Martyrs children's centre	241
Masoud, Hasna Salim	246, 247, 248, 249, 250, 271
Maw'ed, Ahmad	36, 50, 81, 103, 130, 132, 134, 136, 274
Maw'ed, Zahra Hasan	103
Mikhmas	48
Mirror of the East newspaper	205
Mosque of Omar	23
Mount Carmel	25
Muharram, Sana'	8, 128, 129, 130, 143
Murrar, Khazneh Qasem	108
Muslihi, Shahirah Mahmud	268
Mustafa, Amina	50, 103
Mustafa, Zahidah Ahmad	243, 251, 252, 253, 254, 261, 262, 263, 264, 269, 272

N

Nablus	25, 26, 48, 55, 134, 137, 175, 179, 197, 228, 271, 272, 273, 274
Naser, Nabiha	69
Nassar, Najeeb	205
Nassar, Sathej	28, 69, 71, 105, 158
National Front	224
Nawrasi, Alice Elias	62, 116, 122, 133, 136, 137, 274
Nayef, Ahmad	40
Nazareth	43, 95, 122, 130, 131, 196, 202, 271, 272

O

Omar Al-Mukhtar Street (Gaza)	41
Oral history	11, 14, 15, 18, 19, 22, 29, 67, 70, 97, 98, 113, 125, 127, 129
Orthodox community (Bethlehem)	61
Oudeh, Aa'yesha	230
Oudeh, Fatima	101
Oudeh, Na'ilah	8, 131
Oudeh, Rasmeyyieh	230

P

Palestine	8, 18, 19, 20, 39, 40, 42, 45, 56, 57, 64, 66, 67, 68, 69, 71, 74, 76, 78, 93, 94, 103, 104, 107, 108, 112, 120, 121, 127, 141, 147, 158, 162, 163, 174, 175, 177, 178, 179, 180, 181, 182, 189, 190, 191, 193, 196, 197, 198, 201, 203, 204, 206, 207, 208, 210, 211, 214, 216, 222, 223, 224, 226, 229, 232, 235, 236, 246, 259, 264, 266
Palestinian Authority	240
Palestinian cause	75, 93, 181, 183, 198
Palestinian Communist Party	209
Palestinian people	13, 15, 57, 59, 126, 162
Palestinian refugees	217
Partition Plan (1947)	191, 204, 210
PLO	219, 222, 240, 241
Popular memory	14, 32, 126

Q

Qaddourah, Ebtihaj	176, 190
Qalqilya	47

Qanaze', Adele	43, 105
Qaqoun village	32
Qaraman, Su'ad	55, 59, 132, 272
Qasem, Ma'zouzeh	47, 131, 271
Qatannah town	237
Qattamon neighborhood	58
Qiffeen - Tulkarm	131, 132, 271
Quakers	203, 216

R

Radwan, Iman	8, 130, 134, 135, 136, 289
Rafah	129, 272
Ramallah	8, 45, 46, 47, 84, 127, 130, 131, 133, 135, 136, 137, 189, 202, 219, 226, 227, 229, 271, 272
Ramla	50
Ramin - Tulkarm	243, 244, 245, 256, 260, 264, 265, 266, 267, 269, 271, 272, 274
Ras Abu Hamad area	255, 256, 259
Rasheed, Haroun Hashem	24, 26, 28, 41, 76, 92, 106, 128, 129, 130, 134, 136, 274
Recorded history	11, 38
Red Crescent	70, 217
Reemash, Halima	99
Revolution (1936-1939)	12, 14, 51, 88, 89, 206

S

Sa'sa' village	50
Sabbah, Jamila Ahmad	47, 54, 131, 132, 271
Sabra and Shatilla massacre	234, 239
Sabra camp	234, 239
Saeed, Aminah	203

Safad	25, 28, 272, 273
Saffarin village	267
Salah, Munawwar	75, 134, 272
Salamah village	84
Salameh, Hasan	121
Sanour village	112, 256, 257, 262, 263, 265
Saudi Arabia	168
Sayegh, May	217
Sayegh, Rosemary	23, 24
Second Arab women's conference-1944	210
Sha'ab-Acre	271, 272
Sha'rawi, Huda	68, 69, 70, 72, 75, 76, 159
Shafiq, Dorreyah	203
Shalaldeh, Lamia'	8, 129, 137
Shatilla camp	234, 239
Shawar, Yusra	229
Shihabi, Ibrahim Yahya	127, 129
Shneik, Kamleh	32, 47, 113, 129, 131, 137, 272
Sidon	120
Sidon school	120
Site of the unknown soldiers' (Gaza)	204, 211
Stanton Street	64
Sudqi, Jathebeyah	205
Sulaiman, Jaber	127
Suq Al Gharb School	200
Swedenburg, Ted	14, 17
Switzerland	199
Sykes- Picot Agreement	78
Syria	8, 18, 19, 20, 56, 69, 73, 78, 88, 104, 119, 122, 128, 129, 130, 131, 132, 133, 134, 135, 136, 137, 138, 141, 143, 146, 148, 160, 170, 196, 199, 242, 245, 273, 274

T

Taibeh village	39, 179
Tamish, Rabab	8, 132
Tarazy, Virginia	93, 136, 272
Tarazy, Rima	240
Tarazy, Shafiq	216
Tawfiq, Mohammad	49
Teacher's institute	144, 202, 203, 206, 214, 226
Tel Aviv	209
Thafer, Haijar Mustafa	86, 89, 113, 135, 137, 274
The British	41, 48, 66, 70, 83, 94, 147, 246, 249, 251, 252, 265, 268
The Great Mosque (Gaza)	40, 41, 206
The Muslim Youth Association-Haifa	151
The new Arab Marxist Organization	209
The six-month strike of 1936	52, 54, 56, 58, 156, 202, 221
The Society of Women Union in Jerusalem	64
The White Paper (1939)	92, 181
The Women Progress Association	202, 216, 217
The Women's Charity Association	176
The Women's Union	39, 66, 222
The Workers' Union	222
Thinnaba village	39, 112, 129, 179, 184, 185, 244, 245, 255, 256, 257, 258, 263, 265
Tiberias	119, 123, 274
Touqan, Ibrahim	171
Tsipori-Nazareth	274
Tulkarm	34, 39, 43, 44, 47, 48, 51, 52, 65, 66, 88, 271, 272
Turkey	271
Tyre	120, 273

U

Um Ali	25, 28, 108
Um Al-Mu'mineen	97, 98
Um Ezzeinat village	117
Um Irmaih	32
Um Kayed	82, 129, 134, 135
Union of Arab Palestinian Women	175, 176, 177, 179
Union of Barreyyah Association	229
Union of Palestinian Students	222
Union of Women's Society	217
United Nations	203
University of Lebanon	178
UNRWA (The United Nations Relief and Works Agency for Palestine Refugees)	203, 204, 216
Uprising of 1933	23, 24

V

Vietnam	236

W

Wadi Al-Jouz	58
West Bank	18, 185, 219, 226, 229, 232, 237
Women and Memory Forum	20
Women's associations	211
Women's Day	204
World war one	201
World war two	92, 190
Wyes Plantation	240

Y

Yajour village	154
Yalo village	227, 229
Yaseen, Abdul-Qader	41, 68, 94, 130, 133, 136, 274
Yazour-Jaffa	272
Yusef, Ahmad	253

Z

Zahrat Al Oqhuan organization	167, 168
Zionism	93, 94, 182, 201
Zionist gangs	93
Zionist International Congress	224
Zuaiter, Akram	71, 73, 161

Eastern Women's Conference in Cairo (1938)

Names of Women Recognized in the Photo

1. Rifqa Al-Shihabi Al-Taji
2. Aliyyeh Al-Taji AL-Khairi
3. Maymanah Ezzedin Al-Qassam
4. Samiha Al-Taji Al-Huseini
5. Rayya Al-Qasem
6. Eiva Al-Masri (Egyption)
7. Mrs. Shukri Deeb
8. Tarab Abdulhadi
9. Nabiha Naser
10. Sathej Nassar
11. Zulaikha Al-Shihabi
12. Wahida Al-Khalidi
13. Samiha Al-Taji Al-Khalidi

Names of Palestinian Delegation to the Conference

Aliyyeh Al-Taji AL-Khairi, Arnasteen Al-Ghori, Badra Kan'an, Bahira Al-Athmeh, Fatima Al-Nashashibi, Kity Antonios, Malak Al-Shawwa, Malak Halaweh, Maryam Hashem, Mary Kheil, Mrs. Bakr Al-Nashashibi, Mrs. George Salah, Mrs. Hasan Al-Budairi, Mrs. Shukri Al-Muhtadi, Mrs. Shukri Deeb, Mateel Mghnam, Maymanah Al-Qassam, Nabiha Naser, Rayya Al-Qasem, Rifqa Al-Shihabi Al-Taji, Salma Al-Huseini, Samiha Al-Khalidi, Sathej Nassar, Su'ad Al-Huseini, Subhiyyeh Al-Tamimi, Wahida Al-Khalidi, Tarab Abdulhadi, Zahiyyeh Al-Nashashibi, Zulaikha Al-Shihabi.